The Complete Cookie

BY THE SAME AUTHORS

Dip It!

Light Sauces

Quick Breads

The 99% Fat-Free Cookbook

Home Made in the Kitchen

The 99% Fat-Free Book
of Appetizers and Desserts

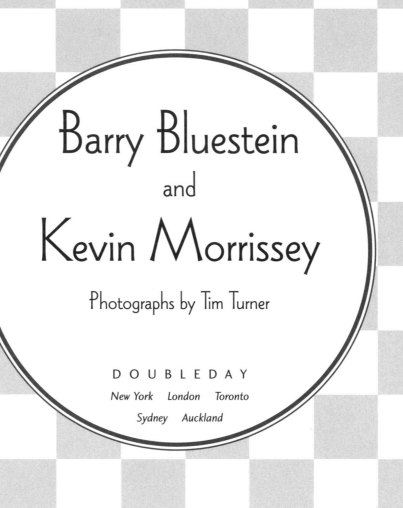

Barry Bluestein
and
Kevin Morrissey

Photographs by Tim Turner

D O U B L E D A Y
New York   London   Toronto
Sydney   Auckland

The Complete Cookie

Cookies for Every Occasion

PUBLISHED BY DOUBLEDAY

a division of Bantam Doubleday Dell Publishing Group, Inc.

1540 Broadway, New York, New York 10036

DOUBLEDAY and the portrayal of an anchor with a dolphin are
trademarks of Doubleday, a division of Bantam Doubleday Dell
Publishing Group, Inc.

Book design by Marysarah Quinn

Library of Congress Cataloging-in-Publication Data
Bluestein, Barry.
The complete cookie : cookies for every occasion / Barry Bluestein
and Kevin Morrissey. — 1st ed.
p.   cm.
Includes index.
1. Cookies.   2. Holiday cookery.   I. Morrissey, Kevin.
II. Title.
TX722.B594   1996
641.8′654—dc20   95-47849
CIP
ISBN 0-385-47773-2

Copyright © 1996 by Barry Bluestein and Kevin Morrissey
Photographs copyright © 1996 by Tim Turner
All Rights Reserved
Printed in the United States of America
September 1996

1   3   5   7   9   10   8   6   4   2

FIRST EDITION

Fondly dedicated to our editor,

Judy Kern,

one smart cookie with whom

it is a thorough joy to work.

Acknowledgments

Thanks are owed so many for their contributions to this book. At Doubleday, we are grateful to Arlene Friedman for her belief in us, Marysarah Quinn for her smashing book design, and Tammy Blake, Tamara Jenkins, Valerie Peterson, Brandon Saltz, and Corrie Silva for their ongoing support of our work. As always, special thanks are due Susan Ramer, our literary agent.

Tim Turner and his capable assistants, Rod La Fleur and Steve Oatley, are responsible for the brilliant photography. For knowledge and assistance graciously shared, we thank Ann Bloomstrand, Cindy Ousterhout of Oh My Goodness, Colin Reeves, and Doris and Jim Stockwell of Spiceland, Inc.

We warmly acknowledge all the folks who lent family recipes, holiday traditions, and inspiration—including Elaine Barlas, Eleanor Bluestein, Sara Bluestein, Sally Cohen, Susan Felber, Ruth Gold, Don Houck, Helen Kalabsa, John Koulias, Marie Koulias, Mary McLaughlin, Mary Ann Morrissey, Jeanne Troxell Munson, Marian Packer, Claudia Clark Potter, Anita Reeves, Martha Schueneman, Lisa Schumacher, Bernice Solomon, Mark Stahr, and Evelyn West.

For enthusiastically consuming untold tins of cookies during months of testing, we acknowledge the role of Sara Bluestein and Elizabeth Morrissey.

Lastly, we thank Jill Van Cleave, the ever present voice of good cheer at the other end of the phone line, for her unfailing erudition and taste and for her unwavering encouragement.

Contents

Introduction   xi

Special Recommendations   1

The Complete Cookie Cupboard
    Selecting the Best Ingredients   5

The Complete Cookie Kitchen
    Choosing the Right Equipment   13

The Complete Cookie Craft
    Mastering Techniques   19

Filled Cookies   23

Shaped, Pressed, and Molded Cookies   55

Bar Cookies   85

Rolled Cookies   115

Refrigerator Cookies   143

Drop Cookies   169

Holiday Cookies   201
    Christmas, Purim, Easter, Passover, Halloween, Thanksgiving

Healthy Cookies   249
    Nonfat, Low-Fat, Sugarless, Gluten-Free

Toppings   289

Source Guide   306

Index   309

Introduction

Barry's mom called a few weeks ago, excited about some news. The story, as it unfolded, was that grandson Dan had recently taken up baking and was busy rediscovering the old family recipes.

Baking's been an avid pursuit in Barry's family for several generations. Grandpa Nigberg worked his culinary alchemy in the kitchens of the Waldorf-Astoria early in the century. He passed on to his children a love of the craft, along with such classic creations as a sugar cookie dough we'll sample in pages to come that makes just about the best apple pie crust around.

Barry's mother, Sara, took her baking seriously enough to keep one room in their Long Island home properly chilled and equipped for preparing doughs for the hamantaschen we also feature, along with dozens of other delights. Barry's been baking since childhood, and now nephew Dan seems to have assumed the mantle.

"He'll do just fine," Sara said. "It's in the genes."

This kind of passion, we used to think, was an isolated phenomenon, a family obsession. But in researching this book we saw a similar pattern emerge over and over again. Canvassing friends around the country for favorite cookies we could replicate and related lore we could share, we encountered a degree of enthusiasm and continuity surprising in an era not reputed for domesticity or custom.

We unearthed recipes and baking rituals passed on from generation to generation and neighbor to neighbor, tracing the subtle transformations in personality that emerged with each new set of hands that touched the dough. We discovered corporate attorneys and university professors joyfully submerged in mounds of flour and sugar on the odd day off, and found siblings in disparate communities and walks of life eagerly swapping family recipe revisions.

Cookies, it would appear, really are a last refuge in a world characterized by too many demands and too much change—the most basic and universal of all the foods that comfort the ravaged spirit.

In *The Complete Cookie*, we've set out to provide everything you need to know to establish, renew, or expand your own cookie traditions. Utilizing modern appliances and techniques, incorporating ingredients not readily available in the past, and employing flavor combinations that reflect today's increasingly sophisticated tastes, we revisit the classics and pursue new directions.

Recipes are organized by basic mode of preparation: bar; drop; filled; refrigerator; rolled; and shaped, pressed, and molded. Individual recipes in each category call for fashioning doughs by the method that will produce the best results for that cookie—in the food processor, with an electric mixer, or, in a few cases, by hand.

A selection of healthy cookies includes nonfat and low-fat offerings, as well as recipes for cookies made without sugar and without flour. Our holiday roundup features all types of cookies and spans seasons and cultures, ranging from Yuletide favorites to sweets prepared according to Passover and Purim conventions, from traditional Thanksgiving and Easter cookies to Halloween novelties.

Included is advice on stocking your baker's pantry; suggestions for selecting cookie sheets and baking pans, mixers and measuring utensils, scoops and spatulas; tips on how to master cookie craft, and a rundown of particularly quick and easy cookies, party cookies, and kids' favorites.

We strive throughout to simplify terminology and technique and to make recipes that will intrigue the experienced baker, as well as be accessible to the determined novice. We use readily available ingredients and minimize the need for specialized equipment.

Cookies, we learned on the odyssey traveled in putting together *The Complete Cookie*, inspire an infectious ardor among their devotees. They're a simple pleasure to be savored in complex times, an equal joy to make, to share, and to consume.

Special Recommendations

QUICK AND EASY COOKIES

Anise Madeleines (page 78)

Apricot-Filled Chocolate Thumbprints (page 34)

Apricot Linzer Cookies (page 48)

Apricot Oatmeal Wheat Fingers (page 104)

Banana Bread Cookies (page 255)

Big, Soft, Chewy Chocolate Chip Cookies (page 176)

Blueberry Streusel Bars (page 105)

Chocolate-Covered Peanut Butter Bars (page 108)

Chocolate Pecan Tartlets (page 45)

Cranberry Orange Oatmeal Cookies (page 198)

Crunchy Granola Chocolate Chip Cookies (page 190)

Elaine Barlas's Mexican Wedding Cookies (page 211)

Fig Port Bars (page 95)

Ginger Pear Biscotti (page 59)

Jill Van Cleave's Currant Shortbread (page 277)

K.C.'s Mom's Date Chews (page 215)

Lemon Poppyseed Wafers (page 192)

Lisa Schumacher's Chocolate Shots (page 218)

Macadamia Macaroons (page 283)

Newfangled Cocoa Brownies (page 253)

No-Bake Chocolate Oat Cookies (page 187)

Parmesan Pepper Rounds (page 119)

Peach Crumb Bars (page 96)

Peanut Butter Chocolate Chip Cookies (page 185)

Pecan Toffee Fingers (page 89)

Ruth Gold's Date Nut Squares (page 99)

Scottish Shortbread (page 81)

Susan's Orange Chippers (page 266)

Viennese Raspberry Sandwiches (page 32)

KID PLEASERS

Almond-Filled Strips (page 42)

Big, Soft, Chewy Chocolate Chip Cookies (page 176)

Caramel Meringue-Filled Oatmeal Sandwich Cookies (page 36)

Carrot Cake Cookies (page 267)

Chocolate-Covered Peanut Butter Bars (page 108)

Chocolate Peanut Butter Thingies (page 131)

Chocolate Rugalach (page 28)

Chocolate "Tuttle" Cookies (page 64)

Cinnamon Swirls (page 159)

Devil's Food Cookies (page 163)

Double Chocolate Fudgies (page 278)

Fig Bars (page 261)

Fruit and Nut Kisses (page 279)

Ginger Bells (page 205)

Gingersnaps (page 182)

Graham Crackers (page 136)

Judy's No-Bake Chocolate and Peanut Butter Cups (page 29)

Lisa Schumacher's Chocolate Shots (page 218)

Mary McLaughlin's Shortbread Ghosts (page 238)

No-Bake Chocolate Oat Cookies (page 187)

Oatmeal Raisin Pecan Cookies (page 275)

Peanut Butter Jack-O'-Lanterns (page 237)

Snickerdoodles (page 69)

Susan's Orange Chippers (page 266)

Very Vanilla Wafers (page 178)

PARTY COOKIES

Amaretti (page 196)

Ann's Key Lime Bars (page 102)

Blackberry Linzer Squares (page 106)

Cappuccino Cream Cheese Bars (page 109)

Cappuccino Tuiles (page 263)

Caraway Cookies (page 142)

Chocolate Madeleines (page 77)

Chocolate Nut Pizzelles (page 72)

Chocolate Raspberry Hazelnut Ribbons (page 168)

Chocolate Rugalach (page 28)

Chocolate Snails (page 271)

Chocolate Walnut Truffles (page 120)

Chocolate–White Chocolate Chunk Cookies (page 181)

Cognac Dreams (page 126)

Double Chocolate Fudgies (page 278)

Doubleday Sweet Potato Dollops (page 246)

Fig Port Bars (page 95)

Fruit Bars (page 272)

Hazelnut Horns (page 141)

John Vranicar's Savory Biscotti (page 254)

Judy's No-Bake Chocolate and Peanut Butter Cups (page 29)

Kevin's Eggnog Cookies (page 214)

Lemon Clove Cookies (page 127)

Licorice Spritz (page 75)

Macadamia Butters (page 122)

Macadamia Florentines (page 173)

Macadamia Macaroons (page 283)

Mini Coconut Meringues (page 281)

Newfangled Cocoa Brownies (page 253)

Nutty Blue Cheese Wedges (page 84)

Oatmeal Lacies (page 186)

Orange Teardrops (page 286)

Parmesan Pepper Rounds (page 119)

Peanut Thumbprints with Chocolate Ganache Filling (page 54)

Pear Caramel Bars (page 90)

Pistachio Pralines (page 199)

Ruth Gold's Date Nut Squares (page 99)

Sesame Wafers (page 177)

Thelma Houston's Vanilla Sugar Tea Cookies (page 147)

Three-Citrus Bars (page 94)

Viennese Raspberry Sandwiches (page 32)

Walnut Bow Ties (page 66)

Yin-Yang Wafers (page 148)

The Complete Cookie Cupboard

Selecting the Best Ingredients

Butter: Always use unsalted butter. Unless chilled (right out of the refrigerator) butter is called for or it is to be melted, allow the butter to warm to room temperature. To soften butter quickly, microwave at 50 percent power for about 30 seconds.

Cut butter into pieces to facilitate creaming or incorporation into a food processor dough. Frozen butter can be grated for easy creaming.

Chocolate: See chart, page 8.

Cocoa Powder: We use unsweetened Dutch-processed (sometimes called European-processed) cocoa powder, which is treated with an alkali and has a rich, full flavor. Those who prefer the taste of carob powder can substitute an equal amount for cocoa powder.

Dried Fruits: We have tried to limit the inventory of dried fruits to those that can be obtained in supermarkets, which now carry a substantial selection. Dried cranberries and dried cherries, for example, are readily available. If you frequent a natural or health foods store with a wider selection, experiment with the substitution of something more exotic, such as dried star fruit or papaya.

Dried fruit should be soft and pliable; it is intended to add moisture as well as flavor to the cookie.

Eggs: Recipes are formulated on the use of Grade A large eggs. In most cases, liquid egg substitute can be used instead for convenience or out of concern for cholesterol. Use $1/4$ cup of the egg substitute to replace 1 whole egg or 2 egg whites. Egg whites cannot, however, be replaced by egg substitute in meringue or macaroon recipes.

In nonfat or low-fat recipes that call for liquid egg substitute, be sure to choose a *nonfat* product and avoid those that contain oil or tofu.

Extracts: For best results, use *pure* flavorings, not imitation. We've found most of the extracts called for (including anise, lemon, orange, peppermint, and vanilla) in pure form in our neighborhood supermarket's spice section. Others can be obtained from spice merchants, some natural foods stores, and some kitchenware stores.

We include recipes for easy homemade vanilla (page 175), and lemon (page 62), and orange (page 62) extracts.

Flour: See chart, page 10.

Fruit Butters: We use natural fruit butters in place of butter in several nonfat and low-fat cookies. They are available from better supermarkets and from natural and health foods stores.

Juice: We prefer to use freshly squeezed orange juice and lemon juice. You'll likely have the lemon on hand anyway, since most recipes that call for lemon juice also call for lemon zest. If you do use prepared orange juice, use the type *not* made from concentrate.

In selecting fruit juice concentrates for use in our sugarless cookies, check labels to ensure you are obtaining a natural or organic fruit juice product with no sweeteners added.

Nut Butters: Recipes are formulated on the use of organic nut butters to which no sugar has been added. They are readily available from natural and health foods stores, as well as from many better supermarkets. Whenever possible, choose the freshly made variety.

Nuts: See chart, page 11.

Salt: We developed the recipes using table salt, rather than coarser grind kosher salt or sea salt.

Spices: Buy the freshest and best quality spices available, store them in tightly sealed opaque containers out of direct sunlight, and replace them at least every 6 months. In recipes that call for nutmeg, freshly ground is always preferable.

Sugar: Never use more sugar than is called for in a recipe; the addition will harden the cookie. If extra sweetness is desired, add a frosting, icing, or glaze.

Granulated sugar, the most common white sugar, is used to sweeten most cookies. For some recipes, we grind it to *superfine* consistency in the food processor. *Confectioners' sugar* is white sugar ground to a powder with a little cornstarch added. We use it for toppings and fillings, to dust cookies, and in a few doughs. *Turbinado sugar,* the coarse raw sugar from which granulated sugar is refined, is sprinkled on top of some cookies to add texture and sheen.

Brown sugar imparts a richness to many cookies (*dark brown sugar* producing a stronger taste than *light brown sugar*) and is combined with butter to produce butterscotch flavor. *Natural raw brown sugar* is rare; most brown sugar on the market is a mixture of granulated sugar and molasses.

Chocolate

Type	Major Components	Characteristics	Forms Readily Available
UNSWEETENED (also called bitter or baking chocolate)	chocolate liquor (cocoa butter and cocoa solids)	very bitter; used only in baking (doughs)	1-ounce squares (usually 8 to a box)
BITTERSWEET or EXTRA BITTERSWEET	chocolate liquor, extra cocoa butter, sugar, vanilla	assertive taste (the choice of chocolate lovers); used in doughs, fillings, and toppings	1-ounce squares (usually 8 to a box), large blocks, and thin bars of various sizes
SEMISWEET	chocolate liquor, sugar, vanilla	slightly sweet; used in doughs, fillings, and toppings	1-ounce squares (usually 8 to a box), large blocks, thin bars of various sizes, and chips
MILK	chocolate liquor, sugar, vanilla, milk solids	creamy and sweet (the basis of most candy bars); used in fillings, in toppings, and in chip form	small blocks, thin bars of various sizes, and chips
WHITE	cocoa butter, sugar, vanilla, milk solids (must contain cocoa butter, not vegetable oil)	not a true chocolate (contains no chocolate liquor); usually used in fillings, in toppings, and in chip form; scorches easily	1-ounce squares (usually 6 to a box), large blocks, thin bars of various sizes, and chips

Preferred Varieties	Shelf Life/Storage	Possible to Substitute
any	indefinite/well wrapped in a cool, dry place (should not be refrigerated or frozen)	(for 1 ounce, melted): 3 tablespoons cocoa powder and 1 tablespoon oil or butter; or 3 tablespoons carob powder and 1 tablespoon oil or butter
French or high-quality American	1 year/well wrapped in a cool, dry place (should not be refrigerated or frozen)	(for 1 ounce, melted): 1 ounce semisweet chocolate; or $^1/_2$ ounce unsweetened chocolate and 2 teaspoons sugar; or $1^1/_2$ tablespoons cocoa powder, $^1/_2$ tablespoon butter, and 1 teaspoon sugar
French or Swiss	1 year/well wrapped in a cool, dry place (should not be refrigerated or frozen)	(for 1 ounce, melted): 1 ounce bittersweet chocolate; or $^1/_2$ ounce unsweetened chocolate and 1 tablespoon sugar; or $1^1/_2$ tablespoons cocoa powder, $^1/_2$ tablespoon butter, and $^1/_2$ tablespoon sugar
any European	3 months/well wrapped in a cool, dry place; 1 year/freezer	(for 1 ounce, melted): 1 ounce white chocolate
French, Swiss, or high-quality American; should be cream-colored	1 month/well wrapped in a cool, dry place; 3 months/freezer	(for 1 ounce, melted): 1 ounce milk chocolate

Flour

Type	Characteristics	Shelf Life/Storage
ALL-PURPOSE (bleached or unbleached)	general purpose baking flour; often *enriched* to replace some of the vitamins lost in refining; amount used determines whether the cookie will be chewy or crisp	6 months/airtight container out of direct sunlight
SELF-RISING	all-purpose flour to which baking powder and salt have been added; no need to add a leavening agent	6 months/airtight container out of direct sunlight
CAKE	fine-textured, low-gluten refined flour; makes a soft, cakey cookie	6 months/airtight container out of direct sunlight
WHOLE WHEAT	full-flavored flour that contains wheat germ and wheat bran; high nutritional and fiber content; makes a dense, chewy cookie; often used in combination with all-purpose flour	3 to 4 weeks/airtight container out of direct sunlight; 1 year/freezer (can be used directly out of freezer)
WHOLE WHEAT PASTRY	more finely ground whole wheat flour; produces a cookie denser than all-purpose flour, but lighter and chewier than regular whole wheat flour; available from natural and health foods stores	3 to 4 weeks/airtight container out of direct sunlight; 1 year/freezer (can be used directly out of freezer)
GRAHAM	more coarsely ground whole wheat flour; used for graham crackers and crusts, or in combination with all-purpose flour; available from natural and health foods stores	3 to 4 weeks/airtight container out of direct sunlight; 1 year/freezer (can be used directly out of freezer)

Nuts

Shelled nuts can be kept for up to 3 months in a cool, dark place and for up to 1 year in the freezer; store in an airtight container. Unshelled nuts will keep somewhat longer, depending on the degree of freshness when purchased. Always select unsalted nuts.

Nut	Variety	Select:			Forms Readily Available*:		
		Blanched	Raw	Roasted	Bulk	Packaged	Vacuum-Sealed
ALMONDS	whole		X		X	X	X
	sliced		X		X	X	
	slivered	X	X		X	X	
	butter				X		X
CASHEWS	whole		X		X		
	pieces		X		X		
	butter				X		X
HAZELNUTS (Filberts)	whole		X		X		
MACADAMIAS	whole			X			X
PEANUTS	whole	X	X		X	X	
	butter				X		X
PECANS	halves		X		X	X	
	pieces		X		X	X	
	chopped		X		X	X	
PISTACHIOS	pieces			X	X		
WALNUTS	halves		X		X	X	
	pieces		X		X	X	
	chopped		X		X	X	

*Bulk refers to goods sold by weight (sometimes prepackaged) in nut shops and in natural and health foods stores. By packaged, we mean brands commonly found in bags on supermarket baking shelves. Also available in supermarkets, vacuum-packed products are commercially prepared by the can or jar.

The Complete Cookie Kitchen

Choosing the Right Equipment

Baker's Parchment: In some recipes, we line cookie sheets or baking sheets with baker's parchment to prevent sticking without adding moisture or fat, or to facilitate the gentle removal of particularly delicate cookies. It can be found in the baking section of most supermarkets or obtained in quantity from many kitchenware stores.

Interchangeable with parchment is *nonstick plastic ovenware liner,* which has the added advantage of being reusable.

Baking Pans: Bar cookies and brownies are baked in baking pans, the most common sizes of which are 9 by 13 by 2 inches and 8 by 8 by 2 inches. We also use the slightly more esoteric 9-by-9-by-2-inch pan, which can be found in many kitchenware stores. For best results, use sturdy pans made of shiny aluminum. We're partial to the type that features a double thickness of aluminum with a pocket of air between the layers; these pans yield particularly soft and moist bars.

Use nonstick pans for easier cleanup if you prefer, but follow the recipe directions for greasing or lining the pan nonetheless.

Avoid glass baking pans unless specified in a particular recipe. Glass pans speed up the baking process, which can easily result in overbaked, dry cookies. If you bake in glass, reduce the oven temperature by 25 degrees and begin to check the cookies at least 5 minutes before the prescribed baking time.

Baking Sheets: We use shallow, rimmed baking sheets for cookies that are baked in loaf form, such as biscotti and mandelbrot. Shiny aluminum sheets are preferred; those fashioned of black steel absorb heat quickly and facilitate burning.

Baking sheets come in a range of sizes. In selecting, always allow for a margin of at least 2 inches on all sides between the sheet and the oven wall. Use nonstick sheets if you wish, but still grease or line the sheets as directed.

Bowls: You'll need a variety of shapes and sizes, ranging from small, shallow bowls for soaking dried fruit to a 4-quart receptacle for mixing dough. We prefer sturdy glass or ceramic mixing bowls.

Cookie Cutters: Cookie cutters come in a seemingly endless array of shapes and sizes. We rely on 2-inch- and 2½-inch-round cutters, with either straight or fluted edges. We also turn often to a population of miniature people, angels, animals, and others that are in residence in our pantry. You can fashion designs of your own as well, using cardboard templates (page 123).

Cookie Presses: We call for a cookie press, or gun—a tube with a trigger release that presses a uniform amount of dough onto the cookie sheet through a decorative disk—to make spritz cookies. In addition to the traditional metal press, the experimenting baker can now choose an inexpensive plastic model.

Cookie Sheets: We highly recommend investing in a supply of good quality cookie sheets, which can make a big difference in the outcome of your baking endeavors. Choose heavy-gauge, shiny aluminum sheets, preferably those with a cushion of air between a double layer of metal. (Two single-layer cookie sheets can be stacked piggyback to approximate this effect.) Select a size that will allow at least a 2-inch border on all sides between the sheet and the oven wall. Avoid black metal sheets, which tend to produce overly browned or burnt cookies.

Nonstick cookie sheets can be used for many recipes; grease or line the sheets according to directions. Do not use coated sheets, however, in preparing recipes that call for *ungreased* cookie sheets.

If you must use thin cookie sheets, check to make sure that they are flat and not warped. Switching sheets between the top and bottom shelves of the oven and rotating them 180 degrees from their original position midway through baking—always recommended when baking more than one sheet at a time—is *essential* with thin sheets. Begin to check the cookies for visual doneness cues a few minutes early to avoid overbaking.

Food Processors: The food processor lends itself to exceedingly quick and easy preparation of many cookie doughs with wonderful results. We use this method in recipes for which the dough can be prepared from start to finish in the processor, those that do not entail a final combination of various components or folding in of whole ingredients. Use a full-size model (ideally, one with a powerful motor) for preparing dough and for chopping and grinding ingredients; a mini processor comes in handy for small quantities.

Graters: A four-sided grater with holes of varying sizes and shapes is an extremely versatile tool. It can be used to grate nutmeg or to zest lemons or oranges, in lieu of more specialized implements.

Madeleine Plaques: Use aluminum or steel madeleine plaques with 3-inch scallop-shaped molds, available from kitchenware stores. The plaques contain from 8 to 24 molds each; our recipes yield 2 dozen madeleines.

Measuring Cups and Spoons: For liquid measures, use *heat-tempered glass measuring cups,* which are easy to gauge visually and microwave-safe. One-cup and 2-cup measures serve most needs; we also find it useful to have a 4-cup measure on hand.

For dry measures, we prefer sturdy *stainless steel measuring cups.* Choose a set with a convenient $1/8$-cup (2-tablespoon) measure.

Although *stainless steel measuring spoons* are the most durable, you may want a set of *plastic measuring spoons* as well for a broader range of measures. You'll need a $1/8$-teaspoon measure; a $1/2$-tablespoon measure eliminates the bother of measuring out $1^{1}/_{2}$ teaspoons.

For accuracy in measurements, never use measuring utensils that are chipped, cracked, or dented.

Mixers: Although most cookie doughs can be prepared manually, electric mixers facilitate such steps as creaming butter that could become cumbersome and time-consuming by hand. In most cases, a good quality hand-held mixer will do the job.

We call for use of a heavy-duty stationary mixer when working with very thick doughs (cream cheese rugalach dough, for example), to lessen the risk that the dough will be overbeaten or that the mixer's motor will burn out, and for a few rolled cookie doughs.

Stationary mixers also work best in the preparation of meringue, for which egg whites need to be well aerated. Making meringue with a hand-held mixer takes a little longer and produces a slightly less airy consistency.

Muffin Tins: A few of our individual cheesecakes and tarts are baked in mini muffin tins. Use tins with 1/4-cup wells that measure about 2 inches across at the top. Grease or line the wells as directed even if using nonstick tins.

Pastry Brushes: Use a pastry brush, available from kitchenware stores, to remove excess flour or to paint dough with a wash. A new *soft-bristled paintbrush* of similar width will do in a pinch.

Rolling Pins: In general, the longer and heavier the rolling pin, the better. Rolling pin covers and pastry cloths are optional for the casual baker; they will make it easier to handle a few of our particularly soft and sticky doughs.

Rulers: Dedicate an easily read and easily washed ruler to cookie baking. You'll use it constantly for accurate rolling, shaping, cutting, and slicing, as well as for spacing cookies on sheets. (This won't sound like superfluous advice the first time you find yourself frantically rummaging through a desk with floured paws.)

Scoops: Stainless steel scoops with squeeze-handle releases facilitate easy preparation of uniform drop cookies. We use a European-manufactured 35-millimeter scoop, which measures 1 1/4 inches in diameter and holds 1 tablespoon of dough.

Sifters: We call for sifting dry ingredients together in preparing some especially dry doughs and for sifting confectioners' sugar in the preparation of toppings. A simple spring-set model—or even a fine-mesh sieve and a spoon—will work just fine. If you do a lot of baking or are as enamored of gadgets as we are, indulge yourself and get a battery-operated sifter.

Spatulas: You'll need different types of spatulas for different steps in the recipes.

A *straight-edged wooden spatula* can be used to level off dry ingredients in measuring cups or spoons for precise measurement.

A *rubber spatula* is useful for scraping ingredients from one receptacle to another, folding ingredients together, turning out dough, working dough into the corners of baking pans or baking sheets, and smoothing and leveling doughs and toppings. A *miniature rubber spatula* has proven to be particularly helpful in placing and shaping drop cookies on cookie sheets.

We use an *offset metal spatula* (technically a turner, the type with an angled handle for greater leverage) to transfer many types of cookies onto cookie sheets and from the sheets to cooling racks, as well as to remove bar cookies from pans. Squared-tip spatulas with beveled edges are the easiest to use. A *flat metal spatula* can be used to level off measures of dry ingredients or to spread toppings evenly.

Thermometers: Use a good quality *mercury oven thermometer* to monitor the accuracy of your oven's calibration and adjust the temperature setting accordingly as needed. We call for an *instant-read thermometer* to register the temperature of water used in making yeast dough and to check that eggs are sufficiently cooked. In addition, a *candy thermometer* is called for when making caramel.

Wax Paper: Although we occasionally line a baking pan with *aluminum foil* or wrap a ball of dough in *plastic wrap,* inexpensive, versatile wax paper is our wrap of choice in preparing cookies.

We often call for lining a work surface with wax paper (to which dough doesn't stick), to facilitate handling and cleanup. Other wraps cannot be substituted for this purpose; if you dispense with the wax paper, use a pastry cloth or put the dough directly on a lightly floured surface.

For chilling, dough can also be wrapped in aluminum foil or plastic wrap. Aluminum foil is particularly useful in wrapping cookies for freezing (page 22).

Whisks: Whisks are indispensable for a range of functions, from beating eggs to combining flour with leavening agents and spices. We keep several small stainless steel sauce whisks on hand; a larger balloon whisk is helpful if you intend to whip egg whites by hand.

Wire Racks: Cookies must be cooled on wire racks. You'll need a few if baking a large batch. Select sturdy racks raised sufficiently on legs to allow air to circulate beneath the cookies.

Wooden Spoons: A wooden spoon is a baker's best friend; always keep a supply nearby. You'll use a wooden spoon from start to finish for doughs prepared manually, to gently stir dry ingredients into wet for many doughs prepared with the aid of an electric mixer, and in individual steps throughout most recipes.

The Complete Cookie Craft

Mastering Techniques

Specific how-to directions for each type of cookie (i.e., how to "drop" cookies, how to cut bar cookies, how to roll and cut out rolled cookies, how to press cookies, etc.) can be found in the respective chapter introductions. Following are a few tips, organized chronologically, that apply to cookies of any persuasion.

Handling Dry Ingredients: To store flour, empty the bag loosely (don't pack the flour down) into a large container with a tight lid. Close and shake to aerate.

To measure flour and other dry ingredients, dip the measuring cup or spoon into the container and scoop out a heaping portion. Do not push down or pack the measure. With a straight-edged wooden spatula, a flat metal spatula, or a knife with a very straight top edge, level the measure evenly and accurately, pushing off the excess. The one exception to this rule is brown sugar, which usually is firmly packed into the measure.

If flour is sufficiently aerated, there is no reason to sift before measuring. (Store as directed above and give the flour a quick stir before scooping to add air.) In most cases, whisking the flour thoroughly with the baking powder, baking soda, salt, and/or spices called for will sufficiently break up and disperse all ingredients. We call for sifting ingredients together only for a few very dry doughs.

Chopping and Grinding Nuts: Many nuts come only whole, halved, or in large pieces and will have to be chopped by hand with a sharp knife. Grinding nuts in the food processor is a fast and easy procedure and the first step in making several of our processor doughs. In some recipes we process a little of the flour or sugar with the nuts to keep them from clumping around the blade.

Creaming: To cream butter (this is sometimes done in combination with sugar) or to cream cream cheese, mash with a wooden spoon or beat with an electric mixer to a very smooth consistency. Start with butter or cream cheese that has been allowed to soften to room temperature and cut it into pieces.

Melting Butter: To melt butter, cut it into pieces. Put it in a glass measuring cup and microwave at full power for about 50 seconds, or warm it over low heat in a small pan, taking care not to burn it.

Melting Chocolate: If you're a purist, melt chocolate in the top of a double boiler over gently boiling water, stirring constantly. Make sure that the water in the bottom does not boil up and touch the underside of the insert.

These days, most of us melt chocolate (sometimes in combination with butter) in a microwave. Simply heat the chocolate at full power for 1 to $2\frac{1}{2}$ minutes (depending upon the amount and type of chocolate) in a glass measuring cup, stirring at the intervals indicated in the individual recipes.

Combining Dry and Wet Ingredients: Once the flour mixture is added to wet ingredients, take care not to overbeat, which will toughen the cookies. As directed in individual recipes, stir with a wooden spoon or beat gently with a mixer just to incorporate, or process just to form a dough ball.

Greasing and Lining Pans and Sheets: We often use *vegetable oil cooking spray* for convenience; in most cases, *butter* can be substituted. To keep the fat content down, use *light vegetable oil cooking spray,* coat very lightly, and rub the oil around the surface to cover evenly.

In some cases, cooking spray can be substituted for butter. However, greasing with butter is necessary to make thin, lacy cookies spread.

When an *ungreased* sheet is indicated, you can't add a spritz for good measure without changing the character of the cookie. Dough baked on a greased sheet will spread more than dough baked on an ungreased sheet, producing a thinner cookie.

We call for *baker's parchment* (page 13) when working with some very dry or delicate cookies. Use parchment or *nonstick plastic ovenware liner.*

Baking: Try to make all cookies in a batch consistent in size and shape. Place them evenly on the cookie sheets, leaving the indicated amount of space between cookies and no large gaps on the sheets. When no specific spacing is indicated (for cookies that won't spread while baking), place them about an inch apart.

Position the racks to divide the oven into thirds. To promote uniform browning when baking more than one sheet at a time, position one of the sheets lengthwise and the other crosswise. Switch the sheets between top and bottom racks and rotate each 180 degrees from its original position midway through baking.

When baking only a single sheet, place it on the top rack with a short end toward the rear oven wall. You shouldn't need to rotate the sheet, but check midway through baking and do so if the cookies do not appear to be browning uniformly.

Every oven is different and ovens can fluctuate suddenly in temperature. Monitor your oven with a thermometer to gauge the accuracy of calibration and make adjustments accordingly. The temperature of the dough and the type of baking sheet used can also affect baking times.

Always set a timer and begin to check for visual doneness cues at least 2 to 3 minutes before the end of the indicated baking time; this is particularly crucial the first time you prepare a recipe. Remember that cookies continue to bake a bit after removal from the oven; underbaking is preferable to overbaking.

When baking multiple batches of cookies, always allow the sheets to cool to room temperature before reusing.

Cooling: Follow specific recipe directions for cooling. Some cookies are removed immediately to wire racks to cool, others are allowed to cool for a minute or two on the sheet first to facilitate removal. Place cookies on the racks so that they aren't touching. Bar cookies are usually cooled in the pan on a rack.

Dusting: When recipes call for dusting with confectioners' sugar, strain the sugar directly onto the cookies through a small, fine-mesh sieve.

Storing: Let's face it, homemade cookies are best fresh. The fresh, home-baked flavor and the absence of all sorts of chemical preservatives are the primary reasons for making them in the first place. Longevity varies by type of cookie (technically, most will keep for weeks if properly stored), but prime flavor and freshness usually last from 3 days to a week.

Most cookies are best stored in cookie jars or cookie tins. Airtight plastic storage bags are not recommended except for short intervals. Very moist cookies (those that contain butter and fruit purees) should never be stored in tightly sealed tins or plastic bags.

Store your crisp cookies and your soft and chewy cookies separately so as not to compromise the texture and taste of either one. Bar cookies are best left uncut in the tin and covered with aluminum foil.

Many cookies can be frozen. Wrap them in aluminum foil and pack in airtight plastic containers with as little headroom as possible, or in heavy-duty plastic storage bags with excess air removed. Thaw in the container (closed) at room temperature for 30 minutes to 1 hour.

Shipping: Most cookies can be shipped, with the obvious exception of very delicate cookies that are likely to crumble in transit and those that need to be kept in the refrigerator.

Pack each type of cookie separately (don't board your vanilla wafers with your brownies or your sandwich cookies) in an individual container, be it a tin, a sturdy plastic storage bag, or the ubiquitous shoe box. Line the bottom and top of the container with crumpled wax paper to keep the cookies from jostling. Put the containers into a sturdy outer box, insulating each on all sides with newspaper, tissue, or Styrofoam pellets.

Filled
Cookies

The filled-cookie category embraces a diverse population—from folksy Amish letter cookies to stylish little linzertortes, from all-American sandwich cookies to such ethnic treats as kolacky and rugalach, from thumbprints holding just a dollop of filling to generously stuffed individual cheesecakes and tarts.

What they have in common is an unfailing ability to surprise and delight with every mouthful; there's always more to savor than first meets the eye.

Filled cookies are prepared in a variety of ways. The doughs for several, including rugalach and kolacky, are rolled and cut prior to filling and assembly. Sandwich cookies and thumbprints are basically drop cookies with an added dimension, while stuffed pillows initially are prepared much like refrigerator cookies. Tartlets, cheese cups, and linzer cookies are miniature renditions of full-scale desserts.

Most filled cookies will remain in their prime for 3 days loosely wrapped with aluminum foil and stored at room temperature, and for 5 days in the refrigerator. Some, such as those with cream cheese fillings, must be refrigerated. They can be frozen for up to 3 months.

Cappuccino-Filled Hazelnut Sandwiches

YIELD = ABOUT 2½ DOZEN SANDWICHES

These elegant little sandwiches pair crisp, nutty cookies with creamy cappuccino filling. For a real treat, serve them with a mug of steaming cappuccino.

DOUGH:
1 cup hazelnuts
½ cup firmly packed light brown sugar
⅔ cup (1⅓ sticks) unsalted butter, at room temperature
2 large egg whites
¾ cup all-purpose flour

FILLING:
3 ounces semisweet chocolate, broken up
1 tablespoon plus 1 teaspoon ground cinnamon
¼ cup (½ stick) unsalted butter, at room temperature

Preheat the oven to 300 degrees.

Butter and lightly flour cookie sheets.

Fit a food processor with the steel blade. With the machine running, add the hazelnuts and brown sugar. Process for about 30 seconds, until the nuts are finely chopped.

In a mixing bowl, cream the butter with an electric mixer at medium speed. Add the nut mixture and continue to beat until well combined, about 1¼ minutes. Add the egg whites and beat for about 45 seconds more, until fluffy. Stir in the flour with a wooden spoon.

Drop the dough onto the prepared cookie sheets by the ½ tablespoonful, leaving about 1½ inches between each one. Lightly flatten with the heel of your hand. Bake for 11 to 12 minutes, until lightly browned.

Remove the cookies from the oven and cool on the sheets for 2 minutes, then transfer them to a wire rack to cool completely.

For the filling, microwave the chocolate in a glass measuring cup at full power for about 2 minutes, until melted, stirring after 1 minute and then after each 30-second interval. Stir until smooth. Whisk in the cinnamon and then the butter. If the butter has not been incorporated into the chocolate after about 1 minute of whisking, heat the mixture in the microwave at full power for 10 seconds.

(You can also make the filling by melting the chocolate in the top of a double boiler over boiling water. Remove the top of the double boiler from the boiling water and whisk in the cinnamon and then the butter.)

Using a pastry bag or a heavy-duty plastic storage bag with a bottom corner snipped off, squeeze about 1 teaspoon of the chocolate mixture onto the flat bottom of each of half the cookies. Spread evenly and top with the remaining cookies, flat side in. Refrigerate for at least 30 minutes, until the filling hardens.

*For Hazelnut Cappuccino Thumbprints,
use about a tablespoonful of batter for each
cookie. Flatten the cookies slightly after dropping
them onto the cookie sheet and make a well in
the center of each with a floured finger.*

*After the cookies have baked, and while they are
still hot, reshape the wells (which may have closed
slightly while baking) with the end of a wooden
spoon. Allow the cookies to cool, then squeeze
the chocolate mixture into the wells,
mounding it slightly.*

YIELD = ABOUT 2¹/₂ DOZEN THUMBPRINTS

Chocolate Rugalach

YIELD = 48 RUGALACH

Rugalach is a Hanukkah treat that can be savored all year. This version is filled with rich and creamy chocolate, along with a bit of tangy apricot as a counterpoint to the sweetness.

Start with very cold butter and cream cheese and mix them with the paddle attachment of a stationary mixer. This will break up and combine the ingredients without generating enough heat to cream them completely. The residual bits of butter and cream cheese in the dough create air pockets while baking, producing an exceptionally flaky crust.

DOUGH:
8 ounces cream cheese, well chilled
1 cup (2 sticks) unsalted butter, well chilled
$\frac{1}{2}$ teaspoon vanilla extract
$\frac{1}{3}$ cup granulated sugar
$2\frac{1}{4}$ cups all-purpose flour

FILLING:
$\frac{1}{2}$ cup plus 1 tablespoon granulated sugar
3 tablespoons firmly packed dark brown sugar
$\frac{1}{4}$ cup plus 2 tablespoons apricot spreadable fruit
$\frac{3}{4}$ cup miniature semisweet chocolate chips

ASSEMBLY:
$\frac{1}{4}$ cup plus 2 tablespoons milk
1 tablespoon granulated sugar mixed with $\frac{3}{4}$ teaspoon ground cinnamon

To make the dough, combine the cream cheese and butter in the bowl of a stationary electric mixer fitted with the paddle attachment. At low speed, mix until smooth, but still dotted with bits of butter and cream cheese. Mix in the vanilla and sugar. Add the flour and continue to mix just until incorporated.

Gather the dough into a ball. Wrap the ball in wax paper and refrigerate for at least 4 hours.

Preheat the oven to 350 degrees.

Lightly grease cookie sheets with butter.

Mix the sugars for the filling in a small bowl and set aside.

Unwrap the dough and cut it into 6 equal pieces. On a lightly floured surface, roll out 1 piece, shaping it into a 12-by-4-inch rectangle. Coat with 1 tablespoon of the spreadable fruit. Sprinkle 2 tablespoons of the sugar mixture and 2 tablespoons chocolate chips on top. Starting with a long end, roll up into a log. Paint the log with 1 tablespoon milk. Dust liberally with the sugar and cinnamon mixture. Cut into 8 pieces.

Repeat the process for each of the 5 remaining pieces of dough. Place the rugalach on the prepared cookie sheets and bake for about 15 minutes, until lightly browned.

Remove the rugalach to a wire rack to cool.

For a more traditional Raisin Nut Rugalach, substitute $\frac{3}{4}$ cup golden raisins and $\frac{3}{4}$ cup chopped walnuts for the chocolate chips.

4 ounces semisweet chocolate, broken up
$^3/_4$ cup creamy peanut butter
$^1/_4$ cup ($^1/_2$ stick) unsalted butter, at room temperature
$^1/_2$ cup confectioners' sugar
$^3/_4$ teaspoon vanilla extract

Microwave the chocolate in a glass measuring cup at full power for about 2 minutes, stirring every 30 seconds, or melt it in the top of a double boiler over boiling water.

Using a small brush, paint the inside of twenty-four 1-inch foil cups with the melted chocolate, taking care to coat the inner surface completely. Refrigerate for at least 20 minutes, until the chocolate has hardened.

Combine the peanut butter, butter, sugar, and vanilla in a mixing bowl. Cream and mix thoroughly by hand, using a wooden spoon. Fill each cup with 2 teaspoons of the mixture. Refrigerate until the filling sets, about 30 minutes. Peel off the foil cups before serving.

Judy's No-Bake Chocolate and Peanut Butter Cups

YIELD = 24 CUPS

These intensely flavorful morsels are a favorite of our editor, Judy Kern. We debated at length as to whether they're really a cookie or a candy—but Judy said skip the philosophical discussion and just whip up another batch!

Chocolate Currant Crescents

YIELD = ABOUT
2 1/2 DOZEN CRESCENTS

Native New Yorkers will recognize elements of two local sweets in this concoction, one of Barry's favorites. The dough brings to mind the chocolate frozen pastries that used to be a favorite in Big Apple bakeries. We achieve the flakiness by adding a little yeast instead of freezing, and we put the chocolate in the filling, which tastes a bit like the ever popular babka.

DOUGH:

1 cup (2 sticks) unsalted butter, at room temperature, cut into 16 tablespoons
3 ounces cream cheese, at room temperature
1/4 teaspoon salt
2 teaspoons granulated sugar
3 cups all-purpose flour
1/4 ounce (1 packet) quick-rise yeast
3 large egg yolks
1 cup sour cream

FILLING:

4 ounces semisweet chocolate, broken up
1/2 cup currants

1 cup granulated sugar

For the dough, combine the butter, cream cheese, and salt in a large mixing bowl. Add the sugar and flour and sprinkle the yeast on top. Beat with an electric mixer at medium speed for about 5 minutes. (The mixture should be crumbly, but without any large pieces of butter intact.)

In a separate bowl, combine the egg yolks and sour cream. Whisk until well blended. Add to the mixture in the large bowl and stir with a wooden spoon until thoroughly incorporated.

Transfer the dough to a sheet of wax paper. Form it into a ball, wrap it in the wax paper, and refrigerate for at least 4 hours. (The dough can remain in the refrigerator overnight.)

Preheat the oven to 350 degrees.

For the filling, in a food processor fitted with the steel blade, process the chocolate until finely chopped. Transfer to a bowl and mix in the currants. Set aside.

Sprinkle 1/4 cup of the sugar onto a work surface.

Divide the dough into quarters. Place a quarter onto the sugar on the work surface. Roll it out to a 1/8-inch-thick circle about 12 inches in diameter. Sprinkle about 1/2 tablespoon of the chocolate and currant filling on top. Using a sharp knife, cut the circle into 8 equal wedges.

Starting at the wide end, roll each wedge up toward the point.

Twist them into semicircles and place them on ungreased cookie sheets.

Repeat the process for the 3 remaining quarters of dough, sprinkling another $1/4$ cup of sugar onto the work surface before rolling out each piece.

Bake for 15 to 16 minutes, until golden.

Remove the cookies to wire racks immediately to cool.

*For Sugar 'n' Cinnamon Crescents,
replace the chocolate in the filling with
1 cup finely chopped walnuts and
1 tablespoon ground cinnamon.*

Viennese Raspberry Sandwiches

YIELD = ABOUT
2 1/4 DOZEN COOKIES

Delicate fruit filling encased in hearty hazelnut fingers. For a special treat, we like to dip them in luscious dark chocolate!

1 cup hazelnuts
1³/₄ cups all-purpose flour
¹/₂ teaspoon baking powder
¹/₈ teaspoon salt
¹/₂ cup firmly packed light brown sugar
³/₄ cup (1¹/₂ sticks) unsalted butter, well chilled,
   cut into 24 pieces
1 large egg
2 teaspoons vanilla extract
1 teaspoon finely grated orange zest
2¹/₂ tablespoons seedless raspberry spreadable fruit or
   homemade Raspberry Jam (page 53)
¹/₂ tablespoon confectioners' sugar

Preheat the oven to 350 degrees.

Grease cookie sheets with butter.

Combine the nuts and ¹/₄ cup of the flour in the bowl of a food processor fitted with the steel blade. Process for about 30 seconds, until the nuts are ground but not yet powdery. Add the baking powder, salt, brown sugar, and the remaining 1¹/₂ cups flour. Process for about 10 seconds, just to combine. Scatter the butter on top and process until crumbly, about 15 seconds.

In a small bowl, combine the egg, vanilla, and orange zest. Beat lightly.

Turn on the food processor and add the egg mixture through the feed tube. The dough should start to stick to the sides of the bowl within a few seconds. Transfer it to a mixing bowl and work in any loose scraps.

Using a tablespoonful of dough for each, shape into fingers 2 inches long and ¹/₂ inch wide on the prepared cookie sheets, leaving about 1 inch between cookies. (You can also squeeze the dough onto the sheets from a heavy-duty plastic storage bag with a bottom corner snipped or from a pastry bag.)

Bake for 10 to 11 minutes, just until lightly browned.

Cool on the sheets for 1 minute. Flip half the cookies over and spread ¹/₄ teaspoon of the raspberry filling on the flat bottom of each. Top with a second cookie, flat side down. Transfer to a wire rack. Cool completely, then dust with confectioners' sugar.

To chocolate-dip the sandwiches, put 2 ounces semisweet chocolate, broken up, into a glass measuring cup. Microwave at full power for 1 minute and stir. Return to the microwave and heat for 20 seconds more. Stir until the chocolate is completely melted and smooth. (You can also melt the chocolate in the top of a double boiler over boiling water.)

Hold each cookie by a short end and submerge it up to halfway in the chocolate. Place the cookies onto a flat sheet or tray lined with a lightly greased piece of wax paper. Refrigerate until the chocolate hardens, about 30 minutes.

Apricot-Filled Chocolate Thumbprints

YIELD = ABOUT
2 $^1/_2$ DOZEN THUMBPRINTS

This stylish cookie is flecked with bits of grated chocolate. With a little supervision, the kids can help by making the thumbprints in the dough after it has been dropped.

$^1/_2$ cup (1 stick) unsalted butter, at room temperature
$^1/_2$ cup firmly packed light brown sugar
1 teaspoon vanilla extract
2 tablespoons milk
$^1/_4$ teaspoon salt
$^1/_3$ cup grated semisweet chocolate (about 2 ounces)
1$^1/_4$ cups all-purpose flour
1 tablespoon plus $^1/_2$ teaspoon confectioners' sugar
$^1/_4$ cup plus 1 tablespoon apricot spreadable fruit

Preheat the oven to 375 degrees.

In a large mixing bowl, combine the butter and brown sugar. Cream with an electric mixer at medium speed. Add the vanilla, milk, and salt and beat to incorporate. Stir in the chocolate and flour with a wooden spoon.

Drop the dough by the tablespoonful onto ungreased cookie sheets, leaving about 1$^1/_2$ inches between cookies. Flatten each lightly with the heel of your hand and make a thumbprint in the center. Bake for 10 minutes.

Remove the cookies from the oven. Reshape the wells with the end of a wooden spoon if they have closed at all while baking. Dust the cookies with confectioners' sugar while still warm. Fill the well of each thumbprint with $^1/_2$ teaspoon of the spreadable fruit. Bake for 4 minutes more.

Cool on the cookie sheets on wire racks.

We make Chocolate Cherry Thumbprints
for festive occasions.

15 glacé cherries, cut in half
3 tablespoons red currant jelly

Prepare as you would Apricot-Filled
Chocolate Thumbprints, but bake with the
wells unfilled. After the thumbprints have
cooled, put a half cherry, cut side down, into
each well.

Heat the jelly in a small saucepan over low
heat for a few seconds, stirring constantly,
until melted. Spoon a generous $^1/_4$ teaspoon
over the cherry in each well. Allow to cool
completely.

Caramel Meringue-Filled Oatmeal Sandwich Cookies

YIELD = ABOUT 3 DOZEN
SANDWICH COOKIES

We fill these thick oatmeal cookies with an unusual caramel meringue, which is frothier than the dense maple buttercream typically used, and more flavorful than plain meringue. When assembled, they're quite a tasty mouthful.

DOUGH:
2 cups all-purpose flour
2 cups rolled oats
2 teaspoons baking soda
1 teaspoon baking powder
$^1/_2$ teaspoon salt
1 teaspoon ground cinnamon
$^3/_4$ cup (1$^1/_2$ sticks) unsalted butter, at room temperature
1 cup firmly packed dark brown sugar
1 cup granulated sugar
2 large eggs
1 teaspoon vanilla extract

FILLING:
1 large egg white
$^1/_4$ cup firmly packed light brown sugar
$^1/_4$ cup granulated sugar
2 tablespoons water
1 tablespoon dark molasses
$^1/_8$ teaspoon cream of tartar
$^1/_2$ teaspoon light rum

Preheat the oven to 350 degrees.

Lightly coat cookie sheets with vegetable oil cooking spray.

Combine the flour, oats, baking soda, baking powder, salt, and cinnamon in a bowl. Whisk and set aside.

In a large mixing bowl, cream the butter and sugars with an electric mixer set at medium speed. Beat in the eggs, one at a time. Beat in the vanilla. Add the flour mixture and stir with a wooden spoon until incorporated.

Drop the dough by the heaping tablespoonful onto the prepared cookie sheets, about 2 inches apart. Bake for 8 to 9 minutes, until the cookies turn light golden.

Remove from the oven and cool the cookies on the sheets for 2 minutes, then transfer to wire racks to cool completely.

For the filling, bring water to a simmer over low heat in the bottom of a double boiler.

Meanwhile, combine the egg white, sugars, water, molasses, and cream of tartar in the detached top of the double boiler. Whisk to blend. Fit the top of the double boiler over the simmering water, making sure that the water doesn't touch the underside. Cook, whisking constantly, until the mixture reaches a temperature of 140 degrees on an instant-read thermometer.

Remove the top of the double boiler from the heat and begin to beat immediately with an electric mixer at medium speed. Continue to mix for about 4 minutes, until light and thick. Add the rum. Increase the speed to high and beat until stiff peaks form, 3 to 4 minutes.

Spread about 2$\frac{1}{2}$ teaspoons of the filling on the flat bottom of a cooled cookie and top with a second cookie, flat side in, to make a sandwich. Repeat the process until all the cookies have been filled.

Blackberry Tarts

YIELD = ABOUT
5 1/2 DOZEN COOKIES

The blackberry filling provides a nice contrast to the plain, intensely buttery dough in these cookies, which resemble miniature tarts.

1 1/4 cups granulated sugar
1 cup whole wheat flour
2 cups all-purpose flour
1/4 teaspoon salt
3/4 cup (1 1/2 sticks) unsalted butter, cold, cut into 24 pieces
1 large egg
1 teaspoon vanilla extract
1/3 cup seedless blackberry spreadable fruit

Process the sugar in a food processor fitted with the steel blade for 1 minute, to superfine consistency. Add the whole wheat flour and process for 30 seconds. Add the all-purpose flour and salt. Process for an additional 15 to 20 seconds. Scatter the butter on top and process just until crumbly.

Combine the egg and vanilla in a small bowl. Beat lightly and pour over the mixture in the bowl of the food processor. Process for about 30 seconds to form a dough.

Turn out onto a sheet of wax paper on a work surface. Work any loose flour into the dough and form it into a ball. Wrap it in the wax paper and refrigerate for at least 2 hours.

Preheat the oven to 350 degrees.

Lightly coat cookie sheets with vegetable oil cooking spray.

Remove the dough from the refrigerator and let it warm to room temperature for about 5 minutes.

Roll the dough into balls by the tablespoonful and place them about 2 inches apart on the prepared cookie sheets. With the end of a wooden spoon (or a pinkie finger), make a deep well in the center of each ball, taking care not to crack the dough. Gently flatten a bit. Put about 1/4 teaspoon of the blackberry filling in each well.

Bake for 14 to 15 minutes, until the cookies are golden around the edges.

Remove from the oven and cool on the sheets for 3 minutes, then transfer the cookies to wire racks to finish cooling.

For Strawberry Tarts or Raspberry Tarts, use an equal amount of strawberry or seedless raspberry spreadable fruit in lieu of the blackberry filling.

½ cup (1 stick) unsalted butter, at room temperature
½ cup firmly packed light brown sugar
¾ cup plus 1 tablespoon apple butter
¼ cup honey
1½ cups all-purpose flour
½ teaspoon baking powder
¼ teaspoon baking soda
¼ teaspoon salt

Cream the butter in a large mixing bowl with an electric mixer at medium speed. Add the brown sugar and ½ cup of the apple butter. Mix thoroughly at low speed. Mix in the honey.

Combine and sift in the dry ingredients, and work into a dough by hand. With a rubber spatula, scrape the dough onto a work surface lined with a sheet of wax paper. Wrap the dough in the wax paper, shaping it into a 7½-by-3¼-inch block about 1¼ inches high. Freeze for 2 hours.

Preheat the oven to 350 degrees.

Cut the dough into ¼-inch-thick slices with a very sharp, lightly floured knife. Place half the slices on ungreased cookie sheets, at least 2 inches apart. If they split while arranging, just work the dough back together.

Spread about 1 teaspoon of the remaining apple butter on each cookie, leaving a thin border. Top each with a second cookie. Crimp the edges of the top and bottom cookies together all around with the tines of a fork to seal. Don't worry if the cookies crack a bit on top.

Bake for about 15 minutes, until lightly browned and firm to the touch.

Cool on the sheets for 5 minutes, then transfer the cookies to wire racks and cool completely.

Apple Honey Pillows

YIELD = ABOUT 1¼ DOZEN PILLOWS

Leave sufficient space between these goodies when you arrange them on the cookie sheets because they blow up into big fluffy pillows while baking. They make a cushy resting place for any sweet tooth in search of solace.

Cocoa Almond Medallions

YIELD = ABOUT
1 3/4 DOZEN MEDALLIONS

Think of a rich, dark chocolate sand dollar with a creamy nut filling. Pack a treasure chest full for your next picnic at the beach! The almond butter can be found in natural or health foods stores, as well as better supermarkets.

1½ cups all-purpose flour
½ teaspoon baking soda
¼ teaspoon salt
¼ cup unsweetened Dutch-processed cocoa powder
½ cup (1 stick) unsalted butter, at room temperature
½ cup plus 7 tablespoons almond butter
½ cup firmly packed light brown sugar
¼ cup light corn syrup
1 tablespoon skim milk

Sift the flour, baking soda, salt, and cocoa powder together into a bowl and set aside.

Combine the butter and ½ cup of the almond butter in a large mixing bowl. Beat with an electric mixer at medium speed for 30 seconds. Scrape down the sides of the bowl.

Add the brown sugar and corn syrup. Mix at low speed until light and fluffy, about 1 minute. Beat in the skim milk. Add the sifted dry ingredients ½ cup at a time, beating after each addition until the mixture is combined and smooth. Turn the dough out onto wax paper, form it into a log, and wrap it in the wax paper. Refrigerate for 4 hours.

Preheat the oven to 350 degrees.

Line cookie sheets with baker's parchment.

Remove the dough from the refrigerator to a floured work surface and cut it into quarters. Roll a quarter out to a ⅛-inch-thick circle about 13 inches in diameter, rewrapping and refrigerating the remaining quarters until ready to use. Cut out cookies with a 3-inch circular cutter and place them on the prepared cookie sheets. Gather and roll out the scraps of dough for additional cookies. Mound 1 teaspoon of almond butter in the center of each circle.

Roll out and cut another quarter of dough. Place a second 3-inch circular cookie on top of each mound of almond butter and crimp the top and bottom cookies together with the tines of a fork to seal. Repeat the process with the remaining pieces of dough.

Bake for about 13 minutes, just until the cookies are beginning to crack on top.

Cool on the sheets for 2 minutes, then remove the cookies to wire racks to finish cooling.

For Cocoa Peanut Medallions or Cocoa Cashew Medallions, substitute an equal amount of peanut butter (the freshly made natural variety, of course) or cashew butter for the almond butter.

Almond-Filled Strips

YIELD = 42 STRIPS

In this variation on an old-time Amish recipe, we substitute an equally light but much simpler dough for the handmade puff pastry originally called for. The delicate almond filling hints of marzipan, but with none of the cloying sweetness of marzipan confections.

DOUGH:
4 cups all-purpose flour
$\frac{1}{4}$ ounce (1 packet) quick-rise yeast
$\frac{1}{4}$ cup granulated sugar
$\frac{1}{4}$ teaspoon salt
8 ounces cream cheese, at room temperature
1 cup (2 sticks) unsalted butter, at room temperature
1 large egg
1 cup milk
1 teaspoon almond extract

FILLING:
7 ounces almond paste
1 tablespoon freshly squeezed orange juice

TOPPING:
2 teaspoons granulated sugar

Combine the flour, yeast, sugar, and salt in a bowl. Whisk and set aside.

In a large mixing bowl, combine the cream cheese and butter. Cream with the back of a wooden spoon. Add the egg, milk, and almond extract. Stir to combine. (Some lumps of butter and cream cheese will remain intact.) Dump in the flour mixture and mix with the wooden spoon to form a dough.

Turn the dough out onto a large sheet of plastic wrap spread on a work surface. Knead in any loose scraps. Flatten the dough and work it into a rectangle about 6 by 10 inches. Fold in the edges of the plastic wrap to cover the dough and refrigerate for 30 minutes.

To prepare the filling, combine the almond paste and orange juice in a bowl. Mix until smooth and spreadable.

Remove the dough from the refrigerator. Unwrap it and transfer it to a lightly floured sheet of wax paper. Roll the rectangle out to 12 by 21 inches. Spread the filling lengthwise over half of the dough. Fold the other half over to encase the filling and press lightly along the seam to seal. Leaving the filled dough on the wax paper, refrigerate for 30 minutes more.

Preheat the oven to 400 degrees.

Lightly coat cookie sheets with vegetable oil cooking spray.

Cut the dough in half lengthwise. Cut each half crosswise into 1-inch strips and place them on the prepared cookie sheets. With a sharp knife, make a diagonal slash from corner to corner on the top of each strip.

Bake for 16 to 18 minutes, until golden.

Dust the cookies immediately with granulated sugar and transfer them to wire racks to cool.

To make Amish Letter Cookies, a personal touch sure to delight your guests, spread the filling over the entire 12-by-21-inch rectangle. (Do not fold the dough in half over the filling.)

After the second refrigeration, cut crosswise into 1-inch strips. Roll each strip up into a 12-inch-long rope and form into the shape of a letter before baking.

YIELD = 21 LETTER COOKIES

Orange Marmalade Triangles

YIELD = 25 TRIANGLES

Little golden triangles puffed up to perfection and prettily adorned with a sugary sheen. Look for the coarse-grained, raw turbinado sugar shelved with the natural or health foods.

1 cup (2 sticks) unsalted butter, at room temperature
$2/3$ cup granulated sugar
2 large eggs, separated
1 tablespoon vanilla extract
$2\frac{1}{2}$ cups all-purpose flour
$1/4$ teaspoon salt
$1/2$ cup plus 1 teaspoon orange marmalade
1 tablespoon water
2 tablespoons turbinado sugar

Cream the butter and sugar in a large bowl, using an electric mixer at low speed. Add the egg yolks. Beat in the vanilla. Add the flour and salt and beat until incorporated.

Gather the dough into a ball, working in any loose scraps. Wrap it in wax paper and refrigerate for 1 hour.

Preheat the oven to 350 degrees.

Coat cookie sheets with vegetable oil cooking spray and flour lightly.

Remove the dough to a well-floured work surface, turning it to coat with flour on all sides. Roll out with a floured rolling pin into a 15-inch square, adding flour to the dough and the pin as needed to prevent sticking. With a pastry or ravioli cutting wheel (preferably fluted) cut into twenty-five 3-inch squares.

Lift each square with a flat spatula and flip it onto the palm of your other hand (holding the cookie while filling and assembling will keep it from sticking to the work surface). Mound 1 teaspoon of the marmalade on a corner and fold the opposite corner over the filling to form a triangle. Crimp the edges together to seal and place on a prepared cookie sheet. Don't worry if the cookies crack a bit in the process.

Prick the tops with the tines of a fork and paint lightly with a mixture of the egg whites and 1 tablespoon water. Sprinkle the cookies with the turbinado sugar.

Bake for about 15 minutes, until golden brown. Remove the cookies to wire racks to cool.

PASTRY:
1½ cups all-purpose flour
2 tablespoons granulated sugar
½ teaspoon salt
¾ cup (1½ sticks) unsalted butter, cold, cut into 24 pieces

FILLING:
1 large egg
1 teaspoon vanilla extract
1 cup firmly packed dark brown sugar
½ cup granulated sugar
1 cup chopped pecans
1 cup semisweet chocolate chips

Preheat the oven to 375 degrees.

Lightly coat a 24-well mini muffin tin (¼-cup wells) with vegetable oil cooking spray.

To make the dough, combine the flour, sugar, and salt in the bowl of a food processor fitted with the steel blade. Process for about 30 seconds to mix. Scatter the butter on top and process for 15 to 20 seconds, until crumbly.

Put 2 tablespoons of the dough in each well of the prepared tin. Press and work it over the bottom and sides of the wells. Refrigerate for 10 minutes.

For the filling, combine the egg, vanilla, and sugars in a small bowl. Whisk until well blended. Stir in the pecans and chocolate chips. Fill each well with 2 tablespoons of the mixture.

Bake for about 15 minutes, until the crust is golden and the filling browned.

Transfer the tin to a wire rack and allow the tartlets to cool for 30 minutes. Remove from the wells gently.

Chocolate Pecan Tartlets

YIELD = 24 TARTLETS

Pecan pie is a joy, but it's so rich one can seldom eat a whole slice. We've solved the problem with these rich little tarts, so perfectly proportioned we even throw in a bit of chocolate to boot. If you desire, serve them à la mode.

Individual Chocolate Chip Cheesecakes

YIELD = 24 CUPS

Overstuffed and overflowing their pastry shells, these treats will grace a dessert board or enliven a lunch box.

BASE:
2 cups all-purpose flour
½ cup confectioners' sugar
½ teaspoon baking powder
¼ teaspoon salt
¾ cup (1½ sticks) unsalted butter, melted

FILLING:
8 ounces cream cheese, at room temperature
¾ cup granulated sugar
1 large egg
1 cup sour cream
¼ cup all-purpose flour
½ cup semisweet mini chocolate chips

Preheat the oven to 325 degrees.

Lightly coat a 24-well mini muffin tin (¼-cup wells) with vegetable oil cooking spray.

Put the flour, confectioners' sugar, baking powder, salt, and melted butter in a bowl and combine thoroughly with a fork. Line the bottom and sides of each well of the prepared tin with a heaping tablespoon of the mixture.

Bake for about 20 minutes, until just beginning to brown.

Remove the tin from the oven and set it aside, leaving the oven on.

For the filling, combine the cream cheese, granulated sugar, and egg in a bowl. Cream with an electric mixer at medium speed. Beat in the sour cream and flour. Stir in the chocolate chips.

Put a heaping 2 tablespoons of the mixture into each well of the prepared tin. Bake for about 20 minutes, until the filling has puffed up.

Cool in the tin for 1 hour. Refrigerate for at least 3 hours, then run a knife around the inside of the wells and gently remove the cups.

BASE:
2 cups quick oats
¼ cup plus 2 tablespoons firmly packed dark brown sugar
¼ cup all-purpose flour
⅓ cup (⅔ stick) unsalted butter, melted

FILLING:
8 ounces cream cheese, at room temperature
¾ cup granulated sugar
1 large egg
2 teaspoons grated orange zest
1 tablespoon orange liqueur
1 teaspoon vanilla extract

Preheat the oven to 325 degrees.

Lightly coat a 24-well mini muffin tin (¼-cup wells) with vegetable oil cooking spray.

Combine the oats, brown sugar, flour, and butter in a bowl. Mix thoroughly with a fork.

Put 2 tablespoons of the mixture into each well of the prepared tin and press and shape to cover the bottom and sides. Bake for about 15 minutes, just until the cups are beginning to look toasty.

Remove the tin from the oven and set it aside, leaving the oven on.

For the filling, combine the cream cheese and granulated sugar in a mixing bowl. Cream with an electric mixer at medium speed. Beat in the egg. Add the orange zest, liqueur, and vanilla. Beat to incorporate.

Put 4 teaspoons of the mixture into each oat cup. Bake for about 20 minutes, until puffy.

Cool the cups in the tin for 1 hour, then refrigerate for at least 3 hours. Run a knife around each well before gently prying out the cups.

Orange Cheese Cups

YIELD = 24 CUPS

Silky bite-size cheesecakes with a refreshing citrus accent, these make a perfect end to a spicy meal. Take care not to crack the delicate oat crust when dislodging them from the tin.

Apricot Linzer Cookies

This exceedingly pretty little sandwich cookie can be made even more festive if you use decoratively shaped miniature cookie cutters to form the hole in the top layer through which the filling mounds.

The cookies soften with age (and the almond taste of the dough becomes stronger) when stored in an airtight tin. If you prefer to keep them crisp, cover loosely with aluminum foil.

3/4 cup blanched, slivered almonds
1 3/4 cups all-purpose flour
1/3 cup granulated sugar
1/4 cup firmly packed light brown sugar
1/8 teaspoon ground allspice
1/4 teaspoon baking powder
1/8 teaspoon salt
1 teaspoon grated orange zest
3/4 cup (1 1/2 sticks) unsalted butter, cold, cut into 12 pieces
1 large egg
1 teaspoon vanilla extract
1 1/2 tablespoons confectioners' sugar
3/4 cup plus 1 tablespoon spreadable apricot fruit

Combine the almonds and flour in the bowl of a food processor fitted with the steel blade. Process until the almonds are finely ground, about 2 minutes. Add the sugars, allspice, baking powder, salt, and orange zest. Process for 1 minute. Scatter the butter over the mixture and process for about 1 minute more, until crumbly.

Lightly beat the egg and vanilla in a small bowl. Add to the mixture in the food processor and process for 30 to 45 seconds to form a dough.

Turn the dough out onto a sheet of plastic wrap. Form it into a ball, wrap it in the plastic, and refrigerate for 1 hour.

Preheat the oven to 350 degrees.

Lightly grease cookie sheets with butter.

Line a work surface with lightly floured wax paper.

Cut the dough into 4 equal pieces. Re-cover 3 pieces and return them to the refrigerator until ready to use. Put the remaining quarter on the prepared work surface and top with a second sheet of wax paper. Roll the dough out to a thickness of 1/8 inch. Peel off the top sheet.

Cut circles with a 2-inch-round cookie cutter, but do not lift the circles out. Using the bottom of a pastry tip, a thimble, or another small round guide, cut small holes (about 1/2 inch) in the center of half of the circles. (Again, do not lift any dough out at this time.) Refrigerate the dough on the wax paper.

Repeat the process until all 4 pieces of dough have been rolled and cut and the last quarter prepared has chilled for at least 10 minutes.

Remove and discard the dough within the small inner circles and the excess dough between the large circles. Place the cookies on the prepared cookie sheets.

Bake for about 10 minutes, until lightly browned around the edges.

Remove from the oven and cool on the sheets for 1 minute. Transfer the cookies with the holes (the top layers) to wire racks. Leave the whole cookies (the bottom layers) on the sheets for 1 minute more, then remove them to wire racks. Dust the top layers with confectioners' sugar. Allow all the cookies to cool a few minutes more.

Spread each bottom layer with about 1 teaspoon of the apricot filling. Place the tops over the filling, dusted side up.

For variety, we top the cookies with chopped almonds instead of confectioners' sugar.

Finely chop ¹/₄ cup slivered, blanched almonds. Before baking, lightly brush the top layers with water and sprinkle about ¹/₂ teaspoon of the nuts on each.

Marie Novosad's Poppyseed Kolacky

YIELD = ABOUT
6 DOZEN KOLACKY

This delightful filled pastry is based on a recipe of the late Marie Novosad, who was a tireless baker. To family and friends, Marie's kolacky were as much a part of every special occasion as the candles on the birthday cake or the Christmas stockings on the fireplace.

PASTRY:
8 ounces cream cheese, at room temperature
1 cup (2 sticks) unsalted butter, at room temperature
3 large egg yolks
2 tablespoons granulated sugar
2 cups all-purpose flour
1 teaspoon baking powder

FILLING:
3/4 cup poppyseed filling (commercially prepared, or see page 223)

TOPPING:
1/4 cup confectioners' sugar

In a large mixing bowl, cream the cream cheese with an electric mixer at medium speed. Add the butter and mix until well blended. One at a time, beat in the egg yolks. Beat in the sugar. Add the flour and baking powder. Mix at low speed until incorporated.

Scrape the dough onto a sheet of wax paper and gather it into a ball. Wrap the ball in the wax paper and refrigerate overnight.

Preheat the oven to 350 degrees.

Allow the dough to warm to room temperature for about 5 minutes.

Cut the dough into quarters. Put 1 quarter on a lightly floured work surface. (Rewrap the remaining pieces in the wax paper to prevent drying out.) Turn the dough in the flour to coat and roll it out to a 1/8-inch-thick rectangle about 10 by 12 inches. Cut out 2 1/2-inch circles. Gather the scraps of dough, roll it out again, and cut out additional circles.

Place 1/2 teaspoon of the poppyseed filling in a thin strip down the center of a circle. Moisten one of the borders parallel to the strip of filling with water. Fold the unmoistened side over the filling and fold up the moistened side to overlap. Secure the kolacky closed by gently inserting half a toothpick into the top. Repeat until all the kolacky are assembled.

Bake on ungreased cookie sheets for about 20 minutes, until browned.

Transfer the kolacky to wire racks and cool for 5 minutes. Carefully remove the toothpicks and dust the kolacky with confectioners' sugar.

For years, Kevin's sister-in-law, Mary Ann, and her siblings tried to duplicate their mother's always perfect kolacky. All too often, some of the carefully formed pastries would burst open in the oven and spill out their filling. (The same thing happened to us on our first try.) When quizzed on her technique, Marie finally revealed to them the seemingly obvious detail omitted in her recipe— toothpicks inserted gently into the kolacky to keep the dough intact while baking.

Raspberry Kolacky

YIELD = ABOUT
6 DOZEN KOLACKY

In this rendition of the popular Eastern European pastry, we fold the dough up over the delicate fruit filling to form a fluffy pillow.

PASTRY:
6 ounces cream cheese, well chilled
1 cup (2 sticks) unsalted butter, well chilled
1 large egg, plus an additional egg yolk
1 tablespoon granulated sugar
1³/₄ cups all-purpose flour
1 teaspoon baking powder

FILLING:
1¹/₂ cups seedless raspberry spreadable fruit

TOPPING:
¹/₄ cup confectioners' sugar

In the bowl of a stationary electric mixer fitted with the paddle attachment, combine the cream cheese and butter. Mix at low speed until smooth, but still dotted with bits of cream cheese and butter. Mix in the egg and egg yolk. Mix in the sugar. Add the flour and baking powder and continue to mix at low speed just until incorporated.

Scrape the dough onto a sheet of wax paper and gather it into a ball. Wrap the ball in the wax paper and refrigerate it overnight.

Preheat the oven to 350 degrees.

Cut the dough into quarters. Put 1 quarter on a lightly floured work surface. (Rewrap the remaining pieces in the wax paper to prevent drying out.) Turn the dough in the flour to coat, and roll it out to a ¹/₈-inch-thick rectangle about 10 by 12 inches. Cut out 2¹/₂-inch circles. Gather the scraps of dough, roll it out again, and cut out additional circles.

Mound 1 teaspoon of the raspberry filling in the center of each circle. Moisten the outer border with water. Fold opposite sides of the circle up over the filling, overlapping them slightly. Repeat with the remaining 2 sides. To secure the kolacky closed, gently insert half a toothpick into the top. Continue the process until all the kolacky are assembled.

Bake on ungreased cookie sheets for about 20 minutes, until browned.

Transfer the kolacky to wire racks and cool for 5 minutes. Carefully remove the toothpicks and dust the kolacky with confectioners' sugar.

Raspberry Kolacky *are even better when you use homemade Raspberry Jam for the filling.*

12 ounces frozen unsweetened raspberries, thawed
3 cups granulated sugar
$^1/_2$ tablespoon freshly squeezed lemon juice
$^1/_2$ teaspoon grated lemon zest

Combine the raspberries and sugar in a wide, nonreactive pan, such as a Dutch oven. Mash the berries with a potato masher. Bring to a boil over medium heat, stirring with a wooden spoon to dissolve the sugar. Lower the heat and gently boil for 15 minutes, periodically scraping the pan to dislodge the sugar crystals. Stir in the lemon juice and lemon zest. Strain the jam through a sieve, pushing the pulp through with the back of a spoon, to remove the seeds.

YIELD = ABOUT 3 CUPS

Peanut Thumbprints with Chocolate Ganache Filling

YIELD = ABOUT
3 DOZEN THUMBPRINTS

We created these cookies for a friend with a weakness for chocolate and peanut butter creations. She makes giant thumbprints, which allow her to double her pleasure with each cookie consumed.

For about 1½ dozen giant thumbprints, use a tablespoonful of dough for each cookie and bake for 12 to 15 minutes.

½ cup (1 stick) plus 2 tablespoons unsalted butter, at room temperature
½ cup creamy peanut butter
1 large egg
½ teaspoon vanilla extract
⅓ cup firmly packed light brown sugar
1 cup all-purpose flour
¾ cup finely chopped, blanched raw peanuts
4 ounces semisweet chocolate, broken up

Preheat the oven to 350 degrees.

Combine ½ cup of the butter, the peanut butter, and the egg in a food processor fitted with the steel blade. Process until the mixture is blended and smooth. Add the vanilla and brown sugar; process until incorporated. Add the flour and pulse until a dough ball begins to form.

Transfer the dough to a mixing bowl. Using ½ tablespoonful for each, form the dough into balls. Roll the balls in the chopped nuts to coat and place about 1 inch apart on ungreased cookie sheets. With your thumb, create a deep well in the center of each.

Bake for 10 to 12 minutes, until firm and lightly browned.

Transfer the cookies to a wire rack to cool.

Place the chocolate in a glass measuring cup and heat for 45 seconds in a microwave oven at full power. Whisk thoroughly, heat for 20 seconds more, and whisk again. (You can also melt the chocolate in the top of a double boiler over boiling water.) Cool until no longer hot to the touch. Whisk in the remaining 2 tablespoons butter.

Transfer the chocolate mixture to a heavyweight plastic storage bag. Carefully snip off a bottom corner of the bag and squeeze the mixture through the hole to fill the well of each thumbprint. Allow the cookies to sit for about 30 minutes, until the filling is firm.

For Peanut Butter and Jelly Thumbprints, substitute 6 tablespoons strawberry spreadable fruit for the chocolate. Put ½ teaspoon into the well of each cookie before baking.

Shaped, Pressed, and Molded Cookies

Carefully sculpted and dressed to the nines, these are high-style denizens of the cookie world. Most are fashioned from firm, thick doughs that hold their form when baked, with little leavening added.

Shaped cookies include such fanciful hand-formed configurations as crescents, pretzels, and bow ties. The shaping is easier if you work with lightly floured fingers. Pizzelles, made with the aid of a specialized pizzelle iron, can be shaped into old-fashioned ice cream or dessert cones while still hot off the iron.

Biscotti and mandelbrot are shaped into loaves, baked, sliced, and baked once more. Mandelbrot, which contains oil, should have a toasty crust and a slightly pliable center. The drier biscotti ranges from merely crisp, if baked the second time standing upright, to downright brittle—and begging to be dunked—when the slices are toasted on their sides.

Rich spritz cookies are made from a buttery dough that's pressed onto sheets using a cookie press fitted with a decorative disk. For best results, make sure the cookie sheets are at room temperature and position the press perpendicular to the sheet. Know that the first cookie or two out of the press will probably be a bit irregular in shape.

We call for fitting the press with a simple star-shaped disk; if you use a more intricate pattern, refrigerate the cookies on the sheet for about 5 minutes to firm before baking. Spritz dough can also be chilled for an hour, rolled out, and cut into decorative shapes with cookie cutters.

Our molded cookies include madeleines, shortbreads, and springles. Crispy shells with spongy centers, madeleines add an elegant finishing touch to any meal. They're baked in the sculpted molds of madeleine plaques. Be sure to grease the molds well; the cakes should pop right out of inverted plaques onto cooling racks.

Shortbreads and shortbread derivatives can be baked either in cake pans or in decorative ceramic, stoneware, or iron molds. The dough is pressed down firmly into the pan or mold, and often is prescored to facilitate cutting. For this type of cookie, position the racks to divide the oven into thirds and place the pan on the upper rack.

Preparation of springles requires a special decoratively carved rolling pin that scores and molds a pattern onto the dough as it is rolled out. The cookies are then cut out along the scores and transferred to sheets for baking.

Store shaped, pressed, or molded cookies in cookie jars or cookie tins. They're in their prime for 5 days. Dry by nature, this type of cookie does not take well to refrigeration, but can be frozen for up to 3 months. Biscotti and mandelbrot will remain fresh and flavorful for weeks in a jar or tin.

3 cups all-purpose flour
$^{1}/_{2}$ tablespoon baking powder
2 teaspoons ground ginger
$^{1}/_{4}$ teaspoon salt
$^{2}/_{3}$ cup granulated sugar
6 ounces dried pears, diced (about $^{3}/_{4}$ cup)
4 large eggs
$^{1}/_{2}$ tablespoon vanilla extract
$^{1}/_{3}$ cup honey

Preheat the oven to 350 degrees.

Line a 12-by-15-inch baking sheet with baker's parchment.

Sift the flour, baking powder, ginger, salt, and sugar together into a large mixing bowl. Mix in the dried pears and make a well in the center.

Whisk the eggs in a small bowl. Add the vanilla and honey, whisking until well blended. Pour into the well of the flour mixture. Stir with a wooden spoon until the flour is completely incorporated. Set aside for 5 minutes.

Divide the dough in half and form each half on the prepared baking sheet into a $^{3}/_{4}$-inch-high loaf about 10 inches long and 3 inches wide. Bake for about 30 minutes, until golden.

Remove the loaves to a work surface. With a serrated knife, cut into $^{1}/_{2}$-inch-thick diagonal slices. For brittle biscotti, lay the slices on their sides on the baking sheet. Return to the oven and toast for about 10 minutes, until lightly browned. For slightly softer biscotti, stand the slices upright and toast for about 15 minutes.

Remove the biscotti to a wire rack and cool completely.

Ginger Pear Biscotti

YIELD = ABOUT
3 DOZEN BISCOTTI

This highly unique biscotti is redolent of ginger and flecked with dried pear. We like to eat it in the classic manner, dipped in port or another dessert wine.

Take care not to overcook these during the second baking. Remove them from the oven as soon as the cookies are very dry to the touch and slightly crisp; like all biscotti, they will continue to crisp while cooling. For more brittle biscotti, lay the cookies on their sides rather than standing them upright during the second baking.

Chocolate Hazelnut Biscotti

YIELD = ABOUT 2 DOZEN 1-INCH-
THICK BISCOTTI OR 2½ DOZEN
¾-INCH-THICK BISCOTTI

Biscotti are crisp Italian cookies baked in a loaf, sliced, and then baked once more. We think of them as just about the ideal snack—they're filling yet not too sweet, lower in fat than the similarly twice-baked mandelbrot, and they keep for weeks.

Try these for breakfast, alongside or dipped into a steaming mug of robust coffee.

1⅓ cups whole hazelnuts
4 large eggs
⅓ cup firmly packed light brown sugar
1½ tablespoons vanilla extract
2 cups all-purpose flour
½ cup granulated sugar
½ cup unsweetened Dutch-processed cocoa powder
1 teaspoon baking powder
½ teaspoon baking soda
¼ teaspoon salt

Preheat the oven to 375 degrees.

Place the hazelnuts on a baking sheet in a single layer. Toast them in the oven for 10 minutes, shaking the pan after the nuts have cooked for 6 minutes.

Remove the baking sheet and turn the oven down to 350 degrees. Put the nuts on 1 end of a clean, dry dish towel. Fold the other end of the towel over to cover the nuts and allow them to cool for 2 to 3 minutes. Rub off as much of the skin as you easily can and set the nuts aside.

Line 1 large or 2 small baking sheets with baker's parchment (if reusing the sheet on which you toasted the nuts, make sure it has cooled completely).

Combine the eggs, brown sugar, and vanilla in a bowl. Whisk until the sugar has dissolved and the mixture is frothy, about 1 minute.

Sift the flour, granulated sugar, cocoa powder, baking powder, baking soda, and salt together into a large mixing bowl. Whisk in the reserved nuts. Make a well in the center and pour in the egg mixture. Stir with a wooden spoon until the flour is fully incorporated.

Divide the dough in half. With lightly floured hands, form each half into a 10-by-3-inch loaf about ¾ inch high (place 1 loaf on each sheet if using 2 small baking sheets). Bake the loaves for about 30 minutes, until well risen and firm to the touch.

Remove the loaves to a work surface. Using a serrated knife, cut diagonal slices ¾ inch or 1 inch thick, as desired. Stand the slices upright on the baking sheet. Bake for about 15 minutes more, until the biscotti are very dry to the touch and slightly crisp.

Cool on the sheet on wire racks.

*Chocolate Hazelnut Biscotti
are good*—Chocolate-Dipped
Chocolate Hazelnut Biscotti
are even better!

*Line a large baking sheet with wax paper lightly
greased with canola oil, and set aside.*

*Put 6 ounces bittersweet chocolate, broken up, into
a glass pie pan or other wide, shallow, microwave-
safe container. Microwave at full power for up to 3
minutes, stirring after 1 minute and then in 30-
second intervals, until the chocolate is melted and
smooth. (You can also melt the chocolate in the top
of a double boiler over boiling water and then
transfer it to a wide, shallow dish or pan
for dipping.)*

*Grasp each biscotti with the tips of your fingers
and dip lengthwise into the chocolate to coat
1 side. Place chocolate side down on the
prepared baking sheet. Refrigerate
until the chocolate hardens.*

Citrus Mandelbrot

YIELD = 24 MANDELBROT

Mandelbrot, or "almond bread," is a crisp, twice-baked Jewish delicacy.

These cookies are filled with whole almonds and topped with a sugar and cinnamon mixture. Orange and lemon extracts provide a light citrus accent.

3 cups all-purpose flour
1 cup plus 2 tablespoons granulated sugar
1 tablespoon baking powder
3 large eggs
$^3/_4$ teaspoon orange extract (see box)
$^3/_4$ teaspoon lemon extract (see box)
$^1/_2$ tablespoon vanilla extract
$^3/_4$ cup canola oil
$^1/_2$ tablespoon grated lemon zest
1 cup whole almonds

TOPPING:
3 tablespoons granulated sugar
$^3/_4$ teaspoon ground cinnamon

Preheat the oven to 350 degrees.

Lightly coat a cookie sheet with vegetable oil cooking spray.

Combine the flour, sugar, and baking powder in a large mixing bowl. Whisk and set aside.

In another bowl, combine the eggs, extracts, oil, and lemon zest. Whisk thoroughly and add to the flour mixture. Add the almonds and stir the mixture with a wooden spoon to incorporate.

Gather the dough into a ball and cut it into 3 pieces. Transfer the pieces to the prepared cookie sheet and work each piece into a $3^1/_2$-by-7-inch loaf about 1 inch high.

Mix the sugar and cinnamon for the topping. Sprinkle it on the loaves and rub it over the surface to coat. Bake for about 35 minutes, until lightly browned.

Remove the sheet from the oven, leaving the oven on. Transfer the loaves to a cutting board and allow them to cool for 8 minutes. (The loaves will spread a bit while cooling.) Using a serrated bread knife, cut each loaf crosswise into eight 1-inch slices.

Stand each slice upright on the cookie sheet and return to the oven for about 20 minutes, until lightly toasted. Remove the cookies to a wire rack to cool.

Orange Extract and Lemon Extract can be made quite easily by combining chopped zest with vodka and water, steeping the mixture for a few days, and straining out the zest. Use 1 cup vodka and $^1/_2$ cup water for the zest of every 1 navel orange or every 2 lemons. Store in tightly sealed jars. The extracts will keep for up to 1 year.

2 large eggs
1 teaspoon vanilla extract
1 teaspoon almond extract
$^2/_3$ cup granulated sugar
$^1/_2$ cup canola oil
2 cups all-purpose flour
$^1/_2$ tablespoon baking powder
$^1/_4$ teaspoon salt
1 cup golden raisins

Raisin Mandelbrot

YIELD = 24 COOKIES

Sweet, delicate golden raisins add a taste twist to this recipe, which derives the almond flavor characteristic of mandelbrot from pure almond extract.

Preheat the oven to 350 degrees.

Combine the eggs, extracts, sugar, and oil in a mixing bowl. Whisk thoroughly. Add the flour, baking powder, salt, and raisins. Stir with a wooden spoon to incorporate.

Divide the dough in half. With lightly floured hands, transfer the halves to an ungreased cookie sheet and form each piece into a $3^1/_2$-by-7-inch loaf about 1 inch high. Bake for about 30 minutes, until lightly browned.

Remove the sheet from the oven, leaving the oven on. Cool the loaves for 5 minutes on the sheet, then transfer them to a work surface and cool for 2 to 3 minutes more. With a serrated bread knife, cut each of the loaves (which will have expanded a bit while cooling) into twelve $^3/_4$-inch slices.

Lay the slices with a cut side up on the cookie sheet and return them to the oven for 8 to 10 minutes, until lightly toasted. Turn the cookies over and toast the other side for another 8 to 10 minutes.

Transfer the cookies to a wire rack to cool.

For Traditional Mandelbrot, substitute an equal amount of chopped, blanched almonds for the raisins, omit the almond extract, and double the amount of vanilla extract used.

Chocolate "Tuttle" Cookies

YIELD = 36 TURTLES

The butter in the batter for this cookie version of the popular candy seeps onto the nuts while baking and glazes the turtles' feet. We've added a luscious white chocolate icing, which looks a little like tiny white backpacks on the army of turtles moving across a platter. Ever since we sent a regiment to our friend Martha in Brooklyn, her two-year-old son, Ray, screams "tuttles" whenever he spies the cookie jar.

180 pecan halves (about $2^2/_3$ cups)
$^1/_2$ cup (1 stick) plus 1 tablespoon unsalted butter, at room temperature
$^1/_2$ cup firmly packed dark brown sugar
$^1/_4$ cup granulated sugar
1 large egg
1 teaspoon vanilla extract
3 tablespoons unsweetened Dutch-processed cocoa powder
$1^1/_2$ cups all-purpose flour
$^1/_4$ teaspoon baking powder
$^1/_8$ teaspoon salt

ICING:
3 ounces white chocolate, broken up
2 teaspoons unsalted butter

Preheat the oven to 350 degrees.

Lightly grease cookie sheets with butter.

On the sheets, make the bases for 36 turtles. For each, create an "X" using 4 pecan halves. Select a shorter half for the head and position it between 2 ends of the "X."

Combine the butter and sugars in a large mixing bowl. Cream with an electric mixer at high speed. Beat in the egg and vanilla at low speed.

In another bowl, combine the cocoa powder, flour, baking powder, and salt. Whisk together and add to the butter and sugar mixture. Mix thoroughly with a wooden spoon.

Carefully place a level tablespoonful of the dough onto each turtle base, flattening the dough slightly and making sure that the pecan extremities are securely embedded into the dough shells. Bake for 10 minutes.

Remove the cookie sheet to a wire rack and let the turtles cool for at least 20 minutes.

For the icing, combine the white chocolate and butter in a glass measuring cup. Melt in a microwave oven at full power, taking care not to burn it—heat for 30 seconds, stir, heat for another 15 seconds, and stir again; if necessary, heat for an additional 10 seconds. (You can also melt

For Chocolate Cashew "Tuttles," substitute whole roasted cashews for the pecan halves.

the white chocolate and butter in the top of a double boiler over boiling water.) With a rubber spatula, spread $1/2$ teaspoon of the mixture over each turtle. Allow about 20 minutes for the icing to set, then carefully remove the cookies from the sheet with a metal spatula.

Walnut Bow Ties

YIELD = 24 BOW TIES

Stylishly shaped cookies that will dress up any dessert board. In this elegant update of an old standby, we add ground nuts to the dough and bake, rather than fry, the cookies.

¾ cup walnut pieces
2 large eggs
¼ cup packed light brown sugar
¼ cup (½ stick) unsalted butter, melted, then cooled to room temperature
1¼ cups all-purpose flour
½ cup granulated sugar
½ teaspoon ground cinnamon

Preheat the oven to 400 degrees.

Lightly grease cookie sheets with butter.

Finely grind the walnut pieces in a food processor fitted with the steel blade. Set aside.

Combine the eggs and brown sugar in a mixing bowl. Beat for about 2 minutes with an electric mixer at low speed, until all the sugar has dissolved and the mixture is frothy. While continuing to beat at low speed, drizzle in the melted butter.

Add the walnuts and flour and mix well with a wooden spoon. Work into a dough ball. Wrap the ball in wax paper and refrigerate for 10 minutes.

Meanwhile, mix the granulated sugar and cinnamon thoroughly and cover a work surface with the mixture. Put the chilled dough atop the sugar mixture, flatten, and roll it out to a ½-inch-thick rectangle about 12 inches long and 6 inches wide. Cut into twenty-four 1-by-3-inch strips.

Coat both sides of the strips with the sugar and cinnamon mixture. Grab each strip by a short end and twist it once (180 degrees) to form a bow tie. Place on the prepared cookie sheets about 1 inch apart. Sprinkle with the excess sugar mixture from the work surface.

Bake for about 20 minutes, until the bow ties are golden brown and beginning to crack on top.

Transfer the cookies to wire racks to cool.

1 cup hazelnuts
1¾ cups all-purpose flour
1 cup (2 sticks) unsalted butter, at room temperature
2 large eggs
½ teaspoon vanilla extract
½ tablespoon water
3 tablespoons turbinado sugar

Combine the hazelnuts and ¼ cup of the flour in the bowl of a food processor fitted with the steel blade. Process for about 30 seconds, until the nuts are finely ground.

In a large bowl, cream the butter with an electric mixer set at medium speed. Mix in 1 egg, the yolk of the other egg (reserving the white), and the vanilla.

With a wooden spoon, stir in the remaining 1½ cups flour and the ground nuts. Gather the crumbly dough into a ball, wrap it in wax paper, and refrigerate for 1 hour.

Preheat the oven to 375 degrees.

Quarter the dough. Roll out each quarter into an 8-by-4-inch rectangle and cut it lengthwise into eight 1-inch strips. Roll the strips over the work surface to form thin ropes. On ungreased cookie sheets, shape the ropes into pretzels (place a rope on the sheet as an upside down "U" and fold the ends up at 45-degree angles).

Paint the pretzels with a mixture of the reserved egg white and the ½ tablespoon of water. Sprinkle with the turbinado sugar.

Bake for 11 to 12 minutes, until light golden.

Carefully transfer the pretzels to wire racks to cool.

Kringlers

YIELD = 32 PRETZELS

These delicate pretzels, fashioned from a rich hazelnut dough, offer a touch of elegance and a bit of the unexpected.

Mary Ann Morrissey's Brandy Almond Crescents

YIELD = ABOUT
4¹/₂ DOZEN COOKIES

These pretty little new moons almost melt in your mouth. They're based on a recipe Kevin's sister-in-law whips up for special occasions.

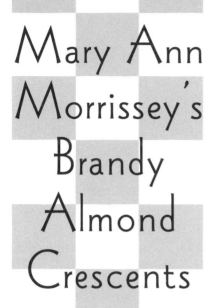

²/₃ cup plus 2 tablespoons confectioners' sugar
1¹/₂ cups almonds
1 cup (2 sticks) unsalted butter, chilled, cut into 8 pieces
2 tablespoons brandy
1 teaspoon vanilla extract
2 cups all-purpose flour

Combine ²/₃ cup of the confectioners' sugar and the almonds in the bowl of a food processor fitted with the steel blade. Process for about 1 minute, until the almonds are finely ground. With the machine on, add the pieces of butter through the feed tube continuously, processing until smooth. Add the brandy and vanilla and process to incorporate. Add the flour and pulse about 30 times, until fully incorporated.

Turn the dough out onto wax paper. Form it into a ball, wrap the ball in the wax paper, and refrigerate for 30 minutes.

Preheat the oven to 350 degrees.

Lightly flour a work surface. Using about a tablespoonful of dough for each cookie, roll with the palm of your hand into ropes about 2¹/₂ inches long and ³/₄ inch thick. Shape the ropes into crescents and place them on ungreased cookie sheets.

Bake for 13 to 15 minutes, until the edges begin to brown.

Remove the cookie sheets to wire racks and cool for 5 minutes. Transfer the cookies directly to the racks and cool for 15 minutes more.

Dust the cooled cookies with the remaining 2 tablespoons confectioners' sugar.

1 cup all-purpose flour
³/₄ cup quick oats
¹/₂ teaspoon baking soda
1 teaspoon cream of tartar
¹/₂ teaspoon ground cinnamon
¹/₄ teaspoon salt
¹/₂ cup (1 stick) unsalted butter, at room temperature,
    cut into 8 pieces
¹/₄ cup firmly packed dark brown sugar
¹/₂ cup granulated sugar
1 large egg
¹/₂ teaspoon vanilla extract

TOPPING:
2 tablespoons granulated sugar
2¹/₂ teaspoons ground cinnamon

Preheat the oven to 400 degrees.

Whisk together the flour, oats, baking soda, cream of tartar, cinnamon, and salt.

Cream the butter and sugars in a large bowl with an electric mixer at medium speed. Add the egg and vanilla. At low speed, beat until fluffy. Stir in the flour mixture with a wooden spoon, just to combine.

Combine the topping ingredients in a large, shallow bowl.

Form the dough into 1-inch balls, using 1 tablespoon for each. Roll the balls in the topping mixture to coat and place them about 2 inches apart on ungreased cookie sheets.

Bake for about 9 minutes, just until the edges are firm to the touch and the tops are brown.

Cool on the sheets for 1 minute before removing the cookies to wire racks to finish cooling.

Snicker-doodles

YIELD = ABOUT
3 DOZEN COOKIES

We make these old-fashioned cinnamon cookies in the old-fashioned manner, using a combination of baking soda and cream of tartar in lieu of baking powder, but add some oats for texture. They're best while still slightly warm and glistening with cinnamon.

Chocolate Grouchos

YIELD = ABOUT
1 1/2 DOZEN CIGARS

Unlike most cigar cookies, these nummy cylinders are dense and spongy, rather than crisp. The rich chocolate dough is spread over circles traced on the sheets of baker's parchment used to line the cookie sheets, baked, and then rolled up while still warm. To keep the parchment from curling up, grease the edges with the residual butter on the paper wrapper of the stick used in the recipe.

3 large egg whites, at room temperature
1/8 teaspoon salt
1/2 cup (1 stick) unsalted butter, at room temperature, cut into pieces
1/4 cup granulated sugar
1/2 cup all-purpose flour
1 ounce semisweet chocolate, grated
1/4 teaspoon vanilla extract
1/2 tablespoon confectioners' sugar
1/2 tablespoon unsweetened Dutch-processed cocoa powder

Preheat the oven to 425 degrees.

Using a cookie cutter or a glass, trace 3½-inch circles on sheets of baker's parchment cut to fit your cookie sheets. (You will need about 18 circles.) Flip the parchment and place traced side down onto the sheets.

Combine the egg whites and salt in a bowl. Beat with an electric mixer at medium speed to soft peaks. Set aside.

In a large mixing bowl, cream the butter and granulated sugar at medium speed. At low speed, add the flour, grated chocolate, and vanilla, beating just until the mixture is crumbly. Stir in a third of the beaten egg whites with a wooden spoon. Fold in the remainder.

Put 1½ tablespoons of the batter into the center of each circle on the parchment. With a small rubber spatula, spread it like frosting to fill the circles.

Bake for about 7 minutes, until the cookies are firm to the touch in the center and lightly browned around the edges.

While the cookies are baking, combine the confectioners' sugar and cocoa powder in a small bowl and mix with a fork.

Remove the sheets from the oven. Gently peel each cookie from the parchment and roll it up into a cigar, working quickly to shape the cigars before the cookies cool. (For any cookies that do not come off the parchment easily, cut

For Chocolate Pancakes, peel the cookies from the baker's parchment, dust with the sugar and cocoa mixture, and allow them to cool flat on wire racks.

around the circle and lift it up to peel.) If the cookies become too brittle to roll, place the sheets back into the oven for a few seconds to warm and soften.

Place the cigars on wire racks. Through a fine sieve dust with the confectioners' sugar and cocoa mixture, and cool.

Chocolate Nut Pizzelles

YIELD = ABOUT
2½ DOZEN PIZZELLES

Pizzelles require specialized pizzelle irons, but the crisp round wafers, impressed with decorative patterns from the disks of the iron, are well worth the modest investment. We particularly like this rendition, which tastes rather like a nutty chocolate ice cream cone.

¼ cup hazelnuts
2 tablespoons plus 1 cup all-purpose flour
⅓ cup (⅔ stick) unsalted butter, melted
3 tablespoons unsweetened Dutch-processed cocoa powder
2 large eggs
½ cup granulated sugar
2 teaspoons vanilla extract
1¼ teaspoons baking powder

Combine the hazelnuts and 2 tablespoons of the flour in the bowl of a food processor fitted with the steel blade. Process until the nuts are finely ground. Set aside.

Whisk together the melted butter and cocoa powder.

In a large mixing bowl, beat the eggs with an electric mixer at low speed. Gradually beat in the sugar, continuing to beat until dissolved. Beat in the vanilla. Add the butter and cocoa mixture. Mix until blended.

Sift in the baking powder and remaining 1 cup flour. Add the ground nut mixture and mix thoroughly with a wooden spoon.

Preheat a pizzelle iron.

Put a rounded teaspoonful of the batter in the center of a disk of the iron (or in the center of each impression if using an electric pizzelle iron that makes more than 1 cookie at a time). Close the iron and bake for 30 to 90 seconds, according to the manufacturer's instructions.

Cool the pizzelles on wire racks.

Still-warm pizzelles right out of
the iron can be shaped into many forms
as long as one works very quickly to fashion
the desired shape before the cookie begins to cool
and harden. Use mitts and take care not to burn yourself.

For a cannoli shell, fold up and overlap opposite sides of
the circle and place it into a champagne flute to
hold the shape while the pizzelle cools.

To make ice cream cones, fold and overlap opposite sides of
the pizzelle in a "V" shape—or shape the cone into a "V"
around a thick-handled wooden spoon—pinch the bottom
closed, and cool in a champagne flute or a large funnel.
(Helpfully, many pizzelle irons come with wooden cones
around which the wafers can be shaped.) Bend the cone
into a cornucopia shape before cooling to make horns in
and around which frozen desserts and custards
can be mounded.

Pizzelles can also be shaped into cookie cups
by draping them while warm inside small
custard cups and allowing
them to cool.

Vanilla Pizzelles

YIELD = ABOUT
2 1/2 DOZEN PIZZELLES

Pizzelles can be served whole, cut into wedges (while still warm) to garnish ice cream or sorbet, or shaped into cones, horns, cups, or cannoli shells. For various ideas, see page 73.

2 large eggs
$^1/_2$ cup granulated sugar
1 tablespoon vanilla extract
$^1/_3$ cup ($^2/_3$ stick) unsalted butter, melted
$1^1/_3$ cups all-purpose flour
$1^1/_4$ teaspoons baking powder

Put the eggs into a large mixing bowl. Beat with an electric mixer at low speed. Gradually add the sugar, beating until incorporated. Beat in the vanilla, then the melted butter. Combine and sift in the flour and baking powder. Stir well with a wooden spoon.

Preheat a pizzelle iron.

Put a rounded teaspoonful of the batter in the center of a disk of the iron (or in the center of each impression if using an electric pizzelle iron that makes more than 1 cookie at a time). Close the iron and bake for 30 to 90 seconds, according to the manufacturer's instructions.

Cool the pizzelles on wire racks.

For Anise Pizzelles, substitute 1 tablespoon anise extract for the vanilla.

1 cup (2 sticks) unsalted butter, at room temperature
$^2/_3$ cup granulated sugar
1 large egg plus 2 additional egg yolks
1 teaspoon anise extract
$2^1/_4$ cups all-purpose flour

Preheat the oven to 375 degrees.

Cream the butter in a bowl with an electric mixer set at high speed. Add the sugar and continue to beat until fluffy. Beat in the whole egg, egg yolks, and anise extract.

Stir in the flour with a wooden spoon. Cover and refrigerate for 15 minutes.

Press the dough onto ungreased cookie sheets, using a cookie press fitted with a star disk and leaving about 1 inch between cookies.

Bake for about 9 minutes, until very lightly browned.

Remove the cookies immediately to wire racks to cool.

Using a cookie press is the quickest and easiest way to make spritz cookies. For each cookie, hold the press upright with the tip touching the cookie sheet and click the lever to "press" out a cookie. (You can also use a pastry bag fitted with a decorative tip.) A star-shaped disk is called for in these recipes, but spritz can be fashioned as rings, hearts, or any of a multitude of fanciful shapes.

To make spritz kisses using only the most rudimentary of kitchen technology, clip $^1/_2$ inch (measured from the point) off a bottom corner of a heavy-duty plastic storage bag and squeeze about a teaspoon of the dough through the bag for each cookie.

Licorice Spritz

YIELD = ABOUT
8 $^1/_2$ DOZEN COOKIES

We like to top each of these anise-flavored morsels with a chocolate coffee bean before baking, for a treat reminiscent of sambuca liqueur. In fact, why not serve them with a pony of sambuca?

Almond Spritz

YIELD = ABOUT
11 DOZEN COOKIES

Make lots of these buttery little gems because no one can seem to eat just one—or two, or even three. They're particularly popular at Christmastime, but we enjoy them all year long because they go so well with a range of ice creams and sorbets.

1 cup almonds
$^2/_3$ cup granulated sugar
$2^1/_4$ cups all-purpose flour
1 cup (2 sticks) unsalted butter, at room temperature
2 large eggs
$^1/_2$ teaspoon almond extract

Preheat the oven to 400 degrees.

Combine the almonds and sugar in the bowl of a food processor fitted with the steel blade. Process until the almonds are finely ground, about 1 minute. Add the flour and process for about 30 seconds to incorporate.

Cream the butter in a bowl with an electric mixer at low speed. Mix in the eggs and almond extract. Add the almond and sugar mixture and beat to incorporate. Cover and refrigerate the dough for 20 minutes.

Fit a cookie press with a star-shaped disk. Press the dough onto ungreased cookie sheets, leaving about 1 inch between cookies. Bake for about 8 minutes, until the cookies are just beginning to brown.

Remove the cookies immediately to wire racks to cool.

For variety, top some of the cookies with chocolate sprinkles or glacé cherries before baking.

2 ounces bittersweet chocolate, broken up
¼ cup (½ stick) unsalted butter, cut into pieces
4 large egg whites
½ cup plus 2 tablespoons granulated sugar
¼ cup plus 2 tablespoons all-purpose flour

Preheat the oven to 350 degrees.

Grease twenty-four 3-inch madeleine molds thoroughly with butter and flour.

In a microwave oven, melt the chocolate and butter in a glass measuring cup at full power for 1 minute and stir with a wooden spoon until smooth (or melt in the top of a double boiler over boiling water).

Put the egg whites in a bowl and beat with an electric mixer at medium speed until frothy. At low speed, beat in the sugar, then the flour. Beat in the chocolate and butter mixture. Fill each mold with a generous tablespoon of the mixture, evening the top a bit with a rubber spatula.

Bake for about 12 minutes, until the madeleines spring back to the touch and are beginning to separate from the edges of the molds.

Unmold by tilting the plaques over a work surface and banging lightly so that the madeleines pop out; gently pry out any that remain with the tip of a knife.

Madeleine plaques, aluminum or steel sheets with shell-shaped molds, are readily available in kitchenware stores. We prefer the plaques that contain molds for 3-inch cakes to those with 1½-inch molds. Three-inch madeleine plaques may contain from 8 to 24 molds.

Chocolate Madeleines

YIELD = 24 MADELEINES

What could be as simple yet as elegant as a madeleine? These tiny little sculpted chocolate cakes should be spongy on the inside and a bit crisp on the outside. The batter can be made hours in advance, put into the molds, and stored in the refrigerator. The madeleines bake in only a few minutes and are perfection still warm from the oven. Serve shell shape up and dust, if desired, with a little confectioners' sugar.

Anise Madeleines

YIELD = 24 MADELEINES

Whenever we smell freshly baked madeleines, it reminds us of those sold every Thursday and Sunday at the street market in the 11th Arrondissement. We might not be able to get to Paris as often as we'd like, but it *is* possible to conjure up the memories.

For these refreshing licorice-flavored cookies, use 2 madeleine plaques, each containing twelve 3-inch molds. Be sure to grease in and around the molds thoroughly to keep the madeleines from sticking. If you have only 1 tin, bake the madeleines in batches, storing the batter in the refrigerator until needed and cooling the tin between each batch.

5 large egg whites
1 cup granulated sugar
$\frac{1}{2}$ cup plus 1 tablespoon all-purpose flour
2 large egg yolks
2 teaspoons finely grated lemon rind
$\frac{1}{4}$ cup plus 2 tablespoons unsalted butter, melted
2 teaspoons anise extract

Preheat the oven to 350 degrees.

Grease twenty-four 3-inch madeleine molds thoroughly with butter and flour.

Beat the egg whites until frothy with an electric mixer at medium speed. At low speed, beat in the sugar, then the flour.

Combine the egg yolks, lemon rind, melted butter, and anise extract in a bowl. Whisk to combine. Whisk into the egg white mixture.

Spoon $1\frac{1}{2}$ tablespoons into each prepared mold. Bake for 12 to 13 minutes, until the madeleines are golden brown around the edges and spring back to the touch.

Cool in the molds for 1 minute, then bang the plaques lightly over a counter to dislodge the madeleines. Pry any remaining madeleines out gently with the tip of a knife.

Even if you don't have any madeleine plaques in your pantry, you can produce tasty little Commercy cupcakes by baking the madeleine batter in mini muffin tins; put a generous 2 tablespoons of the batter into each well.

3 large eggs, at room temperature
2$^1/_2$ cups confectioners' sugar
$^1/_4$ cup ($^1/_2$ stick) unsalted butter, at room temperature,
    cut into 4 pieces
3 cups all-purpose flour
$^1/_4$ teaspoon salt
$^1/_2$ tablespoon Chinese five-spice
    powder
$^1/_4$ teaspoon baking powder

Combine the eggs and sugar in the bowl of a stationary electric mixer fitted with the paddle attachment. Mix at low speed for about 3 minutes, until the sugar has dissolved and the mixture is thick and smooth. Add the butter and continue to beat until well blended, about 4 minutes. Turn the mixer off and sift in the flour, salt, five-spice powder, and baking powder together. Mix for a few seconds to form a dough.

Gather the dough into a ball and place it on a large, lightly floured work surface. Cut into quarters. Flatten and roll out a quarter to a $^1/_4$-inch-thick square, about 8 by 8 inches. Lightly pass a springle rolling pin once over the dough. (Don't press too hard, just enough so that the designs carved into the pin leave an impression on the dough.)

Repeat the process with the remaining 3 dough quarters. Cover the dough with clean, dry dish towels and leave it at room temperature for at least 2 hours to allow the impressions to dry on the surface of the dough.

Preheat the oven to 325 degrees.

Coat cookie sheets with vegetable oil cooking spray.

Cut the dough into squares following the scores made by the springle pin. Transfer with a flat spatula to the prepared cookie sheets.

Bake for about 10 minutes, until the cookies are firm to the touch and have just begun to brown on the bottom.

Remove the cookies to wire racks to cool.

The raised designs baked onto the springles can be colored (dab food coloring on with a paper towel) or lightly glazed when cooled for a festive presentation.

To glaze, mix $^3/_4$ cup confectioners' sugar and 1$^1/_2$ tablespoons milk with a fork until smooth. Add 2 drops food coloring if desired. Brush lightly over the designs and allow to air dry.

Five-Spice Springles

YIELD = ABOUT
6 DOZEN SPRINGLES

Based upon the decoratively embossed German springerle, our version boosts the usual anise flavor with five-spice powder, a blend of the more pungent star anise combined with cinnamon, cloves, fennel, and peppercorn. The designs are created with the aid of a specially carved springle rolling pin, available at kitchenware stores.

Sugar Cookie Squares

YIELD = 18 SQUARES

These buttery sugar cookies are a little thicker than typical and served up as squares rather than rounds. We like to top them while still warm with any of the variety of the different colored sugars that can be found in most supermarkets.

1 cup (2 sticks) unsalted butter, at room temperature
$1^{1}/_{4}$ cups confectioners' sugar
$^{1}/_{4}$ teaspoon salt
2 large eggs
$^{1}/_{2}$ tablespoon vanilla extract
$^{1}/_{2}$ teaspoon almond extract
3 cups all-purpose flour
3 tablespoons colored sugar

Preheat the oven to 350 degrees.

In a large mixing bowl, cream the butter and confectioners' sugar with an electric mixer at medium speed. Add the salt, eggs, and extracts. Mix until well combined.

Add the flour and mix with a wooden spoon to incorporate. Gather the dough into a ball and cut it in half. Press each piece of dough into a nonstick 8-inch-square cake pan, working to cover the bottom of the pan evenly.

Bake for about 12 minutes, until golden brown.

Cool in the pans for 2 minutes, then gently invert the pans over a work surface and unmold. Cut each large square into 9 equal pieces. Sprinkle with colored sugar and cool on wire racks.

This sugar cookie also can be made in a variety of decorative molds. (See Exotic Shortbread, page 82.) Consult the manufacturer's instructions for suggested greasing techniques, oven temperatures, and baking times.

¼ cup confectioners' sugar
1 tablespoon granulated sugar
½ cup (1 stick) unsalted butter, frozen, cut into 8 tablespoons
1 cup all-purpose flour

Preheat the oven to 325 degrees.

Combine the sugars and butter in the bowl of a food processor fitted with the steel blade. Pulse a few times, until incorporated. Add the flour and pulse a few more times, until the mixture has a pebbly consistency.

Mold the dough firmly into the bottom of an ungreased 8-inch-round cake pan. Make fingerprint impressions around the perimeter of the shortbread for a decorative border.

Bake for 40 to 45 minutes, until golden, pricking repeatedly with the tines of a fork after 15 minutes. Take care not to brown.

Cool the shortbread in the pan on a wire rack for 10 minutes. Carefully invert over a cutting board and unmold. With a sharp knife, cut into 8 wedges.

Scottish Shortbread

YIELD = 8 WEDGES

This intensely buttery cookie is prepared in the traditional large round, resembling a Scottish griddle cake, which is cut into wedges before serving.

If desired, serve the shortbread drizzled with Devonshire cream or with a dollop of lightly sweetened whipped cream. For Strawberry Shortbread Cake, a decadent alternative to strawberry shortcake, top each wedge with whipped cream and strawberries.

Exotic Shortbread

We add Chinese five-spice powder for a distinctive, somewhat Eurasian variation on the theme of classic shortbread. This version has a slightly coarser texture than our Scottish Shortbread (page 81) and is a little less dense.

$^1/_4$ cup granulated sugar
$^1/_2$ cup (1 stick) unsalted butter, frozen, cut into 8 tablespoons
1 cup all-purpose flour
1 teaspoon Chinese five-spice powder

Preheat the oven to 325 degrees.

Fit a food processor with the steel blade. Turn the machine on and add the sugar through the feed tube. Process to a superfine consistency, about 1 minute. Add the butter and process for a few seconds more, just until incorporated. Turn the machine off and add the flour and the five-spice powder. Pulse a few times until coarsely granular.

Transfer the dough to an ungreased 8-inch-round cake pan. Press it down to mold evenly over the bottom of the pan. Make a thin border around the outside by pressing lightly with the flat ends of the tines of a fork. Using a sharp knife, score the molded dough about halfway through to form 8 wedges.

Bake for 15 minutes. Prick the shortbread numerous times with the tines of a fork. Return to the oven and bake for 20 to 25 minutes more, until golden, taking care not to brown.

Remove the pan to a wire rack and cool for 10 minutes. Run a knife around the outer edge to loosen the shortbread. Invert the pan and gently unmold. Break the shortbread into wedges along the scores. Serve warm or at room temperature.

In addition to a cake
pan, shortbread can be baked in a variety of
decorative molds. Made of ceramic, stoneware, or even
cast iron, the molds shape the dough into symbols from
ancient Scottish solstice celebrations, patterns that replicate
antique butter plaques, or other fanciful designs.

Molds specifically intended for shortbread are fairly standard
in size and will accommodate most recipes. If using
multipurpose molds, some tinkering with the quantity of
ingredients might be necessary. Most molds come with sample
recipes that suggest the greasing techniques, oven
temperatures, and baking times best suited
to the material from which the mold is made. We've made
shortbread in ceramic molds altering our recipes only
in so far as coating the mold with vegetable oil
cooking spray.

Nutty Blue Cheese Wedges

YIELD = 12 WEDGES

Somewhat akin to shortbread in texture, these sophisticated cookies make a rich, savory snack or a fitting after dinner accompaniment to a mellow dessert wine and a fruit and cheese plate.

$1/3$ cup chopped walnuts
2 tablespoons granulated sugar
2 tablespoons confectioners' sugar
$1/4$ cup crumbled blue cheese
$1/2$ cup (1 stick) unsalted butter, well chilled, cut into 16 pieces
$1^1/4$ cups all-purpose flour

Preheat the oven to 325 degrees.

Combine the walnuts and sugars in the bowl of a food processor fitted with the steel blade. Process for 1 minute and scrape down the sides of the bowl with a rubber spatula. Add the blue cheese and butter. Process for a few seconds to a crumbly consistency. Add the flour and pulse about 20 times until small pebbles form.

Dump the mixture into a nonstick 8-inch-round cake pan. Press it down evenly over the surface of the pan. With a sharp knife, score the top into 12 wedges.

Bake for 15 minutes. Deepen the scoring and prick all over with the tines of a fork. Return to the oven and bake for about 15 minutes more, until light golden on top.

Cool in the pan on a wire rack for 10 minutes. Hold the pan upside down and tap gently to unmold. Cool completely, then break into 12 wedges along the score lines.

Bar Cookies

The bar cookie is the Peter Pan of patisserie—lighthearted, whimsical, given to excess, and determined never to fully grow up. An intrinsic part of everyday life since mid-century, these are what Mom was *really* baking while that apple pie was grabbing all the press.

Bar cookies prompt a wide grin on the face of anyone who has ever devoured a shoe box full of date nut bars in a college dorm or baked brownies on a lazy summer afternoon by the shore. They're fun, almost by definition, a sociable group activity both in the making and in the consuming.

Bars are by far the simplest cookies to make, prepared much like a quick bread and baked whole in a single pan. With a little supervision, these are definitely recipes that the kids can help execute.

We use standard size baking pans, all of which are 2 inches deep. The 9-by-13-inch pan is our workhorse. Know that you can readily substitute a 7-by-9-inch pan when the recipe calls for one 8 inches square.

We prefer metal pans to glass, which cause the bars to cook faster and become too dry. If you do use glass baking pans, reduce the oven temperature by 25 degrees and begin to check for visual doneness cues at least 5 minutes early.

Grease and/or line pans per individual recipe directions. All bar cookies do not dislodge with equal ease. You can have a sticky mess on your hands if, for example, you opt to bake a caramel bar in an ungreased pan.

Spread the dough to coat the pan evenly, working it into the corners. For those doughs that include baking powder as a leavening agent, measure carefully; just a little extra can impart a bitter taste. When the crust is prebaked, allow it to cool before filling. Add the filling in an even layer.

Bake bar cookies in the center of the oven, and cool them completely in the pan on a wire rack. Several bars will cut more easily and hold their shape better if they are chilled after cooling.

We include cutting instructions only by way of suggesting serving sizes and yields; don't feel constrained. Cut only as many bars as you intend to serve at one time. The rest will remain fresher if kept intact in the pan and wrapped with aluminum foil.

See page 97 for decorative cutting tips. For company, we like to cut diamond-shaped bars and serve them in colorful paper muffin cups. When a dusting of confectioners' sugar is called for, sift the sugar through a fine-mesh sieve just before serving.

Much like cakes, bar cookies are at their absolute best the day they're made. They will remain very good for 3 to 4 days if stored at room temperature, or for 5 days in the refrigerator. (A few *must* be refrigerated.) Despite the common practice of freezing brownies, we don't believe that any bar cookie holds up particularly well to freezing, and we don't recommend it.

2 cups all-purpose flour
1 cup firmly packed dark brown sugar
1 cup (2 sticks) unsalted butter, melted
1 large egg, beaten
6 ounces bittersweet chocolate, finely chopped
1 cup finely chopped pecans

Preheat the oven to 350 degrees.

Whisk the flour and brown sugar together in a mixing bowl. Stir in the melted butter with a wooden spoon. Stir in the egg. Scrape the mixture into an ungreased 9-by-13-inch baking pan, spreading it evenly to cover the bottom.

Bake for 18 to 19 minutes, until the edges are lightly browned.

Remove the pan from the oven and sprinkle the chocolate over the base. Allow 3 to 5 minutes for the chocolate to melt, then spread it to coat the base. Sprinkle the pecans evenly over the chocolate. Place the pan on a wire rack to cool completely.

Refrigerate for about 10 minutes, until the chocolate has hardened. To facilitate cutting, dislodge and remove from the pan with a metal spatula. Cut into 1-by-3-inch fingers.

For English Walnut Toffee Fingers, substitute a cup of chopped walnuts for the pecans.

Pecan Toffee Fingers

YIELD = 39 FINGERS

In this variation on a classic confectionery theme, the chocolate and nuts top a thin butterscotch cake instead of the usual brittle candy base.

Pear Caramel Bars

YIELD = 36 BARS

An addictive combination of rich, dense caramel and heavenly pears, these are wonderful served warm with vanilla ice cream or whipped cream, as you would a cobbler. They're a favorite of Kevin's mother, a diminutive Lake Shore Drive octogenarian who can seemingly consume her body weight in cookies.

Lining the baking pan with buttered aluminum foil allows you to transfer the contents easily to a work surface before cutting the bars, a decided advantage when working with sticky caramel.

BASE:
1¼ cups quick oats
1½ cups all-purpose flour
½ cup firmly packed dark brown sugar
½ teaspoon baking soda
¼ teaspoon salt
1 cup (2 sticks) unsalted butter, cold, cut into 16 tablespoons

FILLING:
3 very firm pears (see box)
1 tablespoon lemon juice
⅔ cup firmly packed light brown sugar
⅓ cup granulated sugar
⅔ cup light corn syrup
3 tablespoons unsalted butter, at room temperature
¾ cup heavy cream
½ teaspoon vanilla extract
½ cup pecan pieces

Preheat the oven to 375 degrees.

Line a 9-by-13-inch baking pan with aluminum foil and grease well with butter.

Combine the oats, flour, dark brown sugar, baking soda, and salt in the bowl of a food processor fitted with the steel blade. Process for 1 minute. Add the butter. Pulse about 50 times, to form soft crumbs. Reserve 1¾ cups of the mixture.

Distribute the remainder over the prepared baking pan and press it down to cover the bottom evenly. Bake for about 15 minutes, until lightly browned around the edges.

Meanwhile, peel, quarter, and core the pears. Cut each quarter lengthwise into 4 slices. Toss with the lemon juice and set aside.

When the crust is lightly browned, remove the pan to a wire rack to cool, leaving the oven on.

For the filling, combine the light brown sugar, granulated sugar, and corn syrup in a medium saucepan. Bring to a boil over medium heat, stirring constantly. Stir in the butter and cream. While stirring, bring back to a vigorous boil. Cook for 4 minutes, stirring. Remove from the heat and add the vanilla.

Arrange the pears on the base in a single layer. Scatter the pecans on top. Pour the caramel evenly over the pears and pecans to cover. Top with the reserved oat crumbs. Return to the oven and bake for about 20 minutes, until bubbly and browned.

Cool in the pan on a wire rack for 1 hour, then refrigerate for 2 hours.

Using a moistened knife, cut into bars measuring 1½ inches by a little over 2 inches.

Succulent royal pears are our first choice when available, but several other varieties can be used. Bosc pears hold their shape nicely; Bartlett and Anjou will work as well. Whatever variety you use, be sure to select very firm pears.

Roasted Almond Brownies

YIELD = 36 BROWNIES

In this recipe, we swirl a nut butter mixture and a dense chocolate batter to create a marbleized effect. If you can't find roasted almond butter, use the more readily available plain almond butter. For an optional finishing touch, scatter whole almonds on top before baking.

ALMOND FILLING:
1/2 cup (1 stick) unsalted butter, at room temperature
3/4 cup roasted almond butter
1/4 cup granulated sugar
1 large egg
1 tablespoon milk

BROWNIE BATTER:
2 cups granulated sugar
1/2 tablespoon almond extract
1 cup (2 sticks) unsalted butter, melted
3 large eggs
1/2 cup unsweetened Dutch-processed cocoa powder
1 1/3 cups all-purpose flour
1/2 teaspoon baking powder
1/8 teaspoon salt

1/4 cup whole almonds (optional)

Preheat the oven to 350 degrees.

Lightly grease a 9-by-13-inch baking pan with butter.

Make the filling first by combining the butter, almond butter, sugar, egg, and milk in a mixing bowl. Beat with an electric mixer at medium speed for about 2 minutes, until light-colored and fluffy. Set aside.

For the brownie batter, combine the sugar, almond extract, and melted butter in a large mixing bowl. Beat with an electric mixer at low speed just until incorporated. Beat in 1 egg at a time at medium speed. Add the cocoa powder and beat at medium speed until the cocoa is fully absorbed and the mixture is smooth. Beat in the flour, baking powder, and salt at high speed.

Reserve 1 cup of the brownie mixture. Turn the rest into the prepared baking pan, spreading it over the bottom and working it into the corners. Cover with the almond filling, spread in an even layer.

Scoop the reserved brownie mixture on top in about 6 mounds. With the point of a sharp knife, swirl to marbleize, cutting through all 3 layers. Shake the pan to distribute the batter evenly. If desired, sprinkle the whole almonds on top.

Bake for about 35 minutes, until a toothpick inserted into the center comes out clean.

Cool completely in the pan on a wire rack. Cut into rectangles measuring 1½ inches by a generous 2 inches.

We use this brownie batter as the foundation for Ultimate Brownies, sure to please the purists in your household who prefer their brownies plain and simple, without any newfangled taste twists.

Increase the amount of cocoa powder in the brownie batter to ³/₄ cup. Fold in ³/₄ cup roughly chopped walnuts and ¹/₂ cup semisweet chocolate chips. Pour the entire batter into the prepared baking pan at once, omitting the almond butter filling.

Three-Citrus Bars

YIELD = 24 BARS

We've added orange and lime to jazz up the traditional lemon bar, and served it on a buttery shortbread base. The natural sweetness lent by the orange juice enables us to use less sugar and avoid the too-sweet edge that mars many citrus cookies. The bars should be stored in the refrigerator.

To make hard lemons and limes softer and juicier, microwave them at full power for 20 seconds.

BASE:
1¼ cups all-purpose flour
¼ cup granulated sugar
½ cup (1 stick) unsalted butter, at room temperature, cut into 8 tablespoons

CURD:
2 tablespoons freshly squeezed and strained lemon juice
2 tablespoons freshly squeezed and strained lime juice
2 tablespoons freshly squeezed and strained orange juice
3 large eggs
1 cup granulated sugar
¼ cup all-purpose flour
½ tablespoon finely grated lemon zest

About 1 tablespoon confectioners' sugar

Preheat the oven to 325 degrees.

Lightly coat an 8-by-8-inch baking pan with vegetable oil cooking spray.

To make the base, combine the flour and sugar in a large bowl and mix with a fork. Add the butter, breaking it up and mixing it in with the fork. (You will produce a crumbly mixture dotted with butter.)

Dump the mixture into the prepared baking pan and press it into a firm layer covering the bottom of the pan. Bake for about 20 minutes, until just beginning to brown around the edges.

Remove the pan to a wire rack to cool, leaving the oven on.

Meanwhile, prepare the curd. Combine the juices, eggs, sugar, and flour in a large mixing bowl. Using an electric mixer at medium speed, beat for about 1 minute, until smooth and slightly frothy.

Mix in the lemon zest with a wooden spoon. Pour the curd over the cooled base. Return the pan to the oven and bake for about 30 minutes, until set and lightly browned.

Cool in the pan on a wire rack for 1 hour. Refrigerate for at least 30 minutes.

Top with confectioners' sugar and cut into bars measuring 2 inches by a little over 1¼ inches.

For Chocolate Orange Bars, add 2 tablespoons unsweetened Dutch-processed cocoa powder to the flour mixture, increase the volume of orange juice to 6 tablespoons, and omit the lime juice, lemon juice, and lemon zest.

8 ounces dried Black Mission figs, stemmed and quartered
  (a generous cup)
$1/4$ cup plus 2 tablespoons tawny port
$1/2$ cup (1 stick) unsalted butter, at room temperature
$1/2$ cup firmly packed dark brown sugar
$1/4$ cup all-purpose flour
$1/4$ teaspoon salt
$1/2$ teaspoon baking powder
$3/4$ cup rolled oats
1 cup chopped walnuts
1 teaspoon finely grated orange zest
$1/2$ tablespoon confectioners' sugar

Preheat the oven to 350 degrees.

Coat a 9-by-13-inch baking pan with vegetable oil cooking spray.

Combine the figs and port in a bowl and set aside to soak.

In a large mixing bowl, cream the butter and brown sugar with an electric mixer at medium speed.

Whisk together the flour, salt, baking powder, and oats. Stir into the butter mixture with a wooden spoon until fully incorporated. Stir in the figs and port, the nuts, and orange zest.

Turn the dough into the prepared pan, spread it evenly, and bake for about 15 minutes, until golden.

Remove the pan to a wire rack and cool for 1 hour. Refrigerate for at least 1 hour more, then dust with the confectioners' sugar.

Cut into bars measuring $1^{1}/2$ inches by a little over 2 inches.

Fig Port Bars

YIELD = 36 BARS

One of Kevin's favorites, this delightful cookie is replete with big chunks of chewy, port-infused figs. It's simply wonderful served with an assortment of fruit and cheese—and, of course, a glass of port.

Peach Crumb Bars

YIELD = 24 BARS

These tasty bars are indeed crumbly, as their name should indicate. (We think it's one of their better qualities, along with the addition of slivered almonds in place of the more typical dusting of confectioners' sugar— but be forewarned if you're planning on carting a couple off to bed with a good book.)

They can be made all year long with unsweetened frozen peaches. Use a generous cup of frozen sliced peaches, thawed, drained, and sliced in half lengthwise.

$^3/_4$ cup granulated sugar
$1^1/_2$ cups all-purpose flour
$^1/_4$ cup firmly packed dark brown sugar
$^3/_4$ teaspoon baking powder
$^1/_4$ teaspoon salt
$^3/_4$ cup ($1^1/_2$ sticks) unsalted butter, chilled, cut into 24 pieces
2 large peaches, stoned and thinly sliced
$^1/_2$ tablespoon ground cinnamon
$^1/_2$ cup slivered blanched almonds

Preheat the oven to 375 degrees.

Lightly coat a 9-inch-square baking pan with vegetable oil cooking spray.

Put the granulated sugar in the bowl of a food processor fitted with the steel blade and process for about 1 minute, to superfine consistency. Add the flour, brown sugar, baking powder, and salt. Process for 30 seconds. Scatter the butter over the flour mixture and process for about 15 seconds more, until crumbly.

Dump $2^1/_2$ cups (about two thirds of the mixture) into the bottom of the prepared pan and press it evenly over the bottom. Arrange the peach slices over the base.

Transfer the remaining $1^1/_2$ cups of the sugar and flour mixture to a small bowl. Mix in the cinnamon and almonds with a fork. Sprinkle the mixture evenly over the peaches.

Bake for 30 to 35 minutes, until the top is golden brown and a tester inserted in the center comes out clean.

Cool completely in the pan on a wire rack, about 1 hour. Then refrigerate for at least 1 hour. Cut into $1^1/_2$-by-$2^1/_4$-inch bars.

THE
CUTTING EDGE

Cutting bar cookies is easier with the
aid of a pastry cutting wheel (or a ravioli
cutter or pizza wheel). Some wheels have
scalloped blades that will add a bit of fluting
along the borders. For thinner bar cookies, you can
also use a pastry crimper, which crimps the edges
closed as it cuts. A single-blade wave cutter can add a
sleek Art Deco accent to the bars.

You can also use cookie cutters to make decoratively shaped bars.
If the bar is thick, make an impression with the cutter and finish
the job with a sharp knife. (Of course, someone will have to devour
the bits of bar left between the shapes you've cut out.)

It's easy to cut bars in diamond shapes. To cut 12 diamond-shaped
bars from a square baking pan, first make a diagonal cut from the
top left to the bottom right corner. Make parallel cuts on each side
(halfway between the center cut and the bottom left corner and
between the center and the top right corner). Rotate the pan
90 degrees and repeat the cuts.

To cut 22 diamonds from a rectangular pan, position the pan
lengthwise. Cut a pyramid from the bottom left corner to the
middle of the top and down again to the bottom right corner.
Rotate the pan 180 degrees and repeat the cut. Cut an
"X" to divide the large diamond in the center into 4
equal smaller diamonds, continuing all 4 ends of
the "X" to the long bottom and top sides
of the pan. Cut lines from the
tips of the "X" to the middle
of each short side
of the pan.

White Chocolate Brownies

YIELD = 64 BROWNIES

White chocolate is difficult to bake with and can scorch easily, so it's usually confined to use in frostings and fillings. This recipe contains enough butter to defy the norm. It's so sinfully rich, it almost defies description as well (which is why we cut the brownies into tiny 1-inch squares). Be sure to buy the variety of white chocolate that includes cocoa butter on the ingredient list.

4 ounces white chocolate, broken up into chunks, plus 2 ounces roughly chopped, plus 2 ounces finely chopped
$^1/_2$ cup (1 stick) unsalted butter, cut into pieces
3 large eggs
1 cup granulated sugar
$^1/_2$ tablespoon vanilla extract
$^3/_4$ cup roughly chopped macadamia nuts
$^3/_4$ cup all-purpose flour

Preheat the oven to 350 degrees.

Lightly grease an 8-by-8-inch baking pan with butter.

Combine the broken-up chunks of white chocolate and butter in a glass measuring cup. Heat in a microwave oven at full power for 45 seconds. Stir and microwave for 30 seconds more. Stir until the white chocolate is fully melted and the mixture is smooth. (You can also melt the white chocolate and butter in the top of a double boiler over boiling water.)

In a large mixing bowl, combine the eggs, sugar, and vanilla. Beat with an electric mixer at medium speed for about 1 minute, until the sugar has completely dissolved, leaving a thick, pale mixture. Beat in the melted white chocolate mixture at low speed, until thoroughly combined. Stir in the nuts and flour with a wooden spoon. Stir in the roughly chopped white chocolate.

Turn the batter into the prepared baking pan and shake the pan to distribute it evenly. Bake for about 25 minutes, until the center is firm to the touch and the edges have browned.

Remove the pan from the oven and, while still warm, sprinkle with the finely chopped white chocolate. As the chocolate melts, spread it evenly over the top with a rubber spatula. Transfer the pan to a wire rack and cool completely. Refrigerate for at least 1 hour, then cut into 1-inch squares.

1/4 cup all-purpose flour
2/3 cup granulated sugar
1/3 cup firmly packed light brown sugar
1/4 teaspoon baking powder
1 teaspoon finely grated orange zest
1 cup chopped walnuts
1 cup chopped dates
1/4 cup (1/2 stick) unsalted butter, melted
2 large eggs, well beaten

Preheat the oven to 350 degrees.

Lightly grease an 8-by-8-inch baking pan with butter.

Whisk the flour, sugars, and baking powder together in a mixing bowl. Whisk in the orange zest. With a wooden spoon, stir in the walnuts and dates. Add the butter and eggs and stir until thoroughly blended.

Scrape the mixture into the prepared baking pan and spread it evenly to cover the bottom. Bake for about 25 minutes, until the cake is lightly browned and a tester inserted into the center comes out clean.

Remove the pan to a wire rack and cool completely, about 2 hours.

Cut into 2-by-2-inch squares.

Ruth Gold's Date Nut Squares

YIELD = 16 SQUARES

A staple on Ruth Gold's table, these squares taste a little bit like a cookie version of old-fashioned date nut bread. The brown sugar adds an interesting hint of caramel.

Caramel Cashew Bars

YIELD = 36 BARS

Each bite of this slightly decadent bar delivers a mouthful of caramel, with just an accent of cashew for character. To add texture to the base, we include graham flour, a coarsely ground whole wheat flour high in fiber and nutritional content—but don't tell anyone and spoil their fun.

BASE:

1½ cups all-purpose flour
½ cup graham flour
½ cup granulated sugar
½ teaspoon baking powder
⅛ teaspoon salt
¾ cup (1½ sticks) unsalted butter, melted

FILLING:

½ cup light corn syrup
1 cup firmly packed dark brown sugar
3 tablespoons unsalted butter, cut into pieces
⅔ cup heavy cream
2 teaspoons vanilla extract
2 cups coarsely chopped cashews, toasted (see box)

TOPPING:

1½ ounces bittersweet chocolate, broken up

Preheat the oven to 350 degrees.

Line a 9-by-13-inch baking pan with aluminum foil and grease well with butter.

Combine the flours, granulated sugar, baking powder, and salt in a large mixing bowl. Mix thoroughly with a whisk. Add the melted butter and stir with a wooden spoon for about 1 minute, until the butter is thoroughly combined with the flour, producing a coarse, crumbly mixture.

Turn it into the prepared baking pan and pat it down evenly to cover the bottom and sides. Bake for 10 minutes.

Remove the baking pan to a wire rack, leaving the oven on.

For the filling, combine the corn syrup and brown sugar in a medium saucepan. Bring to a boil over medium heat, stirring constantly. Stir in the butter and cream. Bring back to a boil and reduce the heat to medium-low. Cook for at least 10 minutes, until the mixture is thick and dark and reaches a temperature of 235 degrees on a candy thermometer.

Remove the pan from the heat and stir in the vanilla, then the cashews. Pour the filling into the baked shell and spread it evenly with a rubber spatula or the back of a wooden spoon, working the mixture into the corners. Be sure to keep the caramel inside the pastry to prevent it from sticking to the aluminum foil.

Bake for about 15 minutes, until bubbly.

Cool completely in the pan on a wire rack, for at least 1 hour.

Put the chocolate into a glass measuring cup and microwave at full power for about 1 minute, stirring every 15 seconds. (You can also melt the chocolate in the top of a double boiler over boiling water.) Using a pastry bag or a heavy-duty plastic storage bag with a bottom corner clipped, drizzle the melted chocolate over the top of the bar. Cool for 10 minutes more.

Firmly grasp the aluminum foil along the short sides of the sheet and remove the contents of the pan to a flat work surface. Cut into bars measuring 1½ inches by a little over 2 inches.

To toast the cashews, preheat the oven to 350 degrees.

Spread the nuts in a single layer on a baking sheet lined with aluminum foil. Bake for 8 to 10 minutes, until golden brown, shaking the pan a bit every 2 to 3 minutes.

Ann's Key Lime Bars

YIELD = 36 BARS

A frequent guest in our kitchen, Ann Bloomstrand has offered sage advice and moral support during many a baking binge. We particularly like this Key West–inspired creation. When combined with condensed milk, the key lime juice (found bottled or frozen in many supermarkets) thickens into a custardy filling that we encase between cookie layers. Much like its namesake pie, it's topped with toasted coconut.

One 14-ounce can sweetened condensed milk
$^1/_2$ cup key lime juice
1 cup rolled oats
$^1/_2$ cup granulated sugar
$^1/_2$ cup firmly packed dark brown sugar
$1^1/_2$ cups all-purpose flour
1 teaspoon baking powder
$^1/_2$ teaspoon salt
$^3/_4$ cup ($1^1/_2$ sticks) unsalted butter, well chilled, cut into 24 pieces
$^1/_2$ cup sweetened flaked coconut

Preheat the oven to 350 degrees.

Grease a 9-by-13-inch baking pan with butter.

Combine the condensed milk and key lime juice in a bowl. Whisk until blended and set aside to thicken.

Put the rolled oats in the bowl of a food processor fitted with the steel blade. Process for about 10 seconds, just enough to break up the oats. Add the sugars and process for 20 seconds. Add the flour, baking powder, salt, and butter. Process until combined, about 15 seconds.

Transfer $2^1/_2$ cups of the mixture to the prepared pan and press it evenly over the bottom. Pour the lime filling on top and spread it evenly with a rubber spatula.

Stir the coconut into the remaining oat mixture. Sprinkle it over the lime filling in the baking pan. Bake for about 30 minutes, until light golden.

Remove the pan to a wire rack and cool completely. Then refrigerate for 1 hour.

Cut into bars about $1^1/_2$ inches by a generous 2 inches.

¼ cup golden raisins

¼ cup currants

½ cup mixed candied fruit

¼ cup glacé cherries, quartered

¼ cup brandy

½ cup (1 stick) unsalted butter, at room temperature,
  cut into 8 pieces

1 cup firmly packed dark brown sugar

2 large eggs

1 cup all-purpose flour

1 tablespoon unsweetened Dutch-processed cocoa powder

¼ teaspoon baking soda

¾ teaspoon ground cinnamon

¼ teaspoon ground cloves

¼ teaspoon ground allspice

¼ cup chopped pecans

GLAZE:

½ cup confectioners' sugar

1½ tablespoons brandy

Preheat the oven to 375 degrees.

Coat a 9-by-9-inch baking pan with vegetable oil cooking spray.

Combine the raisins, currants, candied fruit, glacé cherries, and brandy. Set aside to soak.

Combine the butter and brown sugar in a bowl. Cream with an electric mixer at medium speed. Beat in the eggs until the mixture is light and fluffy.

In a large mixing bowl, whisk together the flour, cocoa powder, baking soda, and spices. Add the fruit (and soaking liquid) and the butter mixture. Stir with a wooden spoon until fully incorporated. Fold in the nuts. Turn the dough into the prepared pan.

Bake for about 18 minutes, until a tester inserted in the center comes out clean.

Meanwhile, prepare the glaze. Put the confectioners' sugar in a bowl. Add the brandy, mixing with a fork until the sugar is dissolved and the mixture is smooth.

When baked, remove the pan to a wire rack. Spread the glaze evenly on top and cool completely.

Cut into 2¼-by-1½-inch bars or 1½-inch squares.

Brandied Candied Fruit Bars

YIELD = 24 BARS
OR 36 SQUARES

We once had an acquaintance who liked fruitcake so much that she kept crocks of fruit steeping in brandy scattered about her apartment—on hand at all times for baking or for a potent snack.

We're not quite that gung ho, but we have found that presoaking the fruit in spirits does soften and mellow it nicely. Although slightly evocative of fruitcake, these bars are lighter, less sweet, and good at any time of the year.

Apricot Oatmeal Wheat Fingers

YIELD = 24 FINGERS

This is our retaliation against all those dry, tasteless health food bars. Brimming with healthy whole wheat flour and wheat germ, these cookies are moist, dense, and yummy.

½ cup (1 stick) unsalted butter, melted
¾ cup firmly packed light brown sugar
2 large eggs
1 teaspoon vanilla extract
½ cup all-purpose flour
¼ cup whole wheat flour
2 tablespoons wheat germ
¾ teaspoon baking powder
¼ teaspoon salt
1 teaspoon ground cinnamon
¼ teaspoon ground allspice
1 cup dried apricots (about 6 ounces), chopped
¼ cup chopped walnuts
¼ cup quick oats

Preheat the oven to 350 degrees.

Lightly grease a 9-inch-square baking pan with butter.

Combine the butter, brown sugar, eggs, and vanilla in a small bowl. Beat well with a fork.

In a large mixing bowl, whisk together the flours, wheat germ, baking powder, salt, and spices. Stir in the egg mixture with a wooden spoon. Fold in the apricots, walnuts, and oats. Turn the batter into the prepared baking pan and spread it evenly with the back of the wooden spoon. Bake for about 25 minutes, until a tester inserted in the center comes out clean.

Cool in the pan on a wire rack for at least 30 minutes.

Cut into 2¼-by-1½-inch fingers.

For Apple Oatmeal Wheat Fingers, substitute 2 Granny Smith apples for the dried apricots and an equal amount of chopped pecans for the walnuts. Peel and coarsely grate the apples (core them first if using a food processor to grate). Toss with 2 teaspoons freshly squeezed lemon juice and set aside while preparing the batter.

1 1/3 cups all-purpose flour
3/4 teaspoon baking powder
1/4 cup (1/2 stick) unsalted butter, at room temperature
1/2 cup granulated sugar
2 large eggs
1/2 tablespoon grated lemon zest
1/4 cup buttermilk
1 pint blueberries, picked over

TOPPING:
1/2 cup all-purpose flour
1/4 cup plus 2 tablespoons granulated sugar
1/4 cup plus 2 teaspoon ground cardamom
3/4 teaspoon ground cinnamon
1/4 cup (1/2 stick) unsalted butter, at room temperature

Preheat the oven to 350 degrees.

Lightly coat a 9-by-9-inch baking pan with vegetable oil cooking spray.

Whisk the flour and baking powder together and set aside.

In a large mixing bowl, combine the butter and sugar. Cream with an electric mixer at medium speed. Reduce the speed to low and beat in the eggs. Beat in the lemon zest, then the buttermilk.

Add the flour mixture and stir with a wooden spoon until fully incorporated. Turn the batter into the prepared baking pan and spread it to cover the bottom evenly. Arrange the blueberries on top in a single layer.

For the topping, combine the flour, sugar, and spices in a bowl. Mix well with a fork. Cut in the butter to form crumbs. Scatter the crumbs over the blueberries.

Bake for about 45 minutes, until a toothpick inserted into the center comes out clean.

Cool in the pan on a wire rack for 45 minutes, then cut into 1 1/2-inch squares.

For Blackberry Streusel Bars, use an equal amount of blackberries instead of blueberries.

Blueberry Streusel Bars

YIELD = 36 SQUARES

Cereal is good for kids and pastry is nice for dessert, but we all know that the morning newspaper is supposed to be taken back to bed with a mug of coffee and a handful of cookies. This is the perfect breakfast cookie— filling, not too sweet, and reminiscent of coffee cake.

Blackberry Linzer Squares

YIELD = 36 SQUARES

Each of these thick squares is really an individual linzertorte, containing a generous layer of jam framed by a lattice of the flavorful almond crust that also serves as the base of the cookie.

1 cup almonds
1¼ cups all-purpose flour
½ cup granulated sugar
½ teaspoon baking powder
⅛ teaspoon salt
1 teaspoon ground cinnamon
¼ teaspoon ground cloves
½ tablespoon finely grated lemon zest
½ cup (1 stick) unsalted butter, melted
2 large eggs, well beaten
10 ounces seedless blackberry spreadable fruit
1 teaspoon confectioners' sugar

Preheat the oven to 350 degrees.

Finely chop the almonds in a food processor fitted with the steel blade. Transfer them to a large mixing bowl. Add the flour, sugar, baking powder, salt, cinnamon, cloves, and lemon zest. Whisk thoroughly. Add the butter and eggs. Stir with a wooden spoon to incorporate.

Form the dough into a ball and cut it in half. Wrap one half in wax paper and refrigerate for 15 minutes. Put the other half into an ungreased 9-by-9-inch baking pan and pat it down to cover the bottom completely. Coat the top evenly with the blackberry spreadable fruit, leaving a ½-inch outer border.

Divide the chilled dough into 14 pieces. Work each into a thin rope about 9 inches long. In each direction, lay 5 ropes of dough over the top at 1½-inch intervals, forming a lattice pattern. Place the remaining 4 ropes around the outer border.

Bake for 35 to 40 minutes, until golden and firm to the touch.

Cool in the pan on a wire rack for 1 hour, then refrigerate for at least 1 hour more.

Dust the top with confectioners' sugar and cut into 1½-inch squares.

For Raspberry Linzer Squares, substitute an equal amount of seedless raspberry for the blackberry spreadable fruit.

BASE:
1 cup all-purpose flour
1 cup granulated sugar
½ cup (1 stick) unsalted butter, melted

FILLING:
½ cup firmly packed light brown sugar
¼ cup all-purpose flour
1¼ cups sweetened flaked coconut
¾ cup dried sour cherries
2 large eggs, lightly beaten
1 teaspoon vanilla extract
¾ teaspoon almond extract
¼ teaspoon salt

Preheat the oven to 350 degrees.

Coat a 9-by-13-inch baking pan lightly with vegetable oil cooking spray.

Put the flour and sugar in a bowl. Mix with a fork. Stir in the butter until well combined and crumbly. Transfer the mixture to the prepared pan and press it evenly over the bottom. Bake for 10 to 12 minutes, until the dough is beginning to brown around the edges.

Remove to a wire rack and let the crust cool for 5 minutes.

Combine all the filling ingredients in a large mixing bowl and stir with a wooden spoon until the sugar is completely dissolved. Pour the filling over the crust and spread it evenly. Bake for 20 to 22 minutes, until golden on top.

Transfer the pan to a wire rack and cool completely, about 1 hour.

Cut into 1½-inch squares.

Although dried sour cherries are now stocked by some supermarkets, the canned or frozen varieties of sour cherries, which are found just about everywhere, can be oven-dried easily.

Preheat the oven to 170 degrees.

Rinse and drain the sour cherries (thaw, if frozen). Spread in a single layer on a baking sheet lined with aluminum foil. Bake until the cherries are free of moisture but still pliable, about 10 hours.

Remove from the oven and cool completely before using. Stored in an airtight container, the dried sour cherries will keep for about 3 months.

Sour Cherry Coconut Squares

YIELD = 48 BARS

These juxtapose sweet, rich coconut with tart sour cherries atop a thin crisp sugar cookie base. In the mood to experiment? Try dried cranberries instead of sour cherries, or add a cup of chopped macadamia nuts to the filling in lieu of almond extract.

Chocolate-Covered Peanut Butter Bars

YIELD = 36 BARS

This versatile cookie has something for almost everyone. Some of our friends claim it's gooey enough and sufficiently chock-full of chocolate to remind them of munchies downed while cramming for college exams. Because of the intense peanut flavor, it's also a favorite of Barry's sister-in-law, Eleanor, whose taste normally runs more to classic French.

$\frac{1}{2}$ cup (1 stick) unsalted butter, at room temperature
1 cup creamy peanut butter
$\frac{3}{4}$ cup granulated sugar
$\frac{1}{2}$ cup firmly packed light brown sugar
3 large eggs
$\frac{3}{4}$ teaspoon vanilla extract
1 cup all-purpose flour
$\frac{1}{4}$ cup raw blanched peanuts, coarsely chopped
$\frac{1}{4}$ teaspoon salt
1 cup milk chocolate chips

Preheat the oven to 350 degrees.

Combine the butter and peanut butter in a large mixing bowl. Cream with an electric mixer at high speed. Beat in the sugars at medium speed until incorporated. At low speed, beat in the eggs and vanilla.

Thoroughly stir in the flour, peanuts, and salt with a wooden spoon. Scrape the batter into an ungreased 9-by-13-inch baking pan, spreading it evenly to coat the entire bottom surface of the pan.

Bake for about 25 minutes, until beginning to brown around the edges.

Scatter the chocolate chips on top and return the pan to the oven for about 1 minute to melt the chocolate. With a spatula or knife, spread the melted chocolate evenly to coat the top.

Place the pan on a wire rack and cool for about 2 hours, until the chocolate topping hardens. Cut into rectangles measuring a generous 2 inches by $1\frac{1}{2}$ inches.

For Chocolate-Covered Cashew Butter Bars, substitute equal amounts of cashew butter for the peanut butter and coarsely chopped cashews for the peanuts.

¾ cup all-purpose flour
⅔ cup unsweetened Dutch-processed cocoa powder
1 tablespoon ground cinnamon
½ teaspoon baking soda
¼ teaspoon salt
½ cup (1 stick) unsalted butter, at room temperature
8 ounces cream cheese, at room temperature
1 cup granulated sugar
½ cup firmly packed light brown sugar
3 large eggs, lightly beaten
1 teaspoon vanilla extract
1 cup chopped walnuts

Preheat the oven to 350 degrees.

Lightly grease a 9-inch-square baking pan with butter.

Combine the flour, cocoa powder, cinnamon, baking soda, and salt in a bowl. Whisk and set aside.

In a large mixing bowl, cream the butter and cream cheese with an electric mixer at medium speed. Add the sugars and beat until the mixture is light and fluffy. Mix in the eggs and vanilla. Dump in the flour mixture and stir with a wooden spoon just until well combined.

Pour the batter into the prepared baking pan. Scatter the walnuts over the top. Bake for 30 to 35 minutes, until the edges are slightly puffy and just beginning to pull away from the sides of the pan.

Transfer the pan to a wire rack and cool for about 1 hour. Then refrigerate for 2 hours.

Cut into 2¼-by-1½-inch bars.

Cappuccino Cream Cheese Bars

YIELD = 24 BARS

Sort of a cross between a fudgie brownie and a slice of cheesecake, these bars offer all the trimmings of cappuccino, but none of the java. For those who just can't do without their caffeine, serve the coffee on the side.

Susan Felber's Three-Layer Brownies

YIELD = 16 BROWNIES

This recipe came to us by way of Barry's sister-in-law, Eleanor, who could have sworn she remembered an accent of mint in her sister's brownies. This sounded so good to us that we added a bit of peppermint extract to Susan's recipe. The mint-flavored cream nestles between a thick, fudgie brownie base and a layer of chocolate frosting.

BROWNIE BASE:
1 cup granulated sugar
2 large eggs
2 ounces unsweetened chocolate, broken up
$^1/_2$ cup (1 stick) unsalted butter, cut into pieces
$^1/_2$ teaspoon vanilla extract
$^1/_2$ cup all-purpose flour
$^1/_2$ cup semisweet chocolate chips

FIRST FROSTING LAYER:
1 cup confectioners' sugar
2 tablespoons unsalted butter, at room temperature
1 tablespoon whole milk
$^1/_2$ teaspoon peppermint extract

TOP FROSTING LAYER:
$1^1/_2$ ounces unsweetened chocolate, broken up
$1^1/_2$ tablespoons unsalted butter

Preheat the oven to 350 degrees.

Lightly grease an 8-by-8-inch baking pan with butter.

To make the brownie base, combine the granulated sugar and eggs in a large bowl. Mix with a wooden spoon until well blended and pale yellow.

Combine the unsweetened chocolate and butter in a glass measuring cup. Heat in a microwave oven for 1 minute at full power, stir until smooth and blended. (You can also melt the chocolate and butter in the top of a double boiler over boiling water.) Add to the sugar and egg mixture. Stir in the vanilla. Add the flour and stir until fully incorporated. Fold in the chocolate chips.

Turn the batter into the prepared baking pan and spread it evenly over the bottom with a rubber spatula. Bake for about 20 minutes, until firm.

Remove the pan to a wire rack and cool thoroughly, 30 to 40 minutes.

For the first frosting layer, combine the confectioners' sugar, butter, milk, and peppermint in a mixing bowl. Stir with a wooden spoon until thoroughly combined. Spread the mixture smoothly and evenly over the cooled brownie base, using the back of the wooden spoon.

For the top frosting layer, microwave the chocolate and butter at full power for 1 minute and stir thoroughly, or melt them in the top of a double boiler over boiling water. Pour the frosting over the brownies. Tilt and rotate the pan to disperse the chocolate evenly over the top.

Refrigerate for at least 1 hour, until the top layer is firm. Cut into 2-inch squares.

If your taste runs more to the nutty than the minty, omit the peppermint extract in the first frosting layer and substitute $1/2$ cup chopped pecans in the brownie base.

Apricot Butter Bars

YIELD = 25 BARS

A thick layer of tangy apricot butter atop a crisp sugar cookie base, garnished with a light crumb topping.

FILLING:
16 ounces dried apricots (about 2 cups)
1½ cups granulated sugar
1½ cups water

DOUGH:
2 cups all-purpose flour
½ cup confectioners' sugar
¼ cup granulated sugar
¾ cup (1½ sticks) unsalted butter, melted

Preheat the oven to 375 degrees.

Coat a 10¼-by-15¼-inch baking sheet with vegetable oil cooking spray.

Combine the filling ingredients in a medium saucepan. Bring to a boil over high heat. Lower the heat, cover, and simmer for about 25 minutes, until the fruit is soft enough to mash.

Transfer to the bowl of a food processor fitted with the steel blade and process to a thick, smooth puree, about 20 seconds.

In a mixing bowl, combine the flour and sugars. Mix with a fork. Add the butter and mix to form a crumbly dough (crumbs about the size of peas).

Reserve 1 cup of the dough and transfer the rest to the prepared baking sheet. Press it over the bottom and up the sides. Spread the apricot filling evenly over the crust. Scatter the reserved crumbs of dough over the top.

Bake for about 25 minutes, until the edges are brown.

Cool on the sheet on a wire rack for about 1 hour, then refrigerate for 30 minutes. Cut into 2-by-3-inch rectangles.

For Quick Apricot Bars, we use
prepared piecrusts (the flat dough circles
sold refrigerated in the supermarket, not
the preformed frozen variety) and cook
the apricot filling in the microwave.

8 ounces dried apricots
$^3/_4$ cup granulated sugar
1 cup water
2 prepared refrigerated crusts for 9-inch pies
1 tablespoon milk

Preheat the oven to 350 degrees and coat a
$9^1/_4$-by-$13^1/_4$-inch baking sheet with vegetable oil
cooking spray.

Combine the apricots, sugar, and water in a
microwave-safe container. Cover and cook at full
power for 10 minutes, stirring after 3 minutes and
then again 5 minutes later. Puree the mixture in a
food processor or blender.

Work one of the piecrusts by hand over the
bottom and up the sides of the prepared baking
sheet. Spread the apricot filling evenly over the
crust. On a work surface, shape the remaining
piecrust into a rectangle large enough to cover the
filling. Place it on top and crimp the edges of the
crusts together. Paint with the milk.

Bake for 18 to 20 minutes, until golden brown.

Cool completely on the sheet on a wire rack. Cut
into bars measuring $1^1/_2$ inches by scant $2^1/_4$
inches.

YIELD = 36 BARS

Hazelnut Chocolate Squares

YIELD = 36 SQUARES

For this intense cookie, whole hazelnuts are suspended in a thick, almost custardy caramel spiked with pure maple syrup and bittersweet chocolate. Each 1½-inch square constitutes a more than adequate portion for most folks.

BASE:
¾ cup all-purpose flour
¼ cup confectioners' sugar
2 tablespoons granulated sugar
⅛ teaspoon salt
1 cup (2 sticks) unsalted butter, cold, cut into 16 tablespoons

FILLING:
⅔ cup pure maple syrup
¼ cup granulated sugar
¾ cup firmly packed dark brown sugar
¼ cup (½ stick) unsalted butter, melted
2 large eggs
½ tablespoon vanilla extract
1½ cups hazelnuts
6 ounces bittersweet chocolate, roughly chunked (about 1 cup)

Preheat the oven to 375 degrees.

For the base, combine the flour, sugars, and salt in the bowl of a food processor fitted with the steel blade. Process for 30 seconds. Add the butter and pulse about 40 times, until the mixture is dotted with bits of butter about the size of small peas.

Dump the mixture into an ungreased 9-by-9-inch baking pan and pat it down firmly to cover the bottom. Bake for about 15 minutes, just until beginning to brown around the edges.

Remove the pan to a wire rack to cool for 20 minutes, leaving the oven on.

For the filling, combine the maple syrup, sugars, butter, eggs, and vanilla in a bowl. Mix with an electric mixer at low speed until the sugar is thoroughly dissolved.

Stir in the hazelnuts and chocolate. Pour the filling over the cooled crust. Return the pan to the oven and bake for 30 to 35 minutes, until puffed up and browned.

Cool completely in the pan on a wire rack, for at least 2 hours. Then refrigerate overnight.

Cut into 1½-inch squares.

Rolled Cookies

Rolled cookies bring to mind the archetypal gray-haired grandma, decked out in a ruffled apron, brandishing a well-worn rolling pin and a motley array of cookie cutters. What could be simpler?

The reality is that it's time to give Granny her due. Rolled cookies demand more commitment and skill than most other cookies. In return, they offer the creative baker a great deal of flexibility.

Rolled cookies can be made in a broad and sophisticated spectrum of sweet to savory flavors. They can be artistically crafted in a seemingly endless variety of sizes and shapes, and decorated in critical detail.

Many of our rolled cookie doughs are prepared entirely in the food processor, saving effort up front. Most spend some time in the refrigerator to become firm enough to be rolled. If pressed for time, place the dough in the freezer for about half the specified chilling time. The dough may also be prepared ahead of time and stored in the refrigerator for up to 3 days or in the freezer for up to 1 month before rolling.

When the dough is divided and rolled 1 piece at a time, it's usually best to return unused portions to the refrigerator until you're ready for them.

Roll the dough out to the specified thickness on a lightly floured work surface with a lightly floured pin, working it into the desired shape and approximate size. It's easier to roll very moist and sticky doughs between sheets of wax paper, or with the aid of a pastry cloth and a rolling pin cover. Dough that is too cold may crack when rolled; allow it to soften before proceeding.

Add just enough flour as you work to keep the dough from sticking; too much flour will toughen the cookies. Think of the process as somewhat akin to learning to drive a stick shift—it sounds ominously imprecise in theory, but becomes second nature once you get a feel for the balance.

Cut cookies out with a lightly floured cutter, placing the cutter firmly onto the dough and twisting to make a clean cut. Try to leave as little space as possible between cuts. Transfer the cookies to sheets with a metal spatula, gather the scraps, and reroll gently for additional cookies.

We developed our recipes with a reliance on standard 2-inch- and 2½-inch-round cookie cutters, but the possibilities for variation and experimentation are extensive. For example, 3-inch or 4-inch circles can be quartered, yielding wedges, or doughnut cutters can be used to produce wreaths. You can also fashion cookies of your own design with easily made cardboard templates and a sharp knife (page 123), or you can use any of the hundreds of cutter shapes available.

Just remember not to mix cookies of different sizes on the same cookie sheet, and bear in mind that changes in size, shape, and thickness can alter baking times.

Store rolled cookies in cookie jars or tins. They're at their prime for 5 days and will freeze well for up to 3 months.

1 cup cake flour
¼ cup rye flour
¼ cup freshly grated Parmesan cheese (see box)
⅛ teaspoon ground white pepper
¼ teaspoon salt
¼ teaspoon baking soda
½ cup (1 stick) unsalted butter, at room temperature
¼ cup confectioners' sugar
¼ cup sour cream

Preheat the oven to 350 degrees.

Whisk together the flours, Parmesan cheese, white pepper, salt, and baking soda.

In a large mixing bowl, cream the butter and confectioners' sugar with an electric mixer at low speed. Beat in the sour cream, just to combine. Stir in the flour mixture with a wooden spoon.

Divide the dough in half. Place half on a lightly floured work surface, turning to coat it with flour. Roll it out to a ¼-inch-thick circle about 8 inches across. Cut out 2-inch cookies with a circular cutter and place them about 1 inch apart on ungreased cookie sheets. Prick the top of each cookie 3 times with the tines of a fork. Repeat the process with the remaining piece of dough.

Bake for about 14 minutes, until golden brown.

Transfer the cookies to wire racks to cool.

The type and quality of cheese used in the rounds will make a vast difference in the taste of the finished product. The better the cheese, the better the cookie.

We prefer to do the grating ourselves just before making the cookies, but the variety that is freshly grated on-site at your cheese store or better supermarket will do in a pinch. Avoid bland commercial varieties.

For a slightly sharper flavor, substitute 3 tablespoons pecorino, a sheep's milk cheese, for the Parmesan.

Parmesan Pepper Rounds

YIELD = ABOUT
2½ DOZEN ROUNDS

A savory cross between a cookie and a dessert cracker, these go nicely with fruit or cheese and are perfect for the buffet. Their subtle cheese flavor will be more intense the day after baking.

Chocolate Walnut Truffles

YIELD = ABOUT
4 DOZEN TRUFFLES

This spectacular—if we do say so ourselves—dessert cookie has a rich, fudgy taste and a firm but not crisp consistency.

The chocolate truffle can be put on the cooled cookies using a pastry bag fitted with a star tip or a heavy-duty plastic bag with a bottom corner clipped. You can also use a cookie press with a star-shaped disk; take care to press the truffle on gently so as not to crack the cookie.

DOUGH:

1¾ cups all-purpose flour
¾ cup unsweetened Dutch-processed cocoa powder
¼ teaspoon salt
¾ cup firmly packed light brown sugar
¼ cup granulated sugar
⅓ cup chopped walnuts, plus about 4 dozen walnut halves for decoration (optional)
1 cup (2 sticks) unsalted butter, chilled, cut into pieces
1 teaspoon vanilla extract

TRUFFLE:

8 ounces bittersweet chocolate, chopped
½ cup heavy cream
2 tablespoons unsalted butter, at room temperature
2 tablespoons cognac

Preheat the oven to 300 degrees.

Line cookie sheets with baker's parchment.

Whisk together the flour, cocoa powder, and salt in a mixing bowl.

Combine the sugars and walnuts in a food processor fitted with the steel blade. Process until the nuts are finely ground, about 15 seconds. With the machine running, add the butter continuously through the feed tube. Add the vanilla and continue to process for a few seconds more, until the mixture is smooth and creamy.

Scrape down the sides of the bowl with a rubber spatula. Add the flour mixture and process for about 15 seconds to form a dough ball.

Turn the dough out onto a lightly floured work surface and divide it in half. Roll each half out to a thickness of ⅛ inch, shaping it into an 8-by-8-inch square. Cut out 2-inch circles and place them on the prepared cookie sheets. Repeat the process until all the dough has been used.

Bake for about 10 minutes, until the cookies are beginning to crack lightly on top.

Let the cookies cool on the sheets for 5 minutes. Transfer the cookies to wire racks to finish cooling, and set the baking sheets aside to cool as well.

For the truffle, put the chocolate into a mixing bowl.

Bring the cream to a boil in a small saucepan over medium-low heat. Pour it over the chocolate and stir until the chocolate is fully melted and the mixture is smooth. Stir in the butter, then the cognac. Cover the mixture with plastic wrap and refrigerate it until thick enough to spread, about 15 minutes.

Return the cookies to the cookie sheets. Mound about 1 teaspoon of the chilled truffle mixture in the center of each. Top, if desired, with a half walnut. Put the sheets in the refrigerator and let the cookies chill for about 15 minutes.

For Chocolate Truffle Sandwiches, use half the amount of each ingredient called for in preparing the truffle mixture. Spread about 1 teaspoon on the flat bottom of a cookie, top with a second cookie, and chill.

YIELD = ABOUT 2 DOZEN SANDWICHES

Macadamia Butters

YIELD = ABOUT
4 DOZEN COOKIES

We developed this recipe for a friend, now expecting her second child, who once again has an almost limitless craving for macadamia cookies. It seems like a harmless enough quirk of pregnancy, but with macadamia cookies going for $5.00 a pound, she's been dropping a lot of hints our way.

Macadamias are our one exception to the rule of buying only unsalted nuts, since it's so easy to use the readily available roasted variety, which contain a bit of salt. We have compensated by eliminating the addition of any more salt in the recipe.

1 cup macadamia nuts, plus about
   2 dozen nuts for decoration
$1/2$ cup firmly packed light brown sugar
$1/4$ cup granulated sugar
1 cup (2 sticks) unsalted butter, chilled, cut into pieces
2 large eggs
1 teaspoon vanilla extract
$2 1/4$ cups all-purpose flour
$1/4$ teaspoon baking soda
1 tablespoon water

Combine 1 cup of the macadamia nuts with the sugars in the bowl of a food processor fitted with the steel blade. Process to a fine consistency, about 30 seconds. With the machine on, add the butter a few pieces at a time through the feed tube, continuing to process until the mixture is light and creamy. Add 1 of the eggs and the vanilla; process until blended. Add the flour and baking soda and process to form a smooth dough.

Scrape the dough onto a sheet of wax paper with a rubber spatula. Form the dough into a ball, wrap it in the wax paper, and refrigerate for 1 hour.

Preheat the oven to 375 degrees.

On a floured work surface, roll the dough out into a $1/4$-inch-thick circle about 12 inches in diameter. Cut out $2 1/2$-inch circles and place them about $1 1/2$ inches apart on ungreased cookie sheets.

In a small bowl, thoroughly whisk the remaining egg with the water. Brush the cookies with this wash and place half a macadamia nut in the center of each.

Bake for about 14 minutes, until golden.

Remove the cookies to wire racks to cool.

HOMEMADE COOKIE CUTTERS

Cookie cutters come in a variety of shapes and sizes, and a diligent enthusiast can put together quite a collection. You can also fashion cookies of your own design—initials, trains, trucks, boats, houses, toys, or other decorative shapes—with easily made cardboard templates and a sharp knife.

Draw or trace the desired design on tracing paper, cut it out, and fasten it to a stiff, thin piece of cardboard (the type available from art supply shops). Cut out the design and remove the tracing paper.

After rolling out the dough, lay the template on top, cut the outline of the template into the dough, remove the template, and transfer the cookie with a spatula to a cookie sheet. You can use smaller templates that will produce a yield similar to that of the original recipe, or oversize templates that will yield a few giant cookies. Bake at the temperature called for in the original recipe, watching for visual or textural doneness cues, as baking times may vary with the thickness of the cookie.

Old-Fashioned Sugar Cookies

YIELD = ABOUT
3 1/2 DOZEN COOKIES

We prepare the dough for these cookies in a food processor, yielding old-fashioned taste in a fraction of the time. Using a pastry cloth and rolling pin cover will prevent sticking, overhandling, and the addition of too much extra flour when rolling out the dough.

This thick, rich dough is so versatile it even makes a great piecrust!

2 1/2 cups all-purpose flour
2 teaspoons baking powder
1/2 teaspoon salt
1 cup granulated sugar
1/2 cup (1 stick) unsalted butter, at room temperature, cut into pieces
2 large eggs
2 teaspoons grated lemon zest
1 teaspoon vanilla extract

Sift the flour, baking powder, and salt together into a mixing bowl and set aside.

Put the sugar into the bowl of a food processor fitted with the steel blade. With the machine running, add the butter, a few pieces at a time, through the feed tube. Continue to process for about 1 minute, until the mixture is creamy. Add the eggs, lemon zest, and vanilla and process until blended. Add the flour mixture and pulse just until incorporated.

Gather the dough into a ball, wrap it in wax paper, and refrigerate for at least 3 hours.

Preheat the oven to 350 degrees.

Lightly coat cookie sheets with vegetable oil cooking spray.

Unwrap the dough ball and cut it into quarters. Re-cover 3 of the quarters and return them to the refrigerator until ready to use. Roll out the first quarter on a lightly floured work surface to a thickness of 1/8 inch. Cut out cookies with a 2-inch-round cookie cutter and transfer them with a spatula to the prepared sheets, leaving 2 inches between cookies. Repeat the process with the remaining pieces of dough.

Bake for 8 to 10 minutes, until the cookies have turned a pale gold.

Remove the cookies to a wire rack and cool completely.

Grandpa Nigberg's Apple Pie

This enticing pie, which bakes up much like a German kuchen, has been a favorite in Barry's family for generations. It was created by his grandfather, a baker at the Waldorf-Astoria, in the early 1900s.

FILLING:

6 Granny Smith apples, peeled, cored, and sliced (about 6 cups)
2 Gala apples, peeled, cored, and sliced (about 2 cups)
1 cup granulated sugar
$1/2$ teaspoon salt
3 tablespoons all-purpose flour
$1/4$ teaspoon ground nutmeg
$3/4$ teaspoon ground cinnamon
2 teaspoons freshly squeezed lemon juice

CRUST:

1 recipe Old-Fashioned Sugar Cookies dough, chilled

ASSEMBLY:

1 tablespoon unsalted butter, cut into 3 pats
2 tablespoons whole milk

Preheat the oven to 350 degrees.

Combine the filling ingredients in a large mixing bowl and toss to coat the apples thoroughly.

Cut the dough ball in half. Roll one half out between sheets of lightly floured wax paper to a thickness of $1/8$ to $1/4$ inch. Line a lightly greased and floured 9- or 10-inch glass pie plate with the rolled dough. Pour in the apple mixture and dot with the butter.

Roll out the second half of dough and place it on top. Tightly crimp the crusts together. Cut large vent holes in the center of the crust and brush the top and edges with the milk.

Bake for 45 to 55 minutes, until the bottom crust is lightly browned. Check the pie after about 30 minutes and cover the edge with foil if it appears to be browning too quickly. Remove the plate to a wire rack and cool the pie for at least 1 hour before cutting.

YIELD = 8 TO 10 SERVINGS

Cognac Dreams

YIELD = ABOUT
7 DOZEN COOKIES

Festive little party cookies in fanciful shapes, topped with a creamy cognac frosting.

If you don't have any self-rising flour on hand, use all-purpose flour and add 1 teaspoon cream of tartar and 1 teaspoon baking soda.

1/2 cup granulated sugar
1 cup confectioners' sugar
1 cup (2 sticks) unsalted butter, at room temperature, cut into pieces
1 large egg
1 teaspoon vanilla extract
1 teaspoon cognac
2 1/2 cups self-rising flour, sifted

COGNAC FROSTING:
1 1/2 cups confectioners' sugar
1 teaspoon cognac
2 tablespoons plus 2 teaspoons milk

Put the granulated sugar into the bowl of a food processor fitted with the steel blade. Process to superfine consistency, about 1 minute. Sift with the confectioners' sugar into the bowl of a stationary electric mixer fitted with the paddle attachment. Add the butter. Cream at low speed for about 1 minute, until smooth and pale. Add the egg, vanilla, and cognac. Mix at medium speed for about 1 minute, until fluffy. Reduce the speed to low and beat in the flour, just until incorporated.

Turn the dough out onto wax paper, roll it up, and refrigerate for 3 hours.

Preheat the oven to 375 degrees.

Line cookie sheets with baker's parchment.

Divide the dough in half, returning half to the refrigerator until ready to use. On a lightly floured work surface, roll out 1 piece to a 1/4-inch-thick rectangle about 12 by 10 inches. Cut into small cookies with decorative cutters in various shapes. Place on the prepared cookie sheets. Repeat the process for the remaining piece of dough.

Bake for about 9 minutes, just until the cookies begin to brown.

Remove the cookies to wire racks and cool completely before frosting.

For the frosting, combine all the ingredients and whisk until the mixture is smooth and spreadable.

Lemon Clove Cookies

YIELD = ABOUT
4 DOZEN COOKIES

These pungent cookies are based on an old Danish recipe. They're perfect after dinner, since the clove acts as a palate cleanser. We top each with a pecan half, but you can also use a half walnut or a few slivered blanched almonds.

1½ cups all-purpose flour
½ tablespoon ground cloves
½ teaspoon baking soda
¼ teaspoon salt
½ tablespoon lemon zest
¼ cup firmly packed dark brown sugar
2 tablespoons granulated sugar
6 tablespoons unsalted butter, chilled, cut into pieces
¼ cup dark corn syrup
1 large egg yolk
1 tablespoon water
¾ cup pecan halves

For Orange Clove Cookies, substitute 2 teaspoons orange zest for the ½ tablespoon lemon zest.

Whisk together the flour, cloves, baking soda, salt, and lemon zest in a mixing bowl. Set aside.

Combine the sugars in a food processor fitted with the steel blade and process just to combine. With the machine running, add the butter through the feed tube.

Turn the machine off, scrape down the sides of the bowl with a rubber spatula, and process for a few seconds more until the mixture is creamy. Add the corn syrup and process just to incorporate. Scrape down the sides again and add the flour mixture. Process for about 30 seconds to form a dough.

Turn the dough out onto a large sheet of wax paper and gather it into a ball. Wrap it in the wax paper, and refrigerate for 30 minutes.

Preheat the oven to 375 degrees.

Coat cookie sheets with vegetable oil cooking spray.

Divide the dough in half. Place half on a lightly floured work surface and turn the dough to coat it with flour. Roll it out to a ⅛-inch-thick rectangle, about 9 by 10 inches, adding more flour as necessary to prevent the dough from sticking to the pin. Cut out 2-inch cookies and transfer them with a spatula to the prepared cookie sheets. Repeat the process until all the dough has been used.

Whisk the egg yolk and water thoroughly in a small bowl and paint the cookies with the wash. Press a pecan half gently into the center of each.

Bake for about 8 minutes, until lightly golden.

Remove the cookies to wire racks to cool.

Sour Cream Pillows with Slivered Almonds

YIELD = ABOUT
4 DOZEN COOKIES

While baking, this cookie puffs up to a rich and dense consistency; the slivered almonds scattered on top toast to a golden brown.

2¹/₂ cups all-purpose flour
³/₄ teaspoon baking powder
¹/₄ teaspoon salt
¹/₄ teaspoon baking soda
¹/₂ cup (1 stick) unsalted butter, at room temperature, cut into pieces
1 cup granulated sugar
1 large egg, plus 1 egg white
¹/₂ cup sour cream
1 teaspoon almond extract
1 tablespoon water
1 cup blanched slivered almonds

Whisk together the flour, baking powder, salt, and baking soda.

In a large mixing bowl, cream the butter and sugar with an electric mixer at low speed. Beat in the whole egg until fluffy. Beat in the sour cream and almond extract, then the flour mixture. Scrape the residue from the beaters back into the bowl.

Gather the dough into a ball, wrap it in wax paper, and refrigerate for 1¹/₂ hours.

Preheat the oven to 375 degrees.

Divide the dough in half. Place half on a floured work surface, turning the dough to coat with flour. Roll it out to a thickness of ¹/₈ inch. Cut out 2¹/₂-inch-round cookies and place them 1 inch apart on ungreased cookie sheets. Repeat the process for the remaining dough.

Brush the cookies with a mixture of the egg white and water. Top each with 1 teaspoon slivered almonds, gently pushing the nuts into the dough.

Bake for 10 to 12 minutes, until the cookies are lightly browned around the edges and the nuts are evenly toasted.

Remove the cookies to wire racks and cool.

Rum raisin is a favorite flavor of ours, one we use in everything from tea cakes to quick breads to dessert dips.

To make Rum Raisin Cookies, combine ³/₄ cup seedless raisins and ¹/₄ cup light rum in a small bowl and set aside to soak. Proceed with the recipe directions, substituting 1 teaspoon of the soaking liquid for the almond extract. Just before baking, drain the raisins and top each cookie with ³/₄ teaspoon raisins instead of the slivered almonds.

2 cups all-purpose flour
³/₄ teaspoon ground cinnamon
³/₄ teaspoon ground ginger
¹/₂ teaspoon ground cloves
¹/₂ teaspoon baking soda
¹/₄ teaspoon salt
¹/₄ cup (¹/₂ stick) unsalted butter, at room temperature
¹/₃ cup firmly packed light brown sugar
1 large egg
¹/₂ cup dark molasses

In a mixing bowl, whisk together the flour, spices, baking soda, and salt. Set aside.

Combine the butter and brown sugar in the bowl of a food processor fitted with the steel blade. Process for a few seconds, until creamy. Add the egg and molasses. Process for 15 to 20 seconds, until the mixture is incorporated and smooth. Scrape down the sides of the bowl with a rubber spatula. Add the dry ingredients and process to incorporate.

Scrape the dough out onto a sheet of wax paper, wrap it up, and refrigerate for 1 hour.

Preheat the oven to 375 degrees.

Coat cookie sheets with vegetable oil cooking spray.

Divide the dough in half. On a lightly floured work surface, roll one half out into a 12-inch circle ¹/₈ inch thick. Cut out cookies with a round 2¹/₂-inch cutter and place them on the prepared cookie sheets about 1 inch apart. Repeat the process for the remaining dough.

Bake for about 8 minutes, until firm to the touch.

Transfer the cookies to wire racks to cool.

German Spice Cookies

YIELD = ABOUT
3 DOZEN COOKIES

An Old World favorite, these cookies resemble snaps at first glance, but are soft and chewy inside. We use a minimal amount of sugar to let the aromatic mélange of spices predominate.

White Russians

These tender cookies, which come out of the oven glistening with a sprinkling of coarse turbinado sugar, taste a little like White Russian cocktails. A fluted cookie cutter adds a nice decorative touch.

$^{1}\!/_{2}$ cup granulated sugar
2 tablespoons dark brown sugar
$^{3}\!/_{4}$ cup (1$^{1}\!/_{2}$ sticks) unsalted butter, chilled, cut into pieces
1 large egg plus 1 egg white
$^{1}\!/_{2}$ teaspoon vanilla extract
$^{1}\!/_{2}$ cup Kahlúa liqueur
3 cups all-purpose flour
1 teaspoon baking powder
$^{1}\!/_{2}$ teaspoon baking soda
$^{1}\!/_{4}$ teaspoon salt
1 tablespoon water
3 tablespoons turbinado sugar

For Amaretto Cookies, substitute equal amounts of amaretto liqueur and almond extract for the Kahlúa and vanilla. Instead of sprinkling the cookies with turbinado sugar, place a whole blanched almond in the center of each one.

Preheat the oven to 375 degrees.

Combine the granulated and dark brown sugars in a food processor fitted with the steel blade and process for a few seconds to mix. With the machine running, add the butter piece by piece through the feed tube, continuing to process until it is incorporated and creamy. Scrape down the sides of the bowl with a rubber spatula.

Add the whole egg and the vanilla. Pulse a few times to combine thoroughly, then scrape down the bowl again. Add the liqueur and pulse to combine. (The mixture will appear curdled at this point.)

Combine the flour, baking powder, baking soda, and salt in a bowl and whisk well. Add to the mixture in the food processor. Process to form a dough, 10 to 15 seconds.

Place half of the dough on a lightly floured surface, turning it with flour to coat. Roll it out into a circle about 12 inches across and $^{1}\!/_{4}$ inch thick. Cut out cookies with a 2$^{1}\!/_{2}$-inch circular cutter, pressing down firmly to cut all the way through the dough. Transfer the cookies with a spatula to ungreased cookie sheets. Repeat the process with the remaining half of the dough.

Whisk together the egg white and water and paint the cookies with the wash. Sprinkle turbinado sugar evenly on top.

Bake for about 10 minutes, until lightly colored and slightly puffed. Remove the cookies to wire racks to cool.

1 cup all-purpose flour
$^{1}/_{4}$ cup unsweetened Dutch-processed cocoa powder
1 teaspoon baking powder
$^{1}/_{4}$ teaspoon salt
$^{3}/_{4}$ cup firmly packed light brown sugar
1 large egg
$^{3}/_{4}$ cup fresh natural peanut butter
1 teaspoon vanilla extract
$^{1}/_{2}$ cup (1 stick) unsalted butter, at room temperature,
    cut into pieces
$^{1}/_{2}$ cup raw blanched peanuts, chopped

Whisk together the flour, cocoa powder, baking powder, and salt in a mixing bowl. Set aside.

Combine the brown sugar, egg, peanut butter, and vanilla in a food processor fitted with the steel blade. Process briefly, until blended. With the machine on, add the bits of butter through the feed tube. Add the flour mixture and process for just a few seconds to form a dough.

Remove the dough to a sheet of wax paper, wrap it up, and refrigerate for 1 hour.

Preheat the oven to 350 degrees.

Coat cookie sheets with vegetable oil cooking spray.

Divide the dough in half. On a lightly floured work surface, roll half the dough out to a $^{1}/_{4}$-inch-thick rectangle, about 8 by 10 inches. (Just push the dough back together if it cracks while rolling it out.)

Cut out circles with a 3-inch cutter and transfer to the prepared cookie sheets. Repeat the process for the remaining piece of dough. Top each cookie with a scant $^{1}/_{2}$ tablespoon of the chopped peanuts.

Bake for about 13 minutes, just until the edges are firm to the touch.

Cool on wire racks.

Chocolate Peanut Butter Thingies

YIELD = ABOUT
1 $^{1}/_{2}$ DOZEN THINGIES

Oversize delights, with just the right balance of peanut butter, cocoa powder, and brown sugar! For variety, arrange 6 peanut halves in a starburst pattern in the center of each cookie in place of the chopped peanuts.

Orange Brown-Edge Cookies

YIELD = ABOUT
3 DOZEN COOKIES

Crisp orange wafers with just an edge of golden brown showing around their sugary frosting.

$1\frac{1}{4}$ cups all-purpose flour
$\frac{1}{2}$ teaspoon baking soda
$\frac{1}{2}$ teaspoon salt
$\frac{1}{2}$ cup confectioners' sugar
2 teaspoons chopped dried orange peel (see box)
$\frac{1}{2}$ cup (1 stick) unsalted butter, at room temperature,
    cut into pieces
1 large egg
1 teaspoon orange extract

FROSTING:
1 cup confectioners' sugar
2 tablespoons freshly squeezed orange juice

3 tablespoons orange zest (optional)

Whisk together the flour, baking soda, and salt. Set aside.

Combine the confectioners' sugar and dried orange peel in the bowl of a food processor fitted with the steel blade. Turn the machine on and add the bits of butter through the feed tube.

Turn the processor off and scrape down the sides of the bowl with a rubber spatula. Add the egg and orange extract and process just to a smooth consistency. Add the flour mixture and process until a dough ball forms, about 15 seconds.

Gather the dough, wrap it in wax paper, and refrigerate for 30 minutes.

Divide the dough in half. Put half onto a floured work surface and turn it with flour to coat. Roll it out to a $\frac{1}{8}$-inch-thick circle, with a diameter of about 10 inches. Cut out $2\frac{1}{2}$-inch circles, preferably using a

Dried orange peel is available in the spice section of many supermarkets, but you can also make your own quite easily—just let the peel air dry overnight at room temperature, until brittle. To speed up the process, preheat the oven to 350 degrees. Lay the peel flat on a baking sheet lined with aluminum foil. Turn the oven off and put the baking sheet into the oven for 10 minutes. Remove and set aside for 10 minutes more.

fluted cutter. Transfer to ungreased cookie sheets, leaving about 1 inch between cookies. Repeat the process with the remaining dough.

Bake for about 15 minutes, until the edges are lightly browned. Remove the cookies to wire racks to cool completely.

For the frosting, combine the confectioners' sugar and orange juice in a mixing bowl. Whisk until smooth. Spread evenly over each cookie, leaving a thin border all around. If desired, top with orange zest.

Chewy Honey Cookies

YIELD = ABOUT
5 DOZEN COOKIES

We use these simple yet satisfying cookies to make ice cream sandwiches; they're best paired with vanilla ice cream or lemon frozen yogurt.

3 cups all-purpose flour
$\frac{1}{2}$ teaspoon salt
1 teaspoon ground cinnamon
$\frac{1}{4}$ teaspoon ground cardamom
1 cup (2 sticks) unsalted butter, at room temperature
1 cup firmly packed light brown sugar
$\frac{1}{2}$ cup honey
1 large egg yolk

Sift the flour, salt, and spices together into a bowl and set aside.

Cream the butter and brown sugar at low speed in a stationary electric mixer fitted with the paddle attachment. Raise the speed to medium and beat until light and fluffy, about 1 minute. Add the honey and egg yolk and beat for about 1 minute more until well combined. Fold in the flour mixture, $\frac{1}{2}$ cup at a time, just to combine. Form the dough into a long log, roll it in wax paper, and refrigerate for 4 hours.

Preheat the oven to 350 degrees.

Line cookie sheets with baker's parchment.

Cut the log in half and return half to the refrigerator until ready to use. Roll out to a thickness of $\frac{1}{8}$ inch, working the dough into a 14-inch square. Cut out circles with a 3-inch cookie cutter, transferring them with a spatula to the prepared sheets. Repeat the process with the remaining dough.

Bake for 5 minutes. Rotate the baking sheets and bake for about 5 minutes more, until the edges of the cookies are golden.

Remove them to wire racks to cool.

HONING IN ON HONEY

Like any other recipe that calls for honey as a primary ingredient, this one will yield subtly different results depending upon the type of honey used. While there's nothing wrong with good old clover honey, it's fun to experiment.

There are dozens and dozens of honeys available, ranging from delicate, citrus-tasting orange blossom to assertive buckwheat from California. Generally speaking, honeys darker in hue are more robust in flavor. They range in texture from the very liquid Hungarian acacia to Tasmanian leatherwood from Australia, which may require clarification (boiling and straining) for use in cooking.

Graham Crackers

YIELD = 18 GRAHAM CRACKERS

More tender and less sweet than the commercial variety, and chock full of healthy goodies. You can let the kids eat all they want. And speaking of treats for kids—of all ages—try graham cracker and peanut butter sandwiches!

³/₄ cup graham flour
1¹/₄ cups whole wheat pastry flour
1 cup all-purpose flour
1 teaspoon baking powder
¹/₂ teaspoon baking soda
¹/₄ teaspoon salt
1 teaspoon ground cinnamon
¹/₂ cup (1 stick) unsalted butter, at room temperature
¹/₂ cup firmly packed light brown sugar
¹/₄ cup honey
1 teaspoon vanilla extract
¹/₂ cup skim milk

TOPPING:
3 tablespoons granulated sugar
³/₄ teaspoon ground cinnamon

Combine the graham flour and whole wheat pastry flour in a bowl. On top, sift together the all-purpose flour, baking powder, baking soda, salt, and cinnamon. Whisk and set aside.

Combine the butter and brown sugar in the bowl of a stationary electric mixer fitted with the paddle attachment. Cream at low speed for 1 minute. Mix in the honey and vanilla. With the machine running at low speed, add half of the flour mixture (about 1¹/₂ cups), and then the milk, mixing until combined after each addition. Turn the mixer off and scrape down the sides of the bowl. Add the remaining flour and mix just to incorporate.

Turn a third of the dough out onto 1 side of a 16-inch-long sheet of wax paper. Fold the wax paper crosswise over the dough and press it down to a thickness of about ³/₄ inch. Repeat the process for another third of the dough and then for the remaining third. Stack the wrapped sheets of dough on a baking or cookie sheet and freeze for 1 hour.

Roll each piece of dough out to about 9 by 12 inches and trim with a sharp knife to a neat 8-by-9-inch rectangle. Cut evenly into six 4-by-3-inch crackers and place on ungreased cookie sheets.

Score the top of each cracker in half lengthwise, using the back of the knife. With the tines of a fork, prick 3 diagonal lines about ¹/₂ inch apart into the top of each cracker. Sprinkle with the sugar and cinnamon topping.

Bake for about 13 minutes, until lightly colored.

Remove the crackers to wire racks to cool.

Graham Crackers are ever so versatile!
We use them as a base for scrumptious
Key Lime Pie Napoleons with Coconut Crème Anglaise.

NAPOLEONS:
14 ounces sweetened condensed milk
$1/2$ cup key lime juice
1 cup heavy cream
12 Graham Crackers

COCONUT CRÈME ANGLAISE:
$1/2$ cup coconut milk
1 large egg
$1 1/2$ tablespoons granulated sugar
$1/2$ teaspoon vanilla extract

FOR SERVING:
2 teaspoons toasted coconut
$1/4$ cup confectioners' sugar

Combine the condensed milk and key lime juice in a bowl. Stir and set aside for 5 minutes to thicken.

Whip the heavy cream to soft peaks (by hand or using an electric mixer at medium speed). Fold into the condensed milk mixture.

Put about $1/3$ cup onto a graham cracker and layer with a second cracker, another $1/3$ cup filling, and a third cracker. Repeat the process to assemble 3 more napoleons.

For the crème, bring the coconut milk almost to a simmer in a small saucepan over low heat.

continued

Meanwhile, whisk the egg and sugar together in a mixing bowl. Whisking constantly, add the hot milk. Return the mixture to the saucepan. Cook over low heat for about 5 minutes, stirring constantly with a wooden spoon, just until beginning to thicken. Remove from the heat immediately and stir in the vanilla.

Spoon 2 to 3 tablespoons of the crème on each of 4 dessert plates. Sprinkle with toasted coconut and place a napoleon on each. Dust the top crackers with confectioners' sugar.

YIELD = 4 NAPOLEONS

1 cup granulated sugar
1 cup plus 8 teaspoons unsweetened finely shredded coconut
1 cup (2 sticks) unsalted butter, chilled, cut into pieces
1 large egg
1 teaspoon lemon extract
2 cups all-purpose flour
1 teaspoon baking powder
$^1/_4$ teaspoon salt

Process the granulated sugar for 30 seconds in a food processor fitted with the steel blade. Add 1 cup of the coconut. Turn the machine on and add the butter through the feed tube, a few pieces at a time, processing until the mixture is creamy.

Scrape down the sides of the bowl with a rubber spatula. Add the egg and lemon extract and process just to combine. Add 1 cup of the flour, sprinkle the baking powder and salt on top, and add the remaining 1 cup flour. Process to form a dough, 15 to 20 seconds.

Turn the dough out onto a sheet of wax paper, wrap it up, and refrigerate for about 15 minutes.

Preheat the oven to 400 degrees.

Roll the dough out to a $^1/_4$-inch-thick rectangle, measuring about 12 by 8 inches. Cut out $2^1/_2$-inch circles and place them on ungreased cookie sheets. Brush lightly with water and dust with the remaining coconut, using about $^1/_2$ teaspoon for every 3 cookies.

Bake for 9 to 10 minutes, until the edges of the cookies and the coconut on top are browned.

Remove the cookies to wire racks to cool.

Coconut Crisps

YIELD = ABOUT
4 DOZEN CRISPS

Totally unlike the typical macaroon, this cookie encases coconut in a crispy, generously portioned wafer. Look for the delicate, finer-consistency coconut that's sold in bulk at health and natural foods stores.

New England Farmhouse Cookies

YIELD = ABOUT 4 DOZEN

What would be the flavor of choice in the rural Northeast? Why, maple, of course. Look for grade B maple syrup, which is thicker and more robustly flavored than grade A. In any case, be sure to buy *pure* maple syrup.

2 cups all-purpose flour
$1/2$ teaspoon baking soda
$1/2$ teaspoon salt
$1/2$ cup (1 stick) unsalted butter, at room temperature
$2/3$ cup granulated sugar
$1/3$ cup pure maple syrup
$1/4$ teaspoon maple extract
1 large egg
2 tablespoons maple sugar

Sift the flour, baking soda, and salt together into a bowl and set aside.

Combine the butter and granulated sugar in the bowl of a stationary electric mixer fitted with the paddle attachment. Turn the machine on at low speed. Mix until combined. Mix in the maple syrup and maple extract. Add the egg and continue to mix until combined, about 1 minute. Add the sifted ingredients, $1/3$ cup at a time, mixing just until incorporated after each addition. Take care not to overbeat.

Transfer the dough to a sheet of wax paper. With a rubber spatula, work into a short, thick cylinder. Roll it up in the wax paper and refrigerate for $2^{1}/2$ hours.

Preheat the oven to 375 degrees.

Line cookie sheets with baker's parchment.

Cut the dough in half and return half to the refrigerator until ready to use.

On a lightly floured work surface, shape the dough into a 6-inch circle. Roll it out to a thickness of $1/8$ inch, working the dough into a 12-by-13-inch rectangle. Cut out $2^{1}/2$-inch circles with a straight-edged or scalloped cookie cutter, transferring the cookies with a spatula to the prepared sheets. Sprinkle with maple sugar. Repeat the process with the other half of the dough.

Bake for about 10 minutes, until golden brown.

Remove the cookies to wire racks to cool.

¾ cup hazelnuts
¾ cup plus 2 tablespoons granulated sugar
¾ cup (1½ sticks) unsalted butter, at room temperature,
    cut into pieces
3 ounces cream cheese, at room temperature, cut into pieces
1½ cups all-purpose flour

Combine the hazelnuts and ¾ cup of the granulated sugar in the bowl of a food processor fitted with the steel blade. Process for about 1 minute, until the nuts are finely ground. With the motor running, add the butter through the feed tube. Continue to process for a few seconds more if needed, until well mixed and smooth.

Add the cream cheese and process just to incorporate. Add the flour and pulse about 20 times to form a dough.

Gather the dough into a ball, wrap it in wax paper, and refrigerate for 30 minutes.

Preheat the oven to 350 degrees.

Coat cookie sheets with vegetable oil cooking spray.

Divide the dough in half. Lightly flour half and place it on a work surface that has been sprinkled with the remaining 2 tablespoons sugar. Turn the dough to coat it with sugar. Roll it out (be sure to flour the rolling pin) to a ⅛-inch-thick square, about 9 by 9 inches. Cut out 4-inch circles and quarter the circles.

Starting at the wide end of each wedge, roll the dough up toward the point. Coat with sugar from the work surface, form into a crescent shape, and place on a prepared cookie sheet. Repeat the process until all the dough has been used, adding more sugar to the work surface if necessary.

Bake for about 15 minutes, until lightly browned.

Remove the cookies to wire racks to cool.

For Pecan Cinnamon Horns, substitute an equal amount of pecans for the hazelnuts and mix ½ teaspoon ground cinnamon into the sugar on which the dough will be rolled. Top the cookies with chopped pecans (you'll need about ⅓ cup chopped pecans).

Hazelnut Horns

YIELD = ABOUT
3 DOZEN HORNS

Crunchy, crumbly, sugary little crescents that are sure to please. Leaving the skin on the hazelnuts gives the cookies a pretty flecked appearance and intensifies their nutty taste.

Caraway Cookies

YIELD = ABOUT
3 DOZEN COOKIES

Scandinavian in origin, these cookies were popular at teatime in the Victorian era. Like the classic nineteenth-century jumbles, they derive their texture from the use of sour cream rather than egg.

We include a generous measure of savory caraway, which must be ground for full flavor. This can be done in a spice grinder or a clean coffee mill, using a mortar and pestle, or with the aid of a sturdy rolling pin.

$^1/_2$ tablespoon caraway seeds, ground
1 cup granulated sugar
$^1/_4$ teaspoon ground nutmeg
$^1/_2$ cup (1 stick) unsalted butter, chilled, cut into pieces
$^1/_2$ cup sour cream
$^1/_4$ teaspoon vanilla extract
2 cups all-purpose flour
1 teaspoon baking powder
$^1/_4$ teaspoon salt

Combine the ground caraway seeds, sugar, and nutmeg in the bowl of a food processor fitted with the steel blade. Process for 30 seconds. With the machine running, add the butter piece by piece, through the feed tube, continuing to process until the mixture is fully incorporated and beginning to gather into a ball.

Scrape down the sides of the bowl with a rubber spatula, breaking up the ball. Add the sour cream and vanilla and process for a few seconds, just to mix. Add the flour, baking powder, and salt. Process for about 10 seconds to form a dough.

Turn the dough out onto a sheet of wax paper, wrap it up, and refrigerate for at least 1 hour.

Preheat the oven to 375 degrees.

On a lightly floured surface, roll the dough out to a thickness of $^1/_4$ inch. Cut out cookies with a 2-inch-round cutter and place them on ungreased cookie sheets.

Bake for about 10 to 12 minutes, until beginning to brown around the edges.

Cool on wire racks.

This old-time recipe can be easily adapted to produce Fennel Cookies, which have a pronounced licorice flavor. Use 1 teaspoon of fennel seeds (ground the same way) in place of the $^1/_2$ tablespoon of caraway seeds, and substitute $^1/_4$ teaspoon anise extract for the vanilla.

Refrigerator Cookies

We think everyone should have ready access to freshly baked cookies, even when time is short. Refrigerator cookies are the obvious answer, since the dough can be prepared in advance and stored in the refrigerator for 3 to 5 days or in the freezer for up to a month—allowing you to slice and bake any quantity desired at a moment's notice.

Refrigerator doughs are shaped into logs and refrigerated or frozen for a minimum period of time to firm. A few layered doughs must be rolled up more intricately, like a jelly roll. To shape the rest, just turn the dough out onto a sheet of wax paper about 24 inches long, positioning it crosswise toward 1 end of the sheet. Work the dough into a roughly formed log of the desired size.

Fold the end of the wax paper up over the dough to enclose it with just enough of a lip of paper left over to grasp. Place a straight-edged ruler at a 45-degree angle alongside the dough, grasp the paper lip, and pull the wax paper tightly, shaping the log into a neat round. Roll up in the wax paper and chill as directed.

For extended freezer storage, add an outer layer of aluminum foil. When you're ready to bake, cut off a piece of the log—as much as you want to use—and thaw it in the refrigerator before slicing into cookies. We call for $1/4$-inch slices; thinner slices will produce crisper cookies.

To make stuffed pillows from refrigerator dough, slice thinly. Spread some preserves or a little peanut butter over a slice, place a second slice on top, and crimp the edges together with the tines of a fork. Most refrigerator doughs can also be made as rolled cookies, in which case they need not be chilled before rolling.

Once baked, refrigerator cookies will remain fresh and flavorful for up to 5 days in a cookie jar or cookie tin.

Thelma Houston's Vanilla Sugar Tea Cookies

YIELD = ABOUT
3 DOZEN COOKIES

2¼ cups all-purpose flour
1 teaspoon baking powder
¼ teaspoon salt
1 cup (2 sticks) unsalted butter, at room temperature
¾ cup vanilla sugar (see box)
2 large eggs
½ tablespoon vanilla extract
¼ cup plus 2 tablespoons turbinado sugar

Whisk together the flour, baking powder, and salt.

Cream the butter and vanilla sugar in a large bowl with an electric mixer at medium speed. Beat in the eggs and vanilla. Stir in the flour mixture with a wooden spoon.

Turn the dough out onto a sheet of wax paper. Shape into an 8½-by-2-inch log and roll it up in the wax paper. Refrigerate for at least 3 hours.

Preheat the oven to 400 degrees.

Cut the dough into ¼-inch slices and place on ungreased cookie sheets. Sprinkle ½ teaspoon turbinado sugar on each cookie.

Bake for about 8 minutes, until golden around the edges.

Remove the cookies to wire racks to cool.

To make Vanilla Sugar, use 1 whole vanilla bean cut in half lengthwise for every 2 cups of granulated sugar. Combine in an airtight container for at least 3 to 4 days. We always try to keep a supply on hand in the pantry to use in place of plain sugar whenever a little vanilla accent is desired.

We named this cookie for Barry's friend Thelma, a talented performer and a lovely lady. She spoke recently about a very similar-sounding cookie she hadn't tasted since her childhood in the South. We believe this old-fashioned cross between a butter cookie and a sugar cookie, with a healthy dose of vanilla thrown in for good measure, will prove as award-winning as Thelma.

Yin-Yang Wafers

YIELD = ABOUT
6 1/2 DOZEN WAFERS

Like the opposites of Chinese philosophy, the chocolate and orange sides of this cookie provide complementary visual and flavor contrast. To dress the wafers up for a party, dust lightly with confectioners' sugar.

2 1/2 cups all-purpose flour
2 1/2 teaspoons baking powder
1/8 teaspoon salt
3 ounces unsweetened chocolate, broken up
1 cup (2 sticks) unsalted butter, at room temperature
1 cup confectioners' sugar
1/2 cup firmly packed light brown sugar
1 large egg
1/2 tablespoon orange extract
1 teaspoon orange zest
1/2 teaspoon vanilla extract

Combine the flour, baking powder, and salt in a mixing bowl. Whisk and set aside.

Melt the chocolate in a microwave at full power for 1 1/2 to 2 minutes, stirring every 30 seconds, or in the top of a double boiler over boiling water.

Combine the butter and sugars in a large bowl. Cream until smooth with an electric mixer at medium speed. Mix in the egg. Stir in the flour mixture with a wooden spoon. Take care not to stir too much; leave the mixture crumbly. Remove half (about 2 cups) to another bowl.

To one half, add the orange extract and orange zest, stirring until a dough forms. Transfer to a sheet of wax paper and shape into a 10-by-2-inch log. Roll it up in the wax paper.

To the other half, add the melted chocolate and vanilla. Stir until smooth. Shape and wrap as you did the previous log. Refrigerate both for 20 minutes.

Unwrap the logs and cut each in half lengthwise. Lay an orange half down on a work surface, cut side up. Place a chocolate half, cut side down, on top, positioning it so that it rests about 1/2 inch off center. Wrap in wax paper. Reshape a second two-color log the same way from the 2 remaining dough halves. Wrap. Refrigerate the logs for a minimum of 2 hours.

Preheat the oven to 375 degrees.

Slice the logs into 1/4-inch wafers and place on ungreased cookie sheets. Bake for about 8 minutes, until delicately browned around the edges.

Remove to wire racks to cool.

For separate Orange Wafers and Crispy Chocolate Wafers, leave the two logs of dough intact (do not divide and reassemble) and refrigerate for at least 2 hours before slicing and baking.

For Lemon Yin-Yang Wafers, substitute equal amounts of lemon extract for the orange extract and lemon zest for the orange zest.

Chocolate Nut Swirls

YIELD = ABOUT
3 1/2 DOZEN SWIRLS

Our version of the Victorian snail cookie, named after the spirals in a snail's shell, which the cookies resemble. It's a butter cookie at heart—dense, rich, and creamy.

1 cup (2 sticks) unsalted butter, at room temperature
1 teaspoon vanilla extract
1 cup granulated sugar
1/2 cup finely chopped walnuts
2 cups all-purpose flour
1 teaspoon baking powder
1/2 teaspoon salt
3 ounces unsweetened chocolate, broken up
1 large egg

In a mixing bowl, combine the butter, vanilla, and sugar. Cream with an electric mixer at low speed. Add the walnuts, flour, baking powder, and salt. Continue to mix at low speed until a dough ball begins to form.

Remove half the dough and roll it out on a lightly floured surface to a thickness of 1/4 inch, shaping it into a rectangle.

Melt the chocolate in a glass measuring cup in a microwave oven at full power for 1 1/2 to 2 minutes, stirring every 20 seconds, or in the top of a double boiler over boiling water.

Add the melted chocolate and the egg to the dough remaining in the bowl. Mix thoroughly at low speed. Spread the mixture evenly over the rolled-out dough. Starting with a long side of the rectangle, roll the dough up into a log. Wrap the log in wax paper and refrigerate for 3 to 4 hours.

Preheat the oven to 375 degrees.

Lightly grease cookie sheets with butter.

Unwrap the log and cut it into 1/4-inch rounds. Place the rounds on the prepared cookie sheets. Bake for 8 to 10 minutes, until very lightly browned.

Remove the cookies to a wire rack to cool.

Cookie Cups make nifty edible bowls
for custards and frozen desserts.

Skip the chocolate layer in the Chocolate Nut
Swirls and shape the dough into a thick
6-inch log. Wrap in wax paper and freeze
for at least 1 hour.

Preheat the oven to 350 degrees and coat
the bottom of a muffin tin lightly with
vegetable oil cooking spray.

Cut the dough into $1/2$-inch-thick rounds.
Drape each over an inverted well of the tin.
Bake for 12 to 15 minutes, until golden brown.

Remove from the oven and allow the cups to
cool on the tin for 5 minutes, then remove
to wire racks to finish cooling.

YIELD = 12 CUPS

Orange Walnut Jumbles

YIELD = ABOUT
3 DOZEN JUMBLES

This refreshing cookie has some of the characteristics of buttery shortbread and also bears a resemblance to the delicate jumbles so popular in the 1800s. Like many of the jumbles of yore, it's made with sour cream, but no egg.

2 cups all-purpose flour
1 teaspoon baking powder
1/4 teaspoon salt
3/4 cup chopped walnuts
1/2 cup (1 stick) unsalted butter, at room temperature
1 cup granulated sugar
1/2 cup sour cream
1/2 tablespoon orange extract
1 tablespoon chopped orange zest

Whisk together the flour, baking powder, and salt. Whisk in the nuts.

In a large mixing bowl, cream the butter and sugar with an electric mixer at medium speed. Beat in the sour cream, orange extract, and orange zest.

Add the dry ingredients and stir with a wooden spoon to incorporate. Turn the dough out onto wax paper. Work into a log 9 inches long and 2 1/2 inches in diameter. Wrap in the wax paper and refrigerate for at least 1 hour.

Preheat the oven to 375 degrees.

Cut the dough in 1/4-inch slices and place 2 inches apart on ungreased cookie sheets.

Bake for about 12 minutes, just until the cookies are beginning to brown around the edges.

Remove the cookies to wire racks to cool.

For Old-Fashioned Lemon Jumbles, omit the walnuts and substitute equal amounts of lemon extract and lemon zest for the orange extract and orange zest.

To chocolate-dip Orange Walnut Jumbles or Old-Fashioned Lemon Jumbles, melt 3 ounces semisweet chocolate in a microwave oven at full power for 3 minutes or in the top of a double boiler over simmering water; stir until smooth. Dip each jumble into the chocolate to cover about a third of the cookie.

2 cups all-purpose flour
¹/₂ teaspoon baking soda
¹/₈ teaspoon salt
1¹/₂ tablespoons poppyseeds
1 tablespoon plus 1 teaspoon finely grated lemon zest
3 tablespoons freshly squeezed lemon juice
¹/₂ cup (1 stick) unsalted butter, at room temperature
1 cup granulated sugar
1 large egg
¹/₂ cup sour cream
¹/₄ cup confectioners' sugar (optional, for dusting)

Sift the flour, baking soda, and salt together into a bowl. Stir in the poppyseeds and set aside.

Combine the lemon zest and lemon juice in a small bowl.

In a stationary electric mixer fitted with the paddle attachment, cream the butter and sugar at medium speed. Continue to beat for about 1 minute, until the mixture is pale. Add the egg and beat for about 1 minute more, until fluffy.

With the machine running at low speed, add half the sifted dry ingredients (about ³/₄ cup), mixing until incorporated. Add the sour cream and mix until combined. Turn the mixer off and scrape down the sides of the bowl. Add the remaining dry ingredients and mix at low speed until well combined. Add the lemon zest and lemon juice and mix just to combine.

Turn half of the dough (which will be very soft) out onto a sheet of wax paper. Shape into a 9-inch log about 2 inches in diameter and roll it up in the wax paper. Repeat the process for the remaining dough. Freeze for at least 4 hours.

Preheat the oven to 350 degrees.

Cut the dough into ¹/₄-inch slices and place 2 inches apart on ungreased cookie sheets.

Bake for about 12 minutes, until light golden.

Remove the cookies to wire racks to cool. If desired, dust with confectioners' sugar while still warm.

Lemon Sour Cream Cookies

YIELD = ABOUT
6 DOZEN COOKIES

These tender, cakey cookies pack a pronounced lemon pucker, tempered a bit by the inclusion of soothing sour cream. We've added a poppyseed accent for a favorite flavor combination.

Fig Pinwheels

YIELD = ABOUT
4 DOZEN PINWHEELS

We like the contrast lent by chunks of soft fig encased in a slightly crunchy dough; for a smoother consistency, you can puree the figs after they have cooled to room temperature.

1 cup chopped Calimyrna figs (about 6 ounces)
¼ cup plus 2 tablespoons water
¼ cup granulated sugar
¼ cup chopped walnuts
1½ cups all-purpose flour
½ teaspoon baking soda
¼ teaspoon salt
1 teaspoon ground cinnamon
½ teaspoon ground nutmeg
½ cup (1 stick) unsalted butter,
   at room temperature
¾ cup firmly packed dark brown sugar
¼ cup sour cream
½ teaspoon lemon extract

For Date Pinwheels, substitute an equal amount of chopped dates for the figs.

Combine the figs, water, and granulated sugar in a small saucepan. Cook over medium heat for about 5 minutes, stirring constantly, until the water has been absorbed. Remove from the heat, stir in the walnuts, and set aside to cool.

In a bowl, whisk together the flour, baking soda, salt, and spices.

In a large mixing bowl, cream the butter and brown sugar with an electric mixer at medium speed until pale and smooth. At low speed, beat in the sour cream, and then the lemon extract. Stir in the flour mixture with a wooden spoon.

Turn the dough out onto a small baking sheet that has been lined with wax paper. Shape with a rubber spatula into a rectangle about 8 by 6 inches. Cover with a second sheet of wax paper and refrigerate for 30 minutes.

Roll the dough out on the baking sheet to a 12-by-9-inch rectangle. Remove the top sheet of wax paper. Spread the fig filling evenly on top, leaving a ½-inch border along the long sides.

Fold over the border along one of the long edges and roll the dough up tightly like a jelly roll. Crimp the opposite border closed to seal. Wrap in the wax paper and refrigerate for at least 3 hours.

Preheat the oven to 375 degrees.

Cut the roll into ¼-inch slices and place on ungreased cookie sheets.

Bake for about 12 minutes, until lightly colored and firm to the touch. Cool the cookies for 1 minute on the sheets, then transfer to wire racks to finish cooling.

2 cups all-purpose flour
½ tablespoon baking soda
1 teaspoon baking powder
½ teaspoon salt
1 cup (2 sticks) unsalted butter, at room temperature
½ cup granulated sugar
¼ cup firmly packed light brown sugar
3 large eggs
1 tablespoon plus ½ teaspoon almond extract
½ tablespoon water
½ cup whole blanched almonds

Whisk together the flour, baking soda, baking powder, and salt in a bowl.

In a large mixing bowl, cream the butter and sugars with an electric mixer at medium speed. Add 2 of the eggs and mix to combine. Mix in the almond extract. Stir in the flour mixture with a wooden spoon until incorporated, producing a stiff, but still sticky dough.

Turn out onto a sheet of wax paper. Roll the dough up in the wax paper, working it into a 12-by-2-inch log. Refrigerate for at least 2 hours.

Preheat the oven to 375 degrees.

Coat cookie sheets lightly with vegetable oil cooking spray.

In a small bowl, whisk the remaining egg and the water thoroughly.

Cut the dough into ¼-inch slices and arrange 2 inches apart on the prepared cookie sheets. Put an almond in the center of each. Brush with the egg wash.

Bake for about 10 minutes, until the cookies are golden and firm to the touch.

Remove the cookies to wire racks to cool.

Almond Cookies

YIELD = ABOUT
4 DOZEN COOKIES

These big cookies puff up into gentle domes, each gracefully topped by a single almond. They're much more delicate than those served in Chinese restaurants. Here, the soft golden hue is produced by an egg wash, rather than food coloring.

Chocolate Sour Cherry Pillows

YIELD = ABOUT
2³/4 DOZEN PILLOWS

The taste of sour cherries—which soften and plump up while soaking—really stands out in these big, soft, chewy cookies!

1 cup dried sour cherries
¼ cup boiling water
2 ounces unsweetened chocolate, roughly chopped
½ cup (1 stick) unsalted butter, cut into pieces
2 cups all-purpose flour
½ teaspoon baking soda
¼ teaspoon salt
2 large eggs
½ cup firmly packed light brown sugar
½ cup granulated sugar
1 teaspoon vanilla extract

Mix the sour cherries and boiling water well in a wide, shallow bowl. Set aside.

In a glass measuring cup, microwave the chocolate and butter at full power for 1 minute. Stir, heat for 30 seconds more, and stir until thoroughly melted and smooth. (You can also melt the chocolate and butter in the top of a double boiler over boiling water.) Set aside.

Whisk together the flour, baking soda, and salt.

Combine the eggs and sugars in a large bowl. Mix until smooth with an electric mixer at low speed. Mix in the chocolate mixture and vanilla.

Drain and add the sour cherries. Add the flour mixture and stir with a wooden spoon to form a dough.

Turn the dough out onto a sheet of wax paper. Shape into an 11-by-1½-inch log. Wrap it in the wax paper and refrigerate for at least 3 hours.

Preheat the oven to 350 degrees.

Coat cookie sheets with vegetable oil cooking spray.

Cut the dough into generous ¼-inch slices and place 2 inches apart on the prepared cookie sheets. Bake for about 13 minutes, until firm to the touch.

Remove the cookies to wire racks to cool.

2 1/2 cups all-purpose flour
1/2 cup plus 2 tablespoons unsweetened
   Dutch-processed cocoa powder
1 teaspoon baking soda
1 teaspoon cream of tartar
3/4 cup (1 1/2 sticks) unsalted butter, at room temperature
1 cup confectioners' sugar
2 large eggs
1 teaspoon peppermint extract

Combine the flour, cocoa powder, baking soda, and cream of tartar in a bowl. Whisk thoroughly until incorporated.

In a large mixing bowl, cream the butter and sugar with an electric mixer set at low speed. At medium speed, beat in the eggs and peppermint. Add the dry ingredients and mix thoroughly at medium.

Turn the dough out onto wax paper. Roll into a 10-by-2-inch log and wrap in the paper. Refrigerate for at least 1 hour.

Preheat the oven to 375 degrees.

Slice the log into 1/8-inch rounds and place on ungreased cookie sheets. Bake for about 6 minutes, until the cookies are firm to the touch and beginning to crack around the edge.

Transfer to wire racks to cool.

For Cocoa-Frosted Cocoa Mint Crisps, combine 1 cup confectioners' sugar, 1 tablespoon unsweetened Dutch-processed cocoa powder, and 2 tablespoons hot water in a bowl. Mix thoroughly. Spread a little of the mixture over each cookie after they've cooled.

YIELD = ABOUT 1 CUP
FROSTING

Cocoa Mint Crisps

YIELD = ABOUT
6 1/2 DOZEN CRISPS

Very thin, very delicate, and very minty. We like to serve them alongside Thelma Houston's Vanilla Sugar Tea Cookies (page 147) for an attractive presentation.

Pumpkin Oat Cookies

YIELD = ABOUT
2 1/2 DOZEN COOKIES

These oversize cookies derive their distinctive crunch and variegated appearance from the whole pumpkin seeds mixed into the dough. Chill overnight before cutting to allow the oats to soften and be absorbed into the dough.

Serve with mulled cider on crisp autumnal eves.

1 1/4 cups rolled oats
1 1/4 cups all-purpose flour
1 teaspoon ground cinnamon
1/4 teaspoon salt
1/2 teaspoon baking soda
1 cup pumpkin seeds
1/2 cup (1 stick) unsalted butter, chilled
1/2 cup firmly packed dark brown sugar
2 large eggs
2 tablespoons freshly squeezed orange juice
1 teaspoon vanilla extract

Whisk together the oats, flour, cinnamon, salt, baking soda, and pumpkin seeds.

Combine the butter, brown sugar, eggs, orange juice, and vanilla in a large bowl. Mix with an electric mixer at medium speed until slightly frothy, about 2 minutes. (The mixture will still be flecked with bits of butter.) Stir in the dry ingredients with a wooden spoon.

Turn the dough out onto wax paper and shape into an 8-by-3-inch log. Wrap it in the wax paper and refrigerate overnight.

Preheat the oven to 375 degrees.

Slice the log into 1/4-inch rounds and place 1 1/2 inches apart on ungreased cookie sheets.

Bake for about 10 minutes, until browned and firm to the touch.

Transfer the cookies to wire racks to cool.

FILLING/COATING:
2 tablespoons granulated sugar
1/2 tablespoon ground cinnamon

DOUGH:
1 1/4 cups all-purpose flour
1/2 cup quick oats
1 teaspoon baking powder
1/4 teaspoon salt
1/2 cup (1 stick) unsalted butter, at room temperature
1 large egg
1/2 cup firmly packed light brown sugar
1/2 teaspoon vanilla extract

Combine the granulated sugar and cinnamon in a small bowl. Mix and set aside.

Whisk together the flour, oats, baking powder, and salt.

Combine the butter, egg, brown sugar, and vanilla in a large bowl. Beat until smooth and thick with an electric mixer at medium speed. Stir in the flour mixture with a wooden spoon.

Turn the dough onto a sheet of wax paper with a rubber spatula. Work into a rectangle measuring about 9 by 6 inches. Sprinkle with 2 tablespoons of the sugar and cinnamon mixture and roll up into a log. Roll the log in the remaining sugar and cinnamon mixture to coat. Wrap it in the wax paper and refrigerate for at least 4 hours.

Preheat the oven to 375 degrees.

Coat cookie sheets with vegetable oil cooking spray.

Slice the dough into 1/4-inch rounds and place on the prepared cookie sheets. Bake for about 9 minutes, until lightly browned on top.

Transfer the cookies to wire racks to cool.

Cinnamon Swirls

YIELD = ABOUT
3 DOZEN SWIRLS

These remind us of the cinnamon buns customers line up in droves for at a popular Swedish restaurant in Chicago—transformed into bite-sized cookies. They're soft and chewy, with a slightly crunchy outer edge from the caramelized sugar coating.

For Cinnamon Raisin Swirls, scatter 1/3 cup seedless raisins over the sugar and cinnamon filling before rolling the dough into a log.

Bernice Solomon's Brown Sugar Cookies

YIELD = ABOUT
4 DOZEN COOKIES

We based this cookie on a recipe that has graced the tables of several generations of family and friends on the Eastern seaboard. It was given to expectant mom Bernice in 1953 by a newly married friend, who had received it from her mother. It now resides in the kitchen of Bernice's daughter Sally, who just became a mom herself.

2 cups all-purpose flour
$\frac{1}{2}$ cup firmly packed dark brown sugar
$\frac{1}{8}$ teaspoon salt
1 cup (2 sticks) unsalted butter, chilled, cut into 16 tablespoons
$\frac{1}{2}$ tablespoon pure maple syrup
$\frac{1}{4}$ teaspoon ground cinnamon
1 tablespoon granulated sugar
1 cup chopped walnuts

Combine the flour, brown sugar, and salt in the bowl of a food processor fitted with the steel blade. Process for 1 minute. With the machine running, add half the butter, 1 tablespoon at a time, through the feed tube. Drizzle in the maple syrup. Add the remaining butter, 1 tablespoon at a time, and continue to process until the dough adheres to sides of the bowl.

Turn the dough out onto a work surface. Cut it in half and form each half into a 6-inch log. Wrap the logs separately in wax paper and refrigerate until very firm, about 4 hours.

Preheat the oven to 350 degrees.

Cut the dough logs into $\frac{1}{4}$-inch wafers and place on ungreased cookie sheets. Combine the cinnamon, granulated sugar, and walnuts and sprinkle the mixture over the cookies.

Bake for 12 to 14 minutes, until lightly browned.

Let the cookies cool on the sheets on wire racks.

½ cup (1 stick) unsalted butter, at room temperature
½ cup firmly packed light brown sugar
2 large eggs
½ tablespoon vanilla extract
2 cups all-purpose flour
¼ teaspoon salt
½ cup currants
¾ cup chopped pecans

Combine the butter and brown sugar in a large mixing bowl. Cream with an electric mixer at medium speed. Beat in the eggs and vanilla. Add the flour, salt, currants, and pecans. Stir with a wooden spoon to incorporate.

Turn the dough out onto a sheet of wax paper, shape it into a 9-by-2½-inch log, roll it up in the paper, and refrigerate for at least 2 hours.

Preheat the oven to 375 degrees.

Slice the log into ¼-inch rounds, and transfer the rounds to ungreased cookie sheets.

Bake for about 12 minutes, until the edges begin to brown.

Transfer the cookies to wire racks to cool.

Creole Currant Nut Cookies

YIELD = ABOUT
3 DOZEN COOKIES

A sandy pecan cookie that's crisp outside and just a bit chewy inside. The dough is rich and smooth, but unobtrusive enough to let the tasty mix of nuts and currants predominate. We prefer currants, but you can use seedless raisins instead, if you wish.

Almond Apricot Pillows

YIELD = ABOUT
4 DOZEN PILLOWS

Bits of dried apricot add flecks of color and flavor to these moister-than-typical almond cookies. There's enough butter and egg in the batter so that the cookies almost look glazed when they come out of the oven.

Be sure to add ½ cup of the flour to the bowl of the food processor in the first step. This will keep the dried fruit and nuts from forming a clump around the blade. Take care not to overprocess after drizzling in the egg mixture; a sticky dough will form within a few seconds.

6 ounces dried apricots (about ¾ cup)
½ cup blanched slivered almonds
2 cups all-purpose flour
1 cup granulated sugar
1 teaspoon baking powder
¼ teaspoon salt
3 large eggs
½ teaspoon almond extract
¼ cup (½ stick) unsalted butter,
    melted and cooled to room temperature

Combine the apricots, almonds, and ½ cup of the flour in the bowl of a food processor fitted with the steel blade. Process for about 1 minute, until the nuts are ground and the apricots finely chopped. Add the sugar, baking powder, salt, and remaining 1½ cups flour. Pulse about 20 times to incorporate.

Lightly beat the eggs in a bowl. Whisk in the almond extract, then the melted butter. Turn the food processor on and drizzle the mixture through the feed tube. Continue to process for a few seconds more, just to form a dough.

With a rubber spatula, scrape the dough, which will be very sticky, onto a sheet of wax paper. Shape it into a flat log about 12 inches long, 2½ inches wide, and 1½ inches high. Wrap it in the wax paper and freeze for at least 4 hours.

Preheat the oven to 375 degrees.

Coat cookie sheets with vegetable oil cooking spray.

Cut the dough into ¼-inch slices and place on the prepared cookie sheets.

Bake for about 12 minutes, until the cookies are lightly browned on top.

Remove the cookies to wire racks to cool.

When you just can't wait 4 hours for the dough to freeze, make Almond Apricot Pillows as drop cookies. Prepare the dough according to recipe directions and drop by the tablespoonful 2 to 3 inches apart onto the prepared cookie sheets. Proceed to bake and cool according to directions.

2½ cups all-purpose flour
1¼ teaspoons baking powder
¼ teaspoon salt
½ cup unsweetened Dutch-processed cocoa powder
¼ cup plus 1 tablespoon boiling water
1 cup (2 sticks) unsalted butter, at room temperature
1 cup firmly packed dark brown sugar
2 large eggs

Whisk together the flour, baking powder, and salt. Set aside.

In a small bowl, combine the cocoa powder and boiling water. Whisk until smooth.

Combine the butter and brown sugar in a large mixing bowl. Cream with an electric mixer at medium speed. Mix in the eggs. With a wooden spoon, stir in the cocoa mixture, then the flour mixture.

Turn the dough out onto a sheet of wax paper. Roll it into a log 9 inches long and 3 inches high and wrap it in the wax paper. Refrigerate for at least 2 hours.

Preheat the oven to 375 degrees.

Coat cookie sheets lightly with vegetable oil cooking spray.

Cut the log into ⅛-inch rounds and place at least 2 inches apart on the prepared cookie sheets.

Bake for about 10 minutes, until firm to the touch.

Remove the cookies to wire racks to cool.

Devil's Food Cookies

YIELD = ABOUT
6 DOZEN COOKIES

These bring to mind a hunk of old-fashioned chocolate cake reincarnated in cookie form. Definitely a "glass of milk" sort of cookie.

Prune Pinwheels

YIELD = ABOUT
4 DOZEN PINWHEELS

Luscious prune encased in spirals of cream cheese dough. Bursting with filling by definition, this cookie is somewhat delicate. Take care to spread only a thin layer of filling, even if you have a little left over.

FILLING:

4 ounces pitted prunes (about $^{1}/_{2}$ cup)
$^{1}/_{4}$ cup seedless raisins
$^{1}/_{3}$ cup water
$^{1}/_{4}$ cup granulated sugar
1 tablespoon freshly squeezed orange juice

DOUGH:

$^{1}/_{2}$ cup plus 2 tablespoons (1$^{1}/_{4}$ sticks total) unsalted butter, at room temperature
3 ounces cream cheese, at room temperature
$^{1}/_{2}$ cup granulated sugar
$^{1}/_{2}$ teaspoon lemon extract
1$^{1}/_{2}$ cups all-purpose flour

For the filling, combine the prunes, raisins, water, and sugar in a small saucepan. Bring to a boil. Cover, reduce the heat to low, and simmer for 10 minutes, until slightly thickened.

While the fruit is simmering, prepare the dough. Combine the butter and cream cheese in a large bowl. Cream with an electric mixer at medium speed. At low speed, beat in the sugar and lemon extract. Beat in the flour, just to incorporate. Scrape the beaters and work in the residual bits of dough.

Turn the dough out onto a large sheet of wax paper. Flatten and shape it into a 7-by-5-inch rectangle (about $^{3}/_{4}$ inch thick). Wrap it up in the wax paper and refrigerate until thoroughly chilled, about 30 minutes.

Transfer the prune and raisin filling to the bowl of a food processor fitted with the steel blade. Add the orange juice and puree the mixture. Transfer to a bowl (preferably ceramic) and refrigerate while the dough is chilled and rolled.

Remove the dough from the refrigerator and open the wax paper wrapping. Place a second sheet of wax paper over the dough. Roll out to 12 by 9 inches.

Remove the top sheet of wax paper and spread an even layer of filling over the dough, leaving a $^{1}/_{2}$-inch border along each of the long sides. Fold over the border along 1 of the long edges and roll the dough up tightly like a jelly roll. Crimp the opposite border closed to seal. Wrap in the wax paper and refrigerate for at least 30 minutes.

Preheat the oven to 375 degrees.

Coat cookie sheets with vegetable oil cooking spray.

Slice the dough into ¼-inch rounds and transfer carefully with a spatula to the prepared cookie sheets.

Bake for about 15 minutes, until lightly browned around the edges.

Let the cookies cool for 2 minutes on the sheets, then transfer to wire racks to finish cooling.

The components of Prune Pinwheels can also be assembled and baked as Prune Pastries, filled cookies that bear a strong resemblance to kolacky.

Prepare the dough (to a 7-by-5-inch rectangle) and the filling according to recipe directions and allow them both to chill for at least 30 minutes.

Preheat the oven to 350 degrees.

Transfer the rectangle of dough from the wax paper to a lightly floured work surface. Dust the top with flour and roll out to a thickness of ⅛ inch. Cut out 2½-inch circles. Gather the scraps of dough, roll out again, and cut out additional circles.

Place ½ teaspoon of the filling in a thin strip down the center of a circle. Moisten 1 of the semicircular outer borders with water. Fold the unmoistened side up over the filling. Fold up the moistened side so that it overlaps. To secure closed, gently insert half a toothpick into the top. Repeat until all the cookies are assembled.

Bake on ungreased cookie sheets for about 20 minutes, until browned.

Remove to wire racks and cool for 5 minutes. Carefully remove the toothpicks and dust with confectioners' sugar.

Molasses Spice Cookies

YIELD = ABOUT
3 DOZEN COOKIES

One taste and you'll appreciate why the Far East spice trade so changed Western sensibilities. But don't eat them too quickly. The wonderfully rich blend of molasses, rum, cinnamon, cloves, and ginger—we use fresh, which we find more provocative—mellows on the palate after each bite.

2 cups all-purpose flour
³/₄ teaspoon baking soda
¹/₂ teaspoon salt
1 teaspoon ground cinnamon
1 teaspoon ground cloves
¹/₂ cup slivered blanched almonds, chopped
¹/₄ cup (¹/₂ stick) unsalted butter, at room temperature
¹/₄ cup plus 2 tablespoons granulated sugar
1 large egg
2 tablespoons golden rum
1¹/₂ tablespoons finely grated fresh ginger
¹/₂ cup dark molasses

Combine the flour, baking soda, salt, cinnamon, cloves, and almonds in a bowl and whisk.

In a large bowl, cream the butter and sugar with an electric mixer at medium speed. Beat in the egg and rum. Beat in the ginger and molasses. Add the flour mixture and stir with a wooden spoon to incorporate.

Scrape the dough onto a sheet of wax paper. With a rubber spatula, work it into a 9-by-2-inch log and roll it up in the wax paper. Refrigerate for at least 2 hours.

Preheat the oven to 375 degrees.

Coat cookie sheets lightly with vegetable oil cooking spray.

Cut the dough into ¹/₄-inch slices and place about 1 inch apart on the prepared cookie sheets. Bake for about 10 minutes, until the edges begin to brown.

Transfer the cookies to wire racks to cool.

2¼ cups all-purpose flour
2 teaspoons ground cardamom
½ teaspoon baking soda
¼ teaspoon salt
½ cup (1 stick) unsalted butter, at room temperature
½ cup firmly packed light brown sugar
½ cup granulated sugar
1 large egg
½ cup sour cream
1 teaspoon grated orange zest
1 cup roasted pistachio nuts

Combine the flour, cardamom, baking soda, and salt. Whisk and set aside.

Cream the butter and sugars in a large mixing bowl with an electric mixer at medium speed. Beat in the egg until fluffy. At low speed, mix in the sour cream and orange zest. Stir in the flour mixture with a wooden spoon.

Turn the dough out onto a sheet of wax paper and shape it into a 10-by-2-inch log. Roll the log in the pistachios to coat. Wrap it in wax paper and refrigerate for at least 2 hours.

Preheat the oven to 350 degrees.

Cut the dough into ¼-inch slices and place 2 inches apart on ungreased cookie sheets. Bake for about 15 minutes, until golden.

Transfer the cookies to wire racks to cool.

Cardamom Cookies

YIELD = ABOUT
3¼ DOZEN COOKIES

Subtle spice cookies, generously proportioned and ringed with crunchy pistachios. They're rather unusual in a mild-mannered way and really quite good.

Chocolate Raspberry Hazelnut Ribbons

YIELD = ABOUT
4 DOZEN RIBBONS

This pretty cookie looks a bit like modern art with its squiggly strips of multicolored dough. It's our update of an old icebox cookie that was formed in the metal ice cube trays that used to come with all refrigerator-freezer units; we shape the cookies in the box in which our omnipresent roll of wax paper comes packaged.

$^{1}/_{3}$ cup frozen unsweetened raspberries, thawed
$^{1}/_{2}$ cup (1 stick) unsalted butter, at room temperature, cut into pieces
$^{2}/_{3}$ cup confectioners' sugar
1 large egg
$1^{3}/_{4}$ cups all-purpose flour
$^{3}/_{4}$ teaspoon baking soda
$^{1}/_{2}$ teaspoon salt
1 ounce semisweet chocolate, broken up
$^{1}/_{4}$ cup hazelnuts, chopped

Line a 12-by-2-by-2-inch wax paper box, or another box of similar size, with plastic wrap. (We use wax paper for just about everything else, but it's a bit too stiff to neatly line its own box.) Set aside.

Strain the raspberries through a sieve into a bowl, mashing the berries with the back of a wooden spoon.

Cream the butter and confectioners' sugar in a large bowl with an electric mixer at low speed. Beat in the egg. Add the flour, baking soda, and salt. Stir with a wooden spoon to a crumbly consistency. Divide the dough among 3 bowls, putting about 1 cup into each.

Put the chocolate into a glass measuring cup. Microwave at full power for 45 seconds. Stir. Heat and stir in 15-second intervals, until melted and smooth. (You can also melt the chocolate in the top of a double boiler over boiling water.)

Stir the strained raspberries into 1 bowl of dough, the melted chocolate into another, and the hazelnuts into the remaining bowl.

Press the hazelnut dough evenly over the bottom of the lined box. Layer the raspberry dough over the hazelnut dough, as evenly as possible. Top with the chocolate dough, patting the top smooth and folding the ends of plastic wrap over the dough to cover. Refrigerate for at least 2 hours.

Preheat the oven to 375 degrees.

Remove the dough from the box and peel off the plastic wrap. Cut it into $^{1}/_{4}$-inch slices and transfer to ungreased cookie sheets. Bake for about 8 minutes, until the cookies are lightly browned and beginning to crack on top.

Transfer the cookies to wire racks to cool.

For Checkerboard Cookies, cut the assembled and chilled dough down the middle lengthwise, invert one half, and push the halves back together before slicing the cookies.

Drop
Cookies

When you hear the word cookies, what images first come to mind? Odds are, it's visions of rich chocolate chip concoctions or comforting mouthfuls of oatmeal, of creamy vanilla wafers or crisp gingersnaps, of chewy mounds fashioned from peanut butter or chocolate. Drop cookies all—the classic cookies of our childhood, stuffed by the fistful into lunch boxes, knapsacks, and jacket pockets to fuel that all-too-quick sprint from sandlots to seminars. We loved them then, and we still do.

Drop cookies—so called because the dough is simply prepared and dropped onto cookie sheets—are among the easiest and most basic of cookies. No rolling, cutting, filling, or shaping is required. Drop cookies almost defy fussing of any sort. They're informal and often stubbornly irregular, no matter how purposefully one sculpts the little mounds of dough.

We've picked the size we like best for each cookie, a determination you can, of course, alter as you see fit. In general, medium-sized cookies made from about a tablespoonful of dough are the standard for the family cookie jar. Smaller morsels are ideal for entertaining, and oversize cookies are sure kid pleasers.

In most cases, the dough can be prepared ahead of time, covered with plastic wrap, and stored in the refrigerator for 4 to 6 hours. To freeze the dough for up to 3 months, scrape the dough into a plastic storage bag and seal tightly.

Many doughs lend themselves to the use of spring-action scoops, which enable the easy dropping of uniformly proportioned rations. Scoops manufactured in the United States bear a number pegged to a standardized scale of sizes; the larger the number, the smaller the scoop. We use a European 35-

millimeter scoop, which has a diameter of 1¼ inches and holds 1 tablespoon of dough.

When working with stickier doughs, we use a miniature rubber spatula to dislodge a measure of dough onto the sheet and then to pat it into a smooth, even shape.

Be careful to observe directions for spacing cookies on the sheets; some will spread quite a bit while baking. If no specific spacing is indicated, place the cookies about 1 inch apart.

Most cookies are removed immediately to wire racks to cool, but some are transferred more easily if allowed to cool a bit first on the sheets. In other instances, cookies are moved en masse to cooling racks on the aluminum foil used to line the cookie sheets, or are removed to paper toweling that will absorb excess moisture.

With the exception of a few lacy filigree cookies, which spread into buttery, paper-thin disks while baking, most drop cookies are sturdy creatures that hold up well and can be shipped successfully.

Store them in cookie jars or cookie tins, taking care not to mix moist and crisp cookies. The cookies are in their prime for 5 days. Soft, chewy drop cookies remain fresh and flavorful for at least 1 week in the refrigerator wrapped in aluminum foil. They can be frozen for up to 3 months.

½ cup all-purpose flour
1 teaspoon baking powder
⅛ teaspoon salt
2 tablespoons coarsely grated orange zest
2 tablespoons unsalted butter, at room temperature
2 large eggs, well beaten
1 cup granulated sugar
1 cup firmly packed light brown sugar
1 teaspoon vanilla extract
1 heaping cup chopped macadamia nuts

Preheat the oven to 400 degrees.

Heavily butter and lightly flour cookie sheets.

Whisk together the flour, baking powder, salt, and orange zest. Set aside.

Put the butter in a large mixing bowl and cream it with the back of a wooden spoon. Add the eggs, sugars, and vanilla. Stir until light and fluffy, pushing the lumps of sugar into the sides of the bowl to dissolve them. Stir in the flour mixture and the nuts.

Drop by the heaping teaspoonful onto the prepared cookie sheets, leaving at least 3 inches between cookies. Bake for about 5 minutes, until the cookies are golden and the edges lightly browned.

Remove from the oven and allow the cookies to cool on the sheets for 2 minutes. Carefully peel the cookies from the sheets with a spatula and transfer them to wire racks to finish cooling.

Macadamia Florentines

YIELD = ABOUT
5 DOZEN FLORENTINES

While baking, the dough spreads to form oversize, gossamer wafers with an intriguing trace of orange. This cookie crumbles easily to top ice cream or to decorate a frosted cake.

For Filbert Filigrees, substitute an equal amount of chopped filberts (hazelnuts) for the macadamia nuts and omit the orange zest.

Java Jive Mocha Snaps

YIELD = ABOUT
3¼ DOZEN SNAPS

We created this variation on the classic ginger- or brandy snap in honor of Chicago's coolest coffeehouse and its impresario, Cheryl Blumenthal. Java Jive is where many of the city's jazz and blues musicians go to let their hair down.

These snaps are redolent of coffee, with just a hint of chocolate and cinnamon. Like Cheryl and her gang, they dance to the music.

2 tablespoons instant coffee granules
1 tablespoon boiling water
1½ cups all-purpose flour
¼ teaspoon baking powder
¼ teaspoon baking soda
⅛ teaspoon salt
½ teaspoon ground cinnamon
2 tablespoons unsweetened Dutch-processed cocoa powder
¼ cup (½ stick) unsalted butter, at room temperature
1 cup firmly packed light brown sugar
1 large egg
½ tablespoon vanilla extract
⅓ cup granulated sugar

Preheat the oven to 375 degrees.

In a small bowl, dissolve the coffee granules in the boiling water. Set aside.

Combine the flour, baking powder, baking soda, salt, cinnamon, and cocoa powder in a bowl. Whisk thoroughly.

In a large mixing bowl, combine the butter, brown sugar, and egg. Beat with an electric mixer at medium speed until smooth and fluffy. Beat in the vanilla, then the coffee. Stir in the flour mixture with a wooden spoon.

Drop the dough by the tablespoonful onto ungreased cookie sheets, about 2½ inches apart. Coat the bottom of a glass lightly with vegetable oil cooking spray and dip it in the granulated sugar. Flatten the cookies with the glass, dipping it in the sugar between each cookie.

Bake for about 9 minutes, just until the cookies begin to crack.

Cool on the sheets for 1 minute, then remove the cookies to wire racks to cool completely and crisp.

The quality of the extract can make quite a difference in recipes that call for a large ration of vanilla. Pure vanilla extract's much more pungent than the weak imitation variety; we think the most flavorful of all is that made at home.

Combine in a clear jar $3/4$ cup bourbon, $1/4$ cup water, and 6 vanilla beans that have been cut in half lengthwise and then crosswise. Cover tightly and set aside to steep for 3 to 4 days, until the predominant aroma given off by the mixture is that of vanilla. The extract will keep for up to 1 year.

Big, Soft, Chewy Chocolate Chip Cookies

YIELD = ABOUT
2¹/₂ DOZEN COOKIES

The epitome of the old-fashioned home-baked treats we all recall fondly from childhood, these big, puffy cookies rise (literally) to every occasion.

The cookies are big enough to accommodate giant chocolate chips, if your market stocks them. You can substitute regular whole wheat flour for the whole wheat pastry flour, but process it for 1 minute before adding the other dry ingredients to the food processor.

¹/₃ cup whole wheat pastry flour
1¹/₃ cups all-purpose flour
1¹/₂ cups rolled oats
¹/₂ teaspoon salt
1 teaspoon baking powder
¹/₂ teaspoon baking soda
³/₄ cup (1¹/₂ sticks) unsalted butter, at room temperature
1¹/₃ cups firmly packed light brown sugar
2 large eggs
1 teaspoon orange extract
1¹/₄ cups semisweet chocolate chips

Preheat the oven to 375 degrees.

Combine the flours, oats, salt, baking powder, and baking soda in the bowl of a food processor fitted with the steel blade. Process until fincly ground, about 3 minutes.

In a large mixing bowl, combine the butter and brown sugar. Cream with an electric mixer at medium speed. Add the eggs and orange extract. Beat to mix.

Fold in the chocolate chips. Add the flour mixture and combine with a wooden spoon.

Drop the dough onto ungreased cookie sheets, using 2 tablespoons for each cookie and leaving about 3 inches between cookies. Bake for 8 to 10 minutes, until the cookies are lightly browned and slightly cracked on top.

Remove the cookie sheets to wire racks and allow the cookies to cool.

This cookie is perfect for those special additions bound to earn you at least a few moments' peace, if not eternal gratitude, from the brood. For real kid pleasers, substitute for the semisweet chocolate chips:

1 cup M & M's chocolate mini baking bits; or
³/₄ cup peanut butter chips and ³/₄ cup milk chocolate chips; or
³/₄ cup chocolate toffee chips; or
1 cup chopped chocolate-covered peppermint patties

½ cup plus 2 tablespoons all-purpose flour
¼ teaspoon baking powder
⅛ teaspoon salt
½ cup sesame seeds, toasted (see box)
½ cup firmly packed light brown sugar
¼ cup granulated sugar
¼ cup (½ stick) unsalted butter, melted
1 large egg
½ teaspoon lemon extract

Preheat the oven to 375 degrees.

Lightly coat cookie sheets with vegetable oil cooking spray.

Whisk together the flour, baking powder, salt, and sesame seeds. Set aside.

In a large mixing bowl, combine the sugars and melted butter. Beat until incorporated with a whisk or an electric mixer at medium speed. Add the egg and lemon extract. Beat until light and fluffy. Add the flour mixture and mix with a wooden spoon.

Drop by the teaspoonful onto the prepared cookie sheets, using a small rubber spatula to push the thick dough from the measuring spoon and shape the mounds smoothly.

Bake for about 7 minutes, until the edges begin to brown and air holes begin to appear on top of the cookies.

Let the wafers cool on the sheets for 1 minute, then remove them to wire racks to cool completely.

Sesame Wafers

YIELD = ABOUT
5 DOZEN WAFERS

These diminutive cookies have an intense sesame taste that pairs well with fruit, cheese, or sorbet. We like to serve them alongside anisette-laced cups of espresso.

To toast the sesame seeds, preheat the oven to 350 degrees and line a baking sheet with aluminum foil.

Spread the seeds on the lined sheet in a single layer. Bake for about 15 minutes, shaking the sheet every 5 minutes for even browning. Take care not to scorch the seeds.

Allow the seeds to cool fully before using.

Very Vanilla Wafers

YIELD = ABOUT
4 DOZEN COOKIES

Made with butter instead of shortening, these wafers are richer-tasting and cakier in consistency than the commercial variety, and have a lighter hue.

1^1/$_4$ cups all-purpose flour
^{3}/$_4$ teaspoon baking powder
^{1}/$_8$ teaspoon salt
^{1}/$_2$ cup (1 stick) unsalted butter, at room temperature
^{3}/$_4$ cup granulated sugar
2 large eggs
1 tablespoon vanilla extract

Preheat the oven to 400 degrees.

Lightly coat cookie sheets with vegetable oil cooking spray and dust with flour.

Combine the flour, baking powder, and salt in a mixing bowl. Whisk and set aside.

Cream the butter in a large mixing bowl with an electric mixer at medium speed. Beat in the sugar. Beat in the eggs one at a time, then the vanilla.

Stir in the flour mixture with a wooden spoon. Drop the dough about 2 inches apart onto the prepared cookie sheets, using 2 teaspoons for each cookie.

Bake for about 10 minutes, until golden.

Remove the cookies immediately to wire racks to cool.

For a special treat, use the wafers to make

Chocolate Bourbon Balls.

2 dozen Very Vanilla Wafers
6 ounces semisweet chocolate, broken up
1 cup granulated sugar
3 tablespoons light corn syrup
$\frac{1}{2}$ cup plus 1 tablespoon bourbon
1 cup finely chopped pecans
1 cup dried sour cherries

Finely chop the wafers in a food processor.

Melt the chocolate in the top of a double boiler over simmering water. Remove from the heat and stir in $\frac{1}{2}$ cup of the sugar. Stir in the corn syrup, then the bourbon. Stir until thoroughly combined.

Mix the chopped cookies, nuts, and sour cherries in a large bowl. Scrape in the chocolate mixture and stir well with a wooden spoon.

Using a tablespoonful of the dough for each, roll into balls. Place on a large baking sheet lined with wax paper and refrigerate for 1 hour.

Roll the balls in the remaining sugar. Layer between sheets of wax paper in an airtight tin. Cover and allow the balls to age for 4 days in the refrigerator.

YIELD = ABOUT 4$\frac{1}{2}$ DOZEN BALLS

Orange Spice Crackles

YIELD = ABOUT
5 DOZEN CRACKLES

The day before we opened the cookbook store we used to operate in Chicago, a local newspaper article assured readers that we intended to serve fresh-baked cookies daily. That night Barry was up late baking Orange Spice Crackles. This became a tradition carried on at customers' demand. For months to come, evening telephone calls were invariably answered, "Can't talk . . . I have to make the crackles!"

$^3/_4$ cup (1$^1/_2$ sticks) unsalted butter, at room temperature
$^1/_3$ cup granulated sugar
$^2/_3$ cup firmly packed dark brown sugar
1 large egg
$^1/_2$ cup dark molasses
$^1/_4$ teaspoon vanilla extract
2 teaspoons orange zest
2$^1/_4$ cups all-purpose flour
2 teaspoons baking powder
$^1/_4$ teaspoon salt
$^1/_2$ tablespoon ground cinnamon
2 teaspoons ground ginger
$^1/_8$ teaspoon ground cloves
$^1/_4$ teaspoon ground allspice

TOPPING:
2 teaspoons orange zest
$^2/_3$ cup granulated sugar

Combine the butter and sugars in a large mixing bowl. Cream with an electric mixer at medium speed until light, at least 2 minutes. Add the egg and continue to beat until fluffy. Beat in the molasses and vanilla. Beat in the orange zest.

In a second bowl, combine the flour, baking powder, and salt. Whisk in the spices and add to the mixture in the large bowl. Mix with a wooden spoon until incorporated. Refrigerate for 10 minutes.

Meanwhile, preheat the oven to 350 degrees.

In a shallow bowl, combine the orange zest and the sugar for the topping and mix well.

Form the chilled dough into balls, using 1 tablespoon for each. Roll the balls in the topping mixture to coat and place them at least 2$^1/_2$ inches apart on ungreased cookie sheets. Bake for about 10 minutes, until cracks appear on the tops of the cookies.

Cool on the sheets for at least 5 minutes, then remove the cookies to wire racks to finish cooling.

Macadamia Butters and
Java Jive Mocha Snaps

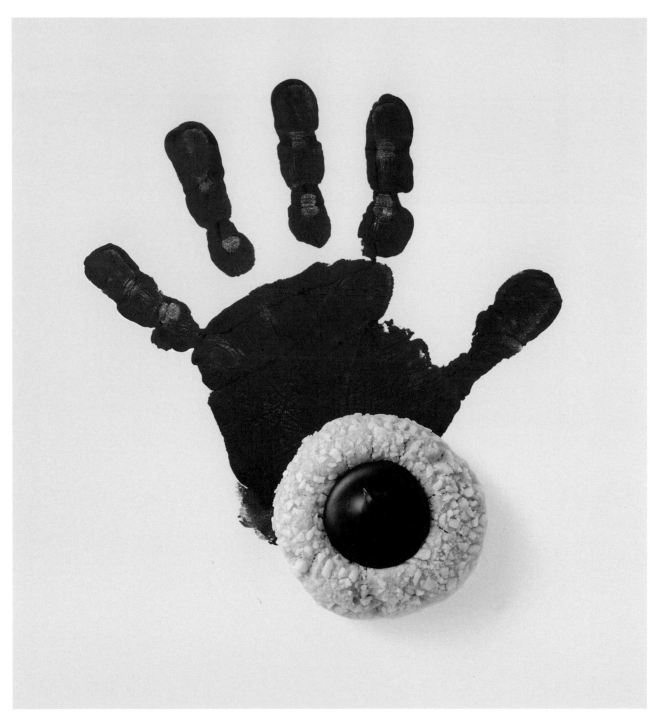

Peanut Thumbprints with
Chocolate Ganache Filling

Left to right:
Yin-Yang Wafers, Orange Walnut Jumbles, and Fig Pinwheels

Amaretti

Assorted Biscotti, including (left to right) Raisin Mandelbrot, Chocolate Hazelnut Biscotti, and John Vranicar's Savory (Nonfat) Biscotti

Doubleday Sweet Potato Dollops

Shortbread Hearts

Nutty Blue Cheese Wedges

1¼ cups rolled oats
1 cup all-purpose flour
¼ teaspoon salt
½ teaspoon baking powder
½ teaspoon baking soda
¼ cup plus 2 tablespoons unsweetened Dutch-
     processed cocoa powder
¾ cup (1½ sticks) unsalted butter, at room temperature
¾ cup granulated sugar
½ cup firmly packed dark brown sugar
1 large egg
1 teaspoon vanilla extract
¾ cup roughly chopped macadamia nuts
1 cup chunked white chocolate (about 6 ounces)

Preheat the oven to 375 degrees.

In a food processor fitted with the steel blade, process the oats to a fine powder, about 1¼ minutes. Add the flour, salt, baking powder, baking soda, and cocoa powder. Process for 1 minute more.

Combine the butter and sugars in a large mixing bowl. Cream with an electric mixer at medium speed. Beat in the egg and vanilla.

Stir in the nuts and white chocolate chunks with a wooden spoon. Add the flour and oat mixture. Mix well with the wooden spoon. Drop by the tablespoonful onto ungreased cookie sheets, leaving about 2 inches between cookies.

Bake for about 6 minutes, until the cookies have spread a bit and begun to crack on top.

Remove the cookies to a wire rack to cool.

For Chocolate Works, substitute ¾ cup dried sour cherries for the white chocolate and ¾ cup chopped pecans for the macadamia nuts.

Chocolate-White Chocolate Chunk Cookies

YIELD = ABOUT
4 DOZEN COOKIES

These cookies are equally at home with a cup of coffee or a glass of milk. The sophisticated look of white chocolate and macadamia nuts in a dark chocolate dough appeals to adult sensibilities, but the cookies are sufficiently gooey to appeal to the kid in all of us.

The rolled oats can be ground in a blender instead of in the food processor. Grind in small batches until powdery and transfer to a bowl. Add the flour, salt, baking powder, baking soda, and cocoa powder. Whisk thoroughly and proceed with the recipe directions.

Gingersnaps

YIELD = ABOUT
3 ½ DOZEN SNAPS

Lots of sugar and spice and everything nice—but little boys love these cookies anyway!

2 cups all-purpose flour
4 teaspoons ground ginger
1 teaspoon ground cinnamon
⅛ teaspoon ground allspice
⅛ teaspoon salt
¾ cup (1½ sticks) unsalted butter, at room temperature
¾ cup plus ⅓ cup granulated sugar
¼ cup firmly packed light brown sugar
1 large egg
2 tablespoons dark molasses

Preheat the oven to 350 degrees.

In a mixing bowl, combine the flour, ginger, cinnamon, allspice, and salt. Mix well with a whisk or a fork and set aside.

Combine the butter, ¾ cup of the granulated sugar, and the brown sugar in a large mixing bowl. Cream with an electric mixer at medium speed. Add the egg and molasses, beating until incorporated. Dump in the flour mixture and combine thoroughly with a wooden spoon.

Form into 1-inch balls, using 1 tablespoon of dough for each. Roll the balls in the remaining granulated sugar to coat and place them at least 2 inches apart on ungreased cookie sheets.

Dip the bottom of a 1-cup glass measuring cup in the sugar and use it to flatten a dough ball into a 2½-inch circle. Repeat the process until all have been flattened.

Bake for 13 to 15 minutes, until lightly browned.

Transfer the cookie sheets from the oven to wire racks and allow the cookies to cool completely, at least 30 minutes. Gently pry the cookies off the sheets with a spatula.

Gingersnaps make a wonderful crust for our favorite
Pumpkin Cheesecake.
If desired, serve with lightly sweetened whipped cream.

CRUST:
10 Gingersnaps
1/2 cup chopped walnuts
1/4 cup (1/2 stick) unsalted butter, melted
FILLING:
16 ounces cream cheese, at room temperature
1 cup granulated sugar
3 large eggs
1 1/4 cups pumpkin puree
1 teaspoon vanilla extract
1/4 cup heavy cream
1/4 teaspoon ground nutmeg
1/4 teaspoon ground cinnamon

Preheat the oven to 325 degrees.
Lightly grease a 9-inch springform pan with butter.
Finely grind the cookies in a food processor. Add the walnuts and process until ground. Transfer to a bowl and stir in the melted butter until the mixture is moist. Press onto the bottom of the prepared pan and work up the sides to form a 1-inch border. Bake for about 10 minutes. Remove the crust from the oven, leaving the oven on.

For the filling, cream the cream cheese until smooth with an electric mixer at medium speed. While beating, slowly add the sugar. Mix thoroughly. Beat in the eggs one at a time. Add the remaining ingredients and mix well. Pour the filling into the crust. Bake for about 1 hour and 15 minutes, until a toothpick inserted into the center comes out almost clean.

Remove to a wire rack and cool in the pan to room temperature, about 1 hour. Chill overnight.

YIELD = 10 TO 12 SERVINGS

Tahini Cookies

YIELD = ABOUT
4 DOZEN COOKIES

The secret ingredient in these unique wafers is tahini, which piqued Barry's interest when he spotted it in a bin alongside the nut butters in our local natural foods store. Intellectual curiosity turned into a challenge that had to be met when a fellow foodie speculated that you couldn't fashion a cookie from tahini.

These cookies have a subtler sesame flavor than our Sesame Wafers (page 177), one more evocative of sweet halvah.

1¼ cups all-purpose flour
1 teaspoon baking soda
¼ teaspoon baking powder
⅛ teaspoon salt
½ cup (1 stick) unsalted butter, at room temperature
¾ cup tahini
¾ cup granulated sugar
1 large egg
1 teaspoon vanilla extract
⅓ cup sesame seeds

Preheat the oven to 375 degrees.

Whisk together the flour, baking soda, baking powder, and salt. Set aside.

Combine the butter and tahini in a large mixing bowl. Cream with an electric mixer at medium speed. Add the sugar and continue to mix until light and fluffy. Beat in the egg and vanilla. Stir in the flour mixture with a wooden spoon.

Put the sesame seeds into a shallow bowl. A tablespoonful at a time, roll pieces of the dough in the sesame seeds to coat and place them about 2 inches apart on ungreased cookie sheets. Flatten the cookies slightly with the heel of your hand, shaping them into circles.

Bake for about 10 minutes, until the edges are lightly browned.

Let the cookies cool for 2 minutes on the sheets, then transfer them to wire racks to finish cooling.

1 cup all-purpose flour
¹/₃ cup rolled oats
³/₄ teaspoon baking soda
¹/₈ teaspoon salt
¹/₂ cup (1 stick) unsalted butter, at room temperature
1 cup peanut butter
³/₄ cup firmly packed light brown sugar
1 large egg
1 teaspoon vanilla extract
1 cup semisweet chocolate chips

Preheat the oven to 350 degrees.

Coat cookie sheets with vegetable oil cooking spray.

Combine the flour, oats, baking soda, and salt in a mixing bowl. Whisk to combine.

In a large mixing bowl, combine the butter, peanut butter, and brown sugar. Using an electric mixer at medium speed, beat until the mixture is light, fluffy, and smooth. Mix in the egg and vanilla.

Stir in the chocolate chips with a wooden spoon. Add the flour mixture and stir to incorporate.

Drop the dough by the tablespoonful onto the prepared cookie sheets, leaving about 1¹/₂ inches between cookies.

Bake for about 15 minutes, until the cookies are golden brown.

Remove from the oven and cool on the sheets for 3 minutes, then transfer to wire racks to finish cooling.

Peanut Butter Chocolate Chip Cookies

YIELD = ABOUT
4¹/₂ DOZEN COOKIES

We double the volume of peanut butter usually called for in cookie recipes for an extra-rich taste. As these cookies don't spread much while baking, they come out of the oven mounded and dense.

The better the peanut butter, the better the cookie. Use natural, freshly made peanut butter rather than the commercial variety in the jar.

Oatmeal Lacies

YIELD = ABOUT
4 DOZEN LACIES

The temptation is strong to nibble these delicate morsels right out of the oven, when they're still slightly chewy and evocative of warm, sweetly seasoned oatmeal on a chilly morn. However, self-discipline is in order. The lacies are best after they've cooled to a crisp. If they soften after storage in the refrigerator or freezer, you can recrisp them before serving by heating for about 5 minutes in a 300-degree oven.

$\frac{1}{2}$ cup (1 stick) unsalted butter, melted
2 cups rolled oats
2 large eggs
1 cup granulated sugar
$\frac{1}{2}$ teaspoon almond extract
$\frac{1}{4}$ teaspoon salt
1 teaspoon baking powder
$1\frac{1}{2}$ tablespoons all-purpose flour

Preheat the oven to 325 degrees.

Line cookie sheets with aluminum foil.

Combine the melted butter and oats in a large bowl, mixing thoroughly. Set aside.

Beat the eggs with a wire whisk until fluffy. Whisk in the sugar, continuing to beat until the mixture has thickened slightly. Add the almond extract, salt, baking powder, and flour. Whisk until completely incorporated and smooth. Add the oat mixture and combine thoroughly.

Drop the dough by the teaspoonful onto the prepared cookie sheets, leaving about 3 inches between cookies. Flatten each one with a rubber spatula.

Bake for 8 to 10 minutes, until golden brown all over.

Transfer the cookies on the aluminum foil to a wire rack; peel them off the foil when cooled.

For about $1\frac{1}{2}$ dozen Large Lacies, use a scant tablespoonful of dough for each cookie.

For about $1\frac{1}{2}$ dozen Oatmeal Lace Cigars, prepare Large Lacies. Carefully peel the cookies from the aluminum foil as soon as they are cool enough to handle, within 1 minute after removal from the oven. Turn each cookie upside down and roll it up around the handle of a wooden spoon. Slip the spoon out and pat the surface of the cigar into an evenly shaped cylinder.

¼ cup natural, unsweetened applesauce
⅓ cup skim milk
¾ cup firmly packed dark brown sugar
2 tablespoons unsweetened Dutch-processed cocoa powder
½ teaspoon vanilla extract
¼ cup creamy peanut butter
1½ cups quick oats
¾ cup chopped dried apricots

Line cookie sheets with wax paper.

Combine the applesauce, skim milk, brown sugar, and cocoa powder in a small, heavy-bottomed saucepan. Bring to a boil over medium heat, stirring constantly. Boil for 1 minute.

Remove the pan from the heat and stir in the vanilla and peanut butter with a wooden spoon. Stir in the oats and dried apricots. Continue stirring until the mixture is thick and blended.

Drop the dough onto the prepared cookie sheets by the heaping tablespoonful. Refrigerate until the cookies have cooled and hardened, about 5 minutes.

No-Bake Chocolate Oat Cookies

YIELD = ABOUT
3 DOZEN COOKIES

When the kids arrive home with the whole Little League in tow, don't panic! It takes only a few minutes to combine the ingredients for these quick and easy crowd pleasers on the stove top, and only 5 minutes to chill them in the refrigerator. No baking, no waiting for the cookies to cool, no threat of a strike. The major leagues should have it so easy.

Cashew Macaroons

YIELD = ABOUT
3 DOZEN MACAROONS

These tiny gems differ from the traditional macaroon in both taste and texture. Their predominant flavor comes from cashews rather than almonds, while the use of nut butter in place of ground nuts lends a smoother consistency. The cashew butter can be found in health or natural foods stores and, increasingly, in better supermarkets.

$1/2$ cup cashew butter
2 tablespoons confectioners' sugar
2 tablespoons all-purpose flour
$1/2$ teaspoon vanilla extract
$1/8$ teaspoon salt
$1/3$ cup granulated sugar
2 large egg whites, at room temperature
$1/4$ teaspoon cream of tartar

Preheat the oven to 325 degrees.

Line baking sheets with baker's parchment.

Combine the cashew butter, confectioners' sugar, flour, vanilla, and salt in a bowl. Mix and set aside.

Process the granulated sugar to superfine consistency in a food processor fitted with the steel blade, about 2 minutes.

Put the egg whites into a bowl. Beat with an electric mixer at medium speed until frothy, about 2 minutes. Add the cream of tartar and beat for about 2 minutes more, just until peaks begin to form. Raise the speed to high and add the superfine sugar gradually. Continue to beat until very stiff, shiny peaks form, about 2 minutes more.

Stir 1 tablespoon of the meringue into the cashew butter mixture until well blended. Add the mixture back to the meringue and whisk thoroughly.

Drop the dough by the $1/2$ tablespoonful onto the prepared sheets, leaving about 1 inch between cookies. Bake for about 15 minutes, until lightly browned.

Cool on the sheets for 1 minute, then peel the cookies from the parchment. Transfer to wire racks and cool completely. Store in an airtight container.

2 cups all-purpose flour
$^3/_4$ teaspoon baking soda
$^1/_4$ teaspoon salt
$^3/_4$ teaspoon ground nutmeg
$^1/_2$ cup (1 stick) unsalted butter, at room temperature
$^2/_3$ cup firmly packed dark brown sugar
$^1/_3$ cup granulated sugar
1 large egg
$^1/_4$ cup strong brewed coffee, cooled to room temperature
$^2/_3$ cup chopped walnuts
$^1/_3$ cup dried sour cherries
$^1/_3$ cup chopped dates
$^1/_3$ cup golden raisins
$^1/_4$ cup chopped dried apricots

Preheat the oven to 375 degrees.

Lightly grease cookie sheets with butter.

Combine the flour, baking soda, salt, and nutmeg in a bowl. Whisk and set aside.

Cream the butter in a large mixing bowl with an electric mixer at medium speed. Beat in the sugars. Add the egg and beat until light and fluffy. Beat in the coffee. (The mixture will look curdled.)

With a wooden spoon, stir in the walnuts, sour cherries, dates, raisins, and apricots. Add the flour mixture and stir until incorporated.

Drop the dough by the tablespoonful onto the prepared cookie sheets. Bake for about 12 minutes, until the cookies are lightly browned and cracked.

Let the cookies cool for 1 minute on the sheets, then transfer them to wire racks to cool completely, 15 to 20 minutes.

Dried Fruit Hermits

YIELD = ABOUT
5 DOZEN HERMITS

These dense little mounds are brimming with flavor. Dried sour cherries are increasingly available on supermarket shelves, but if you can't find them, substitute dried cranberries or seedless raisins.

Crunchy Granola Chocolate Chip Cookies

YIELD = ABOUT
3 DOZEN COOKIES

These generously proportioned cookies feature apple-cinnamon granola, but we like to vary the recipe with any of the other flavored granolas now available in many markets.

2 cups apple-cinnamon granola
1³/₄ cups all-purpose flour
¹/₂ teaspoon baking powder
¹/₂ teaspoon baking soda
¹/₄ teaspoon salt
1 large egg
1 cup firmly packed light brown sugar
1 cup (2 sticks) unsalted butter, melted and cooled to room temperature
¹/₄ cup milk
1 teaspoon vanilla extract
¹/₂ cup mini semisweet chocolate chips

Preheat the oven to 350 degrees.

Whisk together the granola, flour, baking powder, baking soda, and salt. Set aside.

Combine the egg and brown sugar in a large mixing bowl. Beat with an electric mixer set at medium speed until smooth and light. Beat in the melted butter. Beat in the milk and vanilla. Add the chocolate chips and the flour mixture. Stir well with a wooden spoon.

Drop the dough onto ungreased cookie sheets, using about 2 tablespoons for each cookie and leaving 2¹/₂ to 3 inches between cookies. Bake for about 13 minutes, until the cookies are light golden.

Let the cookies cool for 2 minutes on the sheets, then remove them to wire racks to finish cooling.

These cookies can become a bit dry after a few days, particularly if you use a low-fat granola. Their shelf life will be extended by individually shrink-wrapping the cookies.

Preheat the oven to 300 degrees.

Line a large baking sheet with a single layer of paper towels and warm it for at least 5 minutes in the oven.

Place each cookie upside down onto a square of plastic wrap large enough to allow about a 2-inch border all around. Gather the plastic together neatly over the cookie.

Place 2 to 4 cookies at a time right side up on the prepared baking sheet, leaving the oven door open. Watch carefully and remove the cookies after 3 to 5 seconds, as soon as the plastic shrinks onto the cookies, creating an airtight package. Cool on a wire rack.

Lemon Poppyseed Wafers

YIELD = ABOUT
4¼ DOZEN COOKIES

The appealing combination of lemon and poppyseed first appeared in bread and cake recipes featured in *The Settlement Cook Book,* a classic tome that taught generations of young newlyweds how to tame that room with the appliances at the back of their new home.

If you love the taste of poppyseed, increase the volume used in this dainty tea cookie to 1 tablespoon.

1 cup granulated sugar
¾ cup (1½ sticks) unsalted butter, at room temperature, cut into 12 tablespoons
3 ounces cream cheese, at room temperature, cut into 6 pieces
½ tablespoon lemon zest
1 tablespoon freshly squeezed lemon juice
½ teaspoon vanilla extract
1¾ cups all-purpose flour
1¼ teaspoons poppyseeds
3 tablespoons confectioners' sugar

Preheat the oven to 325 degrees.

Process the sugar for about 1 minute in a food processor fitted with the steel blade, to a superfine consistency. Add the butter and cream cheese. Pulse about 10 times, until the mixture is smooth and fluffy. Add the lemon zest, lemon juice, and vanilla. Process for a few seconds, just to combine. Add the flour and poppyseeds. Pulse 8 to 10 times, until the mixture coheres into a mound of dough.

Drop the dough by the tablespoonful onto ungreased cookie sheets, leaving about 1½ inches between cookies. Bake for about 18 minutes, just until the cookies begin to brown around the edges. (Don't let the tops brown.)

Remove the cookies to wire racks immediately to cool. Dust with confectioners' sugar.

For a change of pace, we substitute Lemon Glaze for the dusting of confectioners' sugar. Whisk 1 tablespoon freshly squeezed lemon juice into 1 cup confectioners' sugar until the mixture is smooth. Spread on top of each cookie.

YIELD = ABOUT
½ CUP GLAZE

1/4 cup milk
1/2 teaspoon distilled white vinegar
1 3/4 cups all-purpose flour
1/2 teaspoon baking soda
1/8 teaspoon baking powder
1/4 teaspoon salt
1/2 cup (1 stick) unsalted butter, at room temperature
1 cup firmly packed dark brown sugar
1 large egg
1/2 teaspoon vanilla extract
1/2 cup butterscotch chips

Preheat the oven to 400 degrees.

Lightly coat cookie sheets with vegetable oil cooking spray.

Combine the milk and vinegar in a 1-cup glass measuring cup. Set aside.

Whisk together the flour, baking soda, baking powder, and salt.

In a large mixing bowl, combine the butter, brown sugar, and egg. Beat until light and creamy with an electric mixer at high speed. Add the vanilla and the milk and vinegar mixture, taking care to scrape all the curdled milk from the bottom of the measuring cup with a rubber spatula. Mix at low speed for about 10 seconds to combine. (The batter will appear slightly coarse and curdled.)

Dump in the flour mixture and mix thoroughly with a wooden spoon. Fold in the butterscotch chips. Refrigerate for 15 minutes.

Drop the dough by the teaspoonful onto the prepared cookie sheets, leaving about 2 inches between cookies. Bake for 8 to 10 minutes, until the cookies are lightly browned around the edges.

Transfer the cookie sheets from the oven to wire racks and let the cookies cool.

Double Butterscotch Cookies

YIELD = ABOUT
4 1/2 DOZEN COOKIES

In olden times, frugal cooks used up milk that had soured—which, by the way, is thinner and tangier than buttermilk—when baking. For these little goodies, we duplicate the taste by curdling milk with vinegar. The butterscotch flavor of the dough, derived from the mixture of butter and brown sugar, receives a boost from the addition of butterscotch chips.

Cakey Chocolate Mint Cookies

YIELD = ABOUT
4 DOZEN COOKIES

We've always liked the hint of mint in the popular chocolate wafers sold by the Girl Scouts, but we prefer a somewhat less brittle texture. A bit of tinkering in the old kitchen produced this refreshingly minty rendition, which has the feel of an old-time chocolate cake made with buttermilk.

1³/₄ cups all-purpose flour
¹/₂ teaspoon baking powder
¹/₄ teaspoon baking soda
¹/₄ teaspoon salt
¹/₂ cup (1 stick) unsalted butter, at room temperature, cut into pieces
3 ounces bittersweet chocolate, broken up
¹/₂ cup firmly packed dark brown sugar
¹/₂ cup granulated sugar
1 large egg
¹/₄ cup buttermilk
1 teaspoon peppermint extract

Whisk together the flour, baking powder, baking soda, and salt. Set aside.

Put the butter and chocolate in a glass measuring cup. Microwave at full power for 1 to 1¹/₂ minutes, until melted, stirring every 20 seconds. (You can also melt the butter and chocolate in the top of a double boiler over boiling water.)

Combine the sugars and egg in a large mixing bowl. Beat with an electric mixer at low speed until smooth and blended, about 1 minute. Mix in the buttermilk and peppermint. Beat in the melted chocolate and butter mixture.

Stir in the flour mixture with a wooden spoon. Let the dough sit at room temperature for 15 to 20 minutes to stiffen.

Preheat the oven to 350 degrees.

Drop by the tablespoonful onto ungreased cookie sheets, about 3 inches apart. Bake for 8 to 9 minutes, until the cookies are firm to the touch and the tops have cracked.

Let the cookies cool for 2 minutes on the sheets, then remove them to wire racks to cool completely.

For variety, top the cookies with a Chocolate Glaze.
Put 3 ounces bittersweet chocolate, broken up, into
a glass measuring cup. Microwave at full power for
about 1 1/2 minutes, stirring every 20 seconds. (You
can also melt the chocolate in the top of a double
boiler over boiling water.) Stir 2 tablespoons light
corn syrup and 1 tablespoon unsalted butter,
at room temperature, into the melted chocolate.
Let sit for 2 minutes to thicken. Spread on
top of the cookies, or dip the cookies into the
mixture to coat halfway.

YIELD = ABOUT 1/2 CUP GLAZE

Amaretti

YIELD = ABOUT
5 DOZEN AMARETTI

This Italian cookie was originally made with bitter almonds, the "little bitter things" referred to in a literal translation of the word *amaretti*. Since bitter almonds can't be purchased in the United States, we use almond paste. Sweetened with both granulated and confectioners' sugar, the cookies are essentially crisp macaroons.

For a festive presentation, we like to wrap individual amaretti in squares of brightly colored tissue paper.

3 large egg whites, not combined
Pinch of salt
One 7-ounce tube almond paste
1 cup granulated sugar
1 teaspoon almond extract
1 teaspoon confectioners' sugar

Heavily butter and lightly flour cookie sheets.

In a stationary electric mixer fitted with the whisk, beat 2 of the egg whites at medium speed until frothy, about 2 minutes. Add the salt and continue to beat for about 1½ minutes more, until stiff, but not dry, peaks form.

Transfer the beaten egg whites to another bowl. Wash and dry the bowl of the stationary mixer and fit the mixer with the paddle attachment.

Break the almond paste up into small pieces. Combine with the granulated sugar in the bowl of the mixer. Mix at low speed for about 6 minutes, until all the paste is broken up and the mixture is a fine crumb. Add the remaining egg white and continue to mix until very smooth, about 4 minutes. (The mixture will soften and begin to adhere to the sides of the bowl.)

Add the previously beaten egg whites and mix at low speed for 1½ minutes. Scrape down the sides of the bowl and mix for about 1½ minutes more, until light and fluffy. Mix in the almond extract.

Drop by the teaspoonful onto the prepared cookie sheets. Hold the spoon as close to the cookie sheet as possible and push the dough off with a small rubber spatula. Shape the mounds of dough with the spatula, making each as round as possible. Leave 1 to 1½ inches between cookies. Dust with confectioners' sugar. Set aside for 1 hour at room temperature.

Preheat the oven to 375 degrees.

Bake the cookies for 14 to 15 minutes, until golden brown. Cool on the sheets on wire racks.

*Amaretti are an essential ingredient for Tortoni,
a wonderfully rich Italian frozen dessert.*

1 cup heavy cream
2 tablespoons almond liqueur
1 large egg plus 1 egg white
3 tablespoons granulated sugar
6 Amaretti, roughly crumbled (about 6 tablespoons)

Bring about 2 inches of water to a simmer in a medium saucepan.

Meanwhile, beat the cream in a large mixing bowl with an electric mixer at high speed for a few minutes, until soft peaks form. Add the liqueur and continue to beat for about 1 minute more until the mixture forms stiff peaks.

Combine the egg, the additional egg white, and the sugar in a heatproof glass bowl just big enough to sit atop the saucepan without the water touching the bottom of the bowl. Whisk lightly to combine and place the bowl over the simmering water. Whisking vigorously, heat for 5 to 6 minutes, until the egg mixture reaches a temperature of 140 degrees on an instant-read thermometer. (The mixture will resemble a custard, thick enough to coat the back of a spoon.)

Transfer the bowl from the heat onto a work surface lined with a dish towel. Beat until cool with an electric mixer at medium speed, about 3 minutes. Stir in about $1/3$ cup of the crumbled Amaretti with a wooden spoon. Fold the mixture into the whipped cream. Cover with plastic wrap and freeze for at least 8 hours.

Scoop into individual serving bowls (or paper cups, for authentic presentation), if desired. Garnish with the remaining cookie crumbs.

YIELD = ABOUT 8 SERVINGS

Cranberry Orange Oatmeal Cookies

YIELD = ABOUT
6 DOZEN COOKIES

These slightly crunchy oatmeal cookies derive their distinctive character from the inclusion of tart dried cranberries and the substitution of orange extract for the typical vanilla.

3/4 cup (1 1/2 sticks) unsalted butter, at room temperature
3/4 cup firmly packed dark brown sugar
3/4 cup granulated sugar
2 large eggs
1 teaspoon orange extract
1 cup all-purpose flour
1 teaspoon baking soda
1/4 teaspoon salt
2 3/4 cups rolled oats
1 cup pecan pieces
1 cup dried cranberries

Preheat the oven to 375 degrees.

Coat cookie sheets with vegetable oil cooking spray and flour lightly.

Combine the butter and sugars in a large mixing bowl. Cream with an electric mixer at medium speed. Beat in the eggs and orange extract. Add the flour, baking soda, and salt. Beat just to incorporate. With a wooden spoon, stir in the oats, pecans, and cranberries.

Drop the dough by the tablespoonful onto the prepared cookie sheets, leaving about 2 inches between cookies. Bake for about 8 minutes, until firm and browned.

Remove from the oven and cool on the sheets for 4 minutes, then transfer the cookies to wire racks to finish cooling.

Hard-core oatmeal cookie buffs can boost the oatmeal flavor by toasting the oats first (which will also produce a slightly more crumbly cookie). Scatter the oats in a single layer on a baking sheet lined with aluminum foil. Toast for about 10 minutes in a 300-degree oven.

1 cup roasted pistachio nuts
$\frac{1}{2}$ cup (1 stick) unsalted butter
$\frac{1}{2}$ cup granulated sugar
2 tablespoons all-purpose flour
2 tablespoons sour cream
$\frac{1}{4}$ teaspoon finely grated lime zest

Preheat the oven to 350 degrees.

Line large baking sheets with baker's parchment.

In a food processor fitted with the steel blade or by hand, finely chop the nuts. Set aside.

In a medium saucepan, combine the butter, sugar, flour, sour cream, and lime zest. Bring to a boil over medium heat, stirring constantly. Boil for 1 minute, continuing to stir.

Remove the pan from the heat and stir in the nuts. Drop by the teaspoonful onto the prepared baking sheets, about 3 inches apart.

Bake in the center of the oven for 6 to 7 minutes, just until browned, taking care not to burn.

Cool the cookies on the sheet for about 5 minutes, then transfer them to a paper towel–lined dish and allow to cool completely.

For Almond Pralines, substitute the same quantities of chopped almonds for the pistachios and orange zest for the lime zest.

Pistachio Pralines

YIELD = ABOUT
3 DOZEN PRALINES

Serve these big, crisp cookies at teatime or with ice cream for dessert, but don't send them traveling. (The cookies are so airy that the recipient is likely to end up with a tin of praline crumbs. One of our friends, however, says this is perfect—she can just scoop up mouthfuls from the tin.)

We recommend baking a single sheet at a time. Watch the cookies carefully and remove them from the oven to cool as soon as they are lightly browned.

Holiday Cookies

Cookies are universal—everyone loves them. Every joyful holiday is celebrated with special cookies to mark the occasion; every household has its own favorites.

In this chapter, we tour the nation to join family and friends in the joy of holiday baking. We travel to Florida, where Sara Bluestein makes Prune Hamantaschen to celebrate Purim with neighbors and Anita Reeves bakes Date Chews as Christmas gifts for the ladies in her rug-hooking circle.

Jeanne Troxell Munson's household in the Berkshires of Massachusetts lends a hand with Raspberry Christmas Cookies, while Mark Stahr and Don Houck bake batches of Cranberry Cookies for a Thanksgiving gathering of family and friends in suburban Washington, D.C. In New Jersey, Elaine Barlas prepares Mexican Wedding Cookies for her visiting sister-in-law Martha to take home to Mexico City.

Across the country in California, Eleanor Bluestein bakes Apricot Marmalade Bars in the Passover tradition—following a recipe that originated in the Midwest—for the family seder, while her mother, Ruth Gold, prepares Passover Date Nut Bars.

Deep in the heart of Texas, Claudia Clark Potter's busy baking Mincemeat Bars for Thanksgiving to share with visiting son Scott from San Francisco and daughter Erin from Seattle. Ann Bloomstrand's mom, Evelyn West, is in her Southern Illinois kitchen making Toffee Bars, a Christmas family favorite. Halloween trick-or-treaters in Missouri will get to sample Mary McLaughlin's special Shortbread Ghosts.

Arriving back home in Chicago, we find Lisa Schumacher and her daughter Christina making Aunt Helen's Chocolate Shots for the Christmas buffet. Meanwhile, John Koulias and his mom join forces to bake Greek Easter Cookies, as well as Honey Cakes for Yuletide.

Christmas

¹⁄₂ cup dark molasses
¹⁄₄ cup (¹⁄₂ stick) unsalted butter, at room temperature
2 tablespoons dark brown sugar
1 teaspoon ground ginger
¹⁄₂ teaspoon ground cinnamon
¹⁄₄ teaspoon ground nutmeg
¹⁄₈ teaspoon ground allspice
1 cup all-purpose flour
¹⁄₄ teaspoon baking soda
¹⁄₄ teaspoon salt
3¹⁄₂ dozen small silver dragées or cinnamon candies

Combine the molasses, butter, and brown sugar in a large bowl. Mix thoroughly with a wooden spoon. Stir in the spices. Add the flour, baking soda, and salt. Stir until fully incorporated.

Line a cookie or baking sheet with wax paper. Turn the dough out onto the wax paper and cover with a second sheet. Flatten by hand into a 7-by-9-inch rectangle. Freeze for 30 minutes.

Preheat the oven to 375 degrees.

Coat cookie sheets with vegetable oil cooking spray.

Remove the dough from the freezer and cut it in half crosswise. Return half to the freezer until ready to use and peel the paper from the remaining half.

Cover a work surface with wax paper. Flour lightly. Put the dough onto the wax paper, sprinkle flour over the dough, and cover it with a second sheet of wax paper. Roll it out as thinly as possible, to a thickness of about ¹⁄₁₆ inch. (The rectangle will now measure about 8 by 12 inches.)

Using a miniature bell-shaped cutter, cut out cookies and transfer them with a spatula to the prepared cookie sheets. Reroll the scraps of dough and cut out additional bells. Repeat the process for the second piece of dough. Place a dragée (or a cinnamon candy) at the bottom tip of each bell.

Bake for about 9 minutes, until firm to the touch.

Remove the cookies to wire racks to cool.

Ginger Bells

YIELD = ABOUT
3¹⁄₂ DOZEN BELLS

"Ginger bells, ginger bells, ginger all the way..."

Unlike traditionally stiff and dry gingerbread cookies, these buttery morsels melt in your mouth. The very soft and sticky dough is easier to roll with the aid of a pastry cloth and rolling pin cover. If the dough becomes too soft to work with, return it to the freezer for a few minutes to firm.

In addition to bells, little ginger cookies can be fashioned in a variety of other shapes using miniature cutters. Instead of decorating them with a dragée, pipe them when cool with Royal Icing (page 207), which stands out brilliantly against the dark gingerbread background.

Stained Glass Cookies

The dough for Ginger Bells can do double duty as the base for charming Stained Glass Cookies to adorn your tree.

Prepare the dough through the freezing step according to recipe directions for Ginger Bells. While the dough is in the freezer, crush 7 to 9 rolls of Life Savers candies in a food processor fitted with the steel blade or with a rolling pin (roll between sheets of wax paper). Use candies all of the same color.

Preheat the oven to 375 degrees and coat cookie sheets well with vegetable oil cooking spray.

Cut the dough in half crosswise and return half to the freezer until ready to use.

Place the dough on a work surface lined with lightly floured wax paper. Sprinkle flour over the dough and cover it with a second sheet of wax paper. Roll it out to a thickness of $1/8$ inch, working the dough into a rectangle measuring about 6 by 8 inches.

Cut out $2^1/2$-inch or 3-inch circles and cut the center out of each with a decorative miniature holiday cookie cutter. Using a chopstick (or a Phillips screwdriver), make a hole through the dough in the center of the top of each cookie. Transfer the cookies to the prepared sheets with a spatula. Gather and reroll the scraps of dough and cut out additional cookies. Repeat the process for the second piece of dough.

Bake for about 11 minutes, until firm to the touch. Remove the cookies to wire racks to cool, leaving the oven on.

When cool, transfer the cookies to baking sheets lined with aluminum foil. Mound crushed candy in the center of each to fill the cutout completely. Return to the oven and bake for about 3 minutes more, until the candy has melted and begun to bubble, taking care not to burn it.

Cool on the sheets on wire racks. When cool, thread a color-coordinated ribbon through the hole in each cookie. Don't shrink-wrap, as this could cause the candy to melt.

YIELD = ABOUT 1 1/2 DOZEN ORNAMENTS

To make Royal Icing *for decorating cookies made from Ginger Bells dough (page 205) or Ornament Cookies (page 209), bring 2 inches of water to a boil in the bottom of a double boiler over high heat.*

Reduce the heat to low, insert the top, and put in the whites of 3 large eggs. Cook for 4 to 5 minutes, whisking constantly and making sure the water isn't touching the underside of the insert, until the egg whites register a temperature of at least 140 degrees on an instant-read thermometer.

Transfer to the bowl of a stationary electric mixer fitted with the whisk, or to a large bowl if you will be using a hand-held electric mixer. Add 3 1/2 cups confectioners' sugar. Blend at medium speed until the sugar is incorporated and the mixture is frothy. Increase the speed to high and beat to stiff glossy peaks, about 6 minutes in a stationary mixer and 8 to 9 minutes using a hand-held model. For a festive look, stir in a few drops of food coloring.

Put the icing into a pastry bag fitted with a small decorating tip or into a heavy-duty plastic storage bag with a bottom corner clipped. Pipe the icing along the edges of the cookies after cooled. Excess icing will keep for 3 days refrigerated in an airtight container.

Jeanne Troxell Munson's Raspberry Christmas Cookies

YIELD = ABOUT 2 DOZEN COOKIES

When she's not busy drawing artwork for one or another of our projects, Jeanne likes to bake. Holiday baking's a family project in the Munson household—Jeanne directs operations and prepares dough, while daughter Lindsay and son Matt diligently wield the cookie cutters.

Husband Bill and younger son Eric just as diligently consume the product of the family's labors.

1$^1/_2$ cups all-purpose flour
$^1/_2$ tablespoon baking powder
$^1/_4$ teaspoon salt
6 tablespoons unsalted butter, at room temperature
$^3/_4$ cup confectioners' sugar
1 large egg, well beaten, plus 1 large beaten egg white
2$^1/_2$ tablespoons milk
$^1/_2$ teaspoon vanilla extract
$^1/_2$ cup seedless raspberry spreadable fruit, at room temperature

Preheat the oven to 400 degrees.

Coat cookie sheets with vegetable oil cooking spray.

Whisk together and set aside the flour, baking powder, and salt.

In a large bowl, cream the butter and confectioners' sugar with an electric mixer at low speed. Add the whole beaten egg and mix until light and fluffy. Beat in the milk and vanilla. Add the flour mixture and stir with a wooden spoon to form a dough.

Gather the dough into a ball and cut it in half.

On a lightly floured pastry cloth, roll out half the dough to a thickness of $^1/_8$ inch, working it into a rectangle about 12 by 10 inches. Cut out 2$^1/_2$-inch rounds and transfer them to the prepared cookie sheets. Gather and reroll the dough scraps for additional cookies.

Spread 1 teaspoon of the spreadable fruit over each cookie, leaving a thin border all around the edge.

Roll the remaining piece of dough out to the same thickness and dimensions. Cut out 2$^1/_2$-inch rounds, rerolling the scraps for additional cookies. Using decorative miniature Christmas cookie cutters (in such shapes as trees, stars, and bells), cut the center out of each round.

On top of each cookie layered with filling, place a cookie with a decorative center. Press firmly around the edges to seal the top and bottom cookies together.

Paint the exposed dough with the beaten egg white. Bake for 10 to 12 minutes, until light golden.

Remove the cookies to wire racks to cool.

Ornament Cookies

We've found that Jeanne's dough makes wonderful ornaments for decorating holiday trees.

Preheat the oven to 400 degrees and coat cookie sheets with vegetable oil cooking spray.

Prepare a full recipe of dough. Divide the dough in half and roll each half out into an 8-inch circle about $1/4$ inch thick. Cut out cookies using decoratively shaped holiday cutters (bells, trees, angels, stars, etc.). Make a small hole all the way through the dough in the center of the top of each cookie (for the hanger). Place on the prepared cookie sheets.

Bake for about 13 minutes, until the cookies are just beginning to color. Remove to a wire rack to cool.

Frost the entire top of each cookie with Royal Icing (page 207) to which different shades of food colorings have been added. To give gift ornaments, shrink-wrap according to the directions on page 191.

YIELD: THE NUMBER OF ORNAMENTS DEPENDS UPON THE SIZE OF THE CUTTERS, WITH STANDARD $2^1/_2$-INCH CUTTERS YIELDING ABOUT 2 DOZEN.

Pistachio Spritz Wreaths

YIELD = ABOUT 7 DOZEN

Delicate, diminutive holiday wreaths with an intensely rich pistachio taste. They derive their festive seasonal hue from the nuts rather than food coloring. We use roasted pistachios and skip the extra work involved in shelling them.

DOUGH:
1/3 cup roasted pistachio nuts
2 1/4 cups all-purpose flour
1 cup (2 sticks) unsalted butter, at room temperature
1/2 cup granulated sugar
1/4 cup firmly packed light brown sugar
3 large egg yolks

GLAZE:
1/2 cup confectioners' sugar
2 tablespoons heavy cream

TOPPING:
1/2 cup roasted pistachio nuts, chopped

Preheat the oven to 375 degrees.

To make the dough, put the pistachios and 1/4 cup of the flour in the bowl of a food processor fitted with the steel blade. Process to a fine grind.

In a large mixing bowl, combine the butter, sugars, and egg yolks. Beat with an electric mixer at medium speed until the mixture is smooth and creamy. Add the ground nuts and the remaining 2 cups flour. Stir with a wooden spoon just to incorporate and form a dough.

Press the dough onto ungreased cookie sheets, using a cookie press with a wreath-shaped disk. Bake for about 9 minutes, until golden brown.

Let the cookies cool on the sheets for 1 minute before transferring them to wire racks to finish cooling.

For the glaze, combine the confectioners' sugar and cream in a small bowl. Mix well with a fork or a small whisk.

Line a work surface with aluminum foil or wax paper. Place the racks on which the cookies have cooled onto the lined surface. Brush the wreaths with the glaze and sprinkle with the chopped nuts.

1½ cups walnut pieces
3 tablespoons plus ¼ cup confectioners' sugar
1¼ cups all-purpose flour
¾ cup (1½ sticks) unsalted butter, at room temperature
¾ teaspoon vanilla extract

Preheat the oven to 375 degrees.

Combine the walnuts and 3 tablespoons of the confectioners' sugar in the bowl of a food processor fitted with the steel blade. Process for about 20 seconds, until the nuts are finely chopped. Add the flour and pulse a few times, just to incorporate.

In a bowl, cream the butter with an electric mixer at medium speed. Continue to beat for about 5 minutes, until the butter is very pale. At low speed, mix in the vanilla. Stir in the flour and nut mixture with a wooden spoon.

Using a tablespoonful of dough for each cookie, roll the dough into neatly shaped balls and place them 1 inch apart on ungreased cookie sheets.

Bake for 12 to 14 minutes, until lightly browned. Let the cookies cool on the sheets for 3 minutes, then roll them in the remaining confectioners' sugar and transfer them to wire racks to finish cooling. When cool, roll the cookies again in the confectioners' sugar.

Elaine Barlas's Mexican Wedding Cookies

YIELD = ABOUT
3 DOZEN COOKIES

When her sister-in-law Martha came from Mexico to visit for the holidays, Elaine served this Christmas Eve tradition in the old-fashioned way, individually wrapped in squares of brightly colored tissue paper. Martha liked them so much she had Elaine bake 5 more batches to take home for the family.

Elaine, a native New Yorker devoted to replicating the culinary traditions of her husband Ricardo's family in the authentic manner, chopped the nuts by hand. Barry, a native New Yorker devoted to culinary pragmatism, adapted the recipe to the food processor.

Marie Koulias's Honey Cakes

YIELD = ABOUT
4 DOZEN COOKIES

This traditional Greek dessert is a specialty of John Koulias's mom. Known as *melomakarona,* it's served on Christmas and New Year's Day. These honey cakes are very tasty and rich, but not as overwhelmingly sweet as baklava and other pastries from the same region.

1½ cups canola or vegetable oil
1 cup (2 sticks) unsalted butter, melted
¼ cup confectioners' sugar
¼ cup plus 2 tablespoons honey
1 large egg yolk
1½ tablespoons bourbon
1 teaspoon vanilla extract
½ teaspoon baking powder
¼ cup freshly squeezed orange juice
1 teaspoon finely grated orange zest
½ tablespoon ground cinnamon
4¼ cups all-purpose flour

TOPPING:
1 cup honey
1 cup chopped walnuts
½ tablespoon ground cinnamon

Preheat the oven to 350 degrees.

Lightly coat cookie sheets with vegetable oil cooking spray.

Combine the oil and melted butter in a large bowl. Beat with an electric mixer at low speed until thoroughly blended. Add the confectioners' sugar and honey. Beat at medium speed until the mixture turns pale, about 2 minutes. Beat in the egg yolk, bourbon, and vanilla on low speed.

Dissolve the baking powder in the orange juice. Add to the mixture in the large bowl, along with the orange zest. Beat in at low speed. Beat in the cinnamon. With a wooden spoon, stir in 2 cups of the flour until completely incorporated. Stir in the remaining 2¼ cups flour.

Using 2 tablespoons of dough for each cookie, roll the dough into balls and then flatten them into little cakes. Place them about 1½ inches apart on the prepared cookie sheets. On the top of each cookie, press a fork down flat, turn it 90 degrees, and press down again to form a crosshatch indentation.

Bake for about 20 minutes, until golden brown.

Remove the cookies to wire racks to cool.

For the topping, bring the honey to a boil in a small saucepan over medium-low heat. Remove from the heat and cool completely. In a small bowl, mix the walnuts and cinnamon.

Transfer the cookies on the racks to a work surface lined with aluminum foil. Pour 1 teaspoon honey over each cookie, then sprinkle with 1 teaspoon of the cinnamon-nut mixture.

Kevin's Eggnog Cookies

YIELD = ABOUT
3 DOZEN COOKIES

Kevin, who thinks eggnog is just about the niftiest concoction one can imbibe, has been known to consume substantial amounts during the holiday season (loosely interpreted as Thanksgiving to New Year's). Given the fat and calorie content of this liquid time bomb, it came down to weaning Kevin off eggnog or endowing Saks every January.

This cookie is our solution. Now Kevin just nibbles a couple whenever the eggnog craving strikes.

2 cups all-purpose flour
1/2 teaspoon baking soda
1/4 teaspoon salt
1 teaspoon plus 1 tablespoon freshly grated nutmeg
2 large eggs
1 cup granulated sugar
6 tablespoons (3/4 stick) unsalted butter, at room temperature
1/2 tablespoon rum extract
1/2 cup heavy cream
1/4 cup confectioners' sugar

Preheat the oven to 350 degrees.

Lightly coat cookie sheets with vegetable oil cooking spray.

Whisk together the flour, baking soda, salt, and 1 teaspoon of the nutmeg.

In a large mixing bowl, beat the eggs and sugar with an electric mixer at high speed until the mixture is smooth and thick.

Add the butter, rum extract, and cream. Mix at low speed until thoroughly blended. Increase the speed to high and mix for 15 seconds more. Add the flour mixture, beating just to incorporate.

Drop by the tablespoonful onto the prepared cookie sheets, leaving 2 inches between cookies. Bake for about 12 minutes, until light golden and firm to the touch.

Remove from the oven. Dust them with confectioners' sugar, sprinkle each with a pinch of the remaining nutmeg, and remove to wire racks to cool.

Why not spike the Eggnog cookies with a bit of Brandy Frosting?

In a bowl, soften 2 tablespoons unsalted butter at room temperature with an electric mixer at low speed. Sift in 1 cup confectioners' sugar. Add 1 tablespoon plus 1 teaspoon brandy, and beat until smooth. Spread the icing on the cookies while they're still warm and dust with ground nutmeg.

1 cup chopped dates
1 cup chopped walnuts
³/₄ cup granulated sugar
³/₄ cup all-purpose flour
1 teaspoon baking powder
¹/₂ teaspoon salt
2 large eggs, beaten
¹/₄ cup confectioners' sugar

Preheat the oven to 325 degrees.

Lightly grease a 7-by-9-inch baking pan with butter.

In a large mixing bowl, combine the dates, walnuts, granulated sugar, flour, baking powder, and salt. Whisk thoroughly. Add the beaten eggs and stir with a wooden spoon to incorporate.

Press the dough evenly into the prepared baking pan, and bake for 20 to 25 minutes, until the cake is lightly browned and a tester inserted in the center comes out clean.

Remove the pan to a wire rack. Cut the cookies into 1³/₄-by-1¹/₂-inch bars and allow them to cool in the pan. Once cooled, roll the bars in the confectioners' sugar to coat.

K.C.'s Mom's Date Chews

YIELD = 24 CHEWS

Culinary wiz K. Colin (aka K.C.) Reeves's mother, Anita, makes these scrumptious bars at Christmastime for the ladies in her rug-hooking circle. They're K.C.'s favorite cookie, and Anita says her "hookers" like them too!

Use additional confectioners' sugar if needed. However, Anita cautions not to roll the bars in the confectioners' sugar until they're completely cooled; they'll absorb too much sugar if rolled hot.

Cinnamon Puffs

YIELD = ABOUT
2 1/2 DOZEN PUFFS

Based on a very old recipe, these cookies have a nutty, spicy base topped with a meringue dome.

8 ounces almonds
4 large egg whites, at room temperature
1 3/4 cups confectioners' sugar
1 teaspoon orange zest
1 teaspoon ground cinnamon

Preheat the oven to 300 degrees.

Line cookie sheets with baker's parchment.

Finely grind the almonds in a food processor fitted with the steel blade.

Put the egg whites in a stationary electric mixer fitted with the whisk. Beat at medium speed until soft peaks form, about 4 minutes. Gradually add the confectioners' sugar, beating for about 2 minutes more to stiff peaks. Fold in the orange zest. Remove and reserve about 1/2 cup of the mixture. Stir the cinnamon and ground almonds into the mixing bowl.

Drop by the tablespoonful onto the prepared sheets. Top each cookie with 1/2 teaspoon of the reserved egg white mixture, adding a little extra if needed to cover the cookie completely.

Bake for about 20 minutes, until cookies are beginning to crack around the edges.

Let the cookies cool on the sheets for 30 minutes.

We drop the puffs onto cookie sheets, but for a more elaborate presentation you can use a pastry bag fitted with a star tip, creating mounds about 1 1/2 inches in diameter.

1 cup (2 sticks) unsalted butter, at room temperature
1 cup firmly packed dark brown sugar
1 large egg yolk
1 teaspoon vanilla extract
2 cups all-purpose flour
¼ teaspoon salt
8 ounces milk chocolate, chopped
1 cup chopped pecans

Preheat the oven to 350 degrees.

In a large mixing bowl, cream the butter and brown sugar with an electric mixer. Add the egg yolk and vanilla and beat at medium speed until the mixture is light and fluffy. Stir in the flour and salt, just to incorporate.

Pat the dough evenly into an ungreased 13-by-10-inch baking sheet.

Bake for 20 to 25 minutes, until lightly browned.

Remove from the oven and scatter the chopped chocolate over the base while it is still warm. As the chocolate melts, spread it evenly with a rubber spatula. Scatter the nuts on top.

Allow the toffee to cool completely. Cut into diamond-shaped bars (page 97).

Evelyn West's Toffee Bars

YIELD = 22 BARS

Ann Bloomstrand's mom, Evelyn West, made these every Christmas unfailingly. Traditional toffee bars cut into pretty diamond shapes, they consist of a thin butterscotch base topped with creamy milk chocolate and pecans.

Lisa Schumacher's Chocolate Shots

YIELD = ABOUT
4 DOZEN SHOTS

These buttery gems are named for the chocolate shots, or sprinkles, that adorn them. For years, Lisa's aunt, Helen Kalabsa, made enough for the entire clan each Christmas. The toque has now been passed to Lisa, who's cheerfully taken over holiday baking with the aid of her daughter Christina.

1¼ cups all-purpose flour
1 cup confectioners' sugar
½ teaspoon baking soda
1 cup rolled oats
1 cup (2 sticks) unsalted butter
2 teaspoons vanilla extract
3 tablespoons chocolate sprinkles

Whisk together the flour, confectioners' sugar, and baking soda in a large bowl. Mix in the oats.

Melt the butter in a small saucepan over medium-low heat. Stir in the vanilla and pour over the oat mixture. With a wooden spoon, stir to form a dough.

Remove the dough to a work surface and divide it into thirds. Form each piece into a log 4 inches long and 2 inches in diameter.

Scatter 1 tablespoon of the sprinkles onto a sheet of wax paper. Roll a log in the sprinkles to coat and wrap it up in the wax paper. Repeat the process with the remaining sprinkles and the remaining 2 logs. Freeze the logs for 1 hour.

Preheat the oven to 350 degrees.

Using a large serrated knife, cut each log into ¼-inch rounds. Place them 2 inches apart on ungreased baking sheets.

Bake for about 20 minutes, until golden brown.

Remove the cookies to wire racks to cool.

In lieu of chocolate sprinkles, decorate the shots with an equal quantity of seasonal red and green sprinkles or festive multicolored sprinkles. For variety, try whole chocolate toffee chips or M & M's chocolate mini baking bits; for either, use double the quantity of sprinkles called for.

6 ounces semisweet chocolate, chopped
1 cup chopped pecans
1 cup (2 sticks) unsalted butter, at room temperature
²/₃ cup granulated sugar, plus ²/₃ cup for finishing
¹/₄ teaspoon salt
1 teaspoon vanilla extract
1³/₄ cups all-purpose flour

Preheat the oven to 350 degrees.

Heat the chocolate in the top of a double boiler over boiling water, stirring until melted and smooth. Stir in the pecans. Remove from the heat and set the top of the double boiler aside for the mixture to cool.

In a large bowl, cream the butter with an electric mixer at low speed. Mix in ²/₃ cup of the sugar, the salt, and the vanilla. Add the flour and stir with a wooden spoon just to incorporate.

Add the chocolate mixture and "revel" with a fork to produce a marbleized effect.

Drop by the teaspoonful onto ungreased cookie sheets, leaving 2 inches between cookies. Lightly coat the bottom of a 1¹/₂-inch-diameter glass with vegetable oil cooking spray and dip it in granulated sugar. Flatten each cookie to a thickness of ¹/₄ inch with the glass, dipping it into the sugar between each cookie.

Bake for about 10 minutes, until the cookies are firm to the touch.

Let the cookies cool on the sheets for 2 minutes before removing them to wire racks to finish cooling.

For Chocolate Raspberry Revels, reduce the amount of chocolate to 4 ounces. When the chocolate is melted, stir in ¹/₃ cup seedless raspberry spreadable fruit along with the pecans.

Helen Kalabsa's Chocolate Nut Revels

YIELD = ABOUT
10 DOZEN REVELS

Helen's recipe calls for the baker to "revel"—or stir with a fork to marbleize—melted chocolate with a butter and sugar mixture. These little gems have brought smiles to the faces of generations of Kalabsa kids and their cousins, the Schumachers. We're sure you'll revel—in the more common sense of the word—in their consumption as well.

Sara Bluestein's Prune Hamantaschen

YIELD = ABOUT
4 DOZEN HAMANTASCHEN

Luscious prune filling encased in a sugar dough, this Purim pastry is based on a recipe that Barry's mom developed herself. Sara has always been such an enthusiastic baker that she kept one room of the house unheated for years—the room was dedicated to preparing doughs and kept cool to prevent them from overheating.

Make your own prune butter (see box) or use prepared prune filling—the *lackva* found in Jewish grocery stores or a similar Bohemian kolacky filling.

Purim

$\frac{1}{2}$ cup granulated sugar
$\frac{1}{2}$ cup (1 stick) unsalted butter, at room temperature
1 teaspoon lemon extract
3 large eggs
$\frac{1}{4}$ teaspoon salt
2 teaspoons baking powder
$2\frac{2}{3}$ cups all-purpose flour
2 tablespoons water
2 cups prune butter filling (see box)

Combine the sugar, butter, lemon extract, and 2 of the eggs in a large mixing bowl. Beat with an electric mixer at medium speed for 2 minutes. (The resulting mixture will be slightly lumpy.) Add the salt, baking powder, and flour. Beat at low speed for about 1 minute, until all the flour is incorporated.

Turn the dough out onto wax paper, gather it into a ball, wrap it in the paper, and refrigerate for 30 minutes.

Preheat the oven to 350 degrees.

Lightly butter and flour cookie sheets.

Whisk together the remaining egg and the water in a small bowl and set aside.

Remove the chilled dough to a lightly floured work surface and cut it in half. Re-cover 1 piece in the wax paper to keep it from drying out. Roll the other piece out to $\frac{1}{8}$ inch thick and about 12 inches square. Cut out $2\frac{1}{2}$-inch circles with a cookie cutter.

Put 2 teaspoons of the prune filling in the center of each circle. Paint the exposed dough with the egg and water wash. Fold the dough up around the filling to form a triangle and pinch the 3 corners closed. Paint the sides of the cookies with the wash and place on the prepared cookie sheets.

Gather up the scraps of dough, work them back into a ball, and roll out again. Cut out additional $2\frac{1}{2}$-inch circles and continue to fill and assemble the hamantaschen.

Repeat the process for the second half of the dough.

Bake for about 15 minutes, until lightly browned. Cool on the sheets on wire racks.

If you're going to make the hamantaschen from scratch, why not make your own Prune Butter as well?

Combine 24 ounces pitted prunes and $^2/_3$ cup water in a saucepan. Bring to a boil. Reduce the heat, cover, and simmer for 20 to 25 minutes, until fork tender.

Mash the prunes to a smooth consistency with a fork. Drop a teaspoonful onto a small plate. If a ring of water forms around the edge, return the prune butter to the pan and cook for about 3 minutes more over low heat, stirring constantly. Allow to cool completely before filling the hamantaschen.

Poppyseed Hamantaschen

YIELD = ABOUT
2 DOZEN HAMANTASCHEN

Barry's dad, who consumed sweets very sparingly, was the only member of the Bluestein household to prefer poppyseed hamantaschen. The prune or apricot varieties were favored by Barry and his mother, both dedicated sweet eaters— so every year she baked four poppyseed and bushels of prune and apricot hamantaschen.

This version is made from yeast dough. The pastries have a delicate texture and a deep, rich brown color. A sprinkling of poppyseeds on the outside adds visual interest and a little crunch.

$^{1}/_{4}$ ounce (1 packet) quick-rise yeast
2 tablespoons lukewarm water
  (105 to 115 degrees on an instant-read thermometer)
$^{1}/_{4}$ cup plus 2 tablespoons milk
2$^{1}/_{4}$ cups all-purpose flour
$^{3}/_{4}$ teaspoon salt
$^{1}/_{2}$ cup granulated sugar
$^{1}/_{2}$ cup (1 stick) unsalted butter, at room temperature,
  cut into pieces
1 large egg plus 1 egg white
$^{1}/_{2}$ cup poppyseed filling, homemade (see box)
  or commercially prepared
1 tablespoon water
1 teaspoon poppyseeds

Combine the yeast and lukewarm water in a small bowl. Set aside for about 5 minutes until bubbly.

Meanwhile, scald the milk in a small saucepan over medium-low heat, just until bubbles begin to form around the edge. Remove from the heat.

In the bowl of a food processor fitted with the steel blade, combine the flour, salt, and sugar. Process for 10 seconds. Scrape in the yeast mixture with a rubber spatula. Scatter the pieces of butter on top and process for about 10 seconds to combine. Scrape down the sides of the bowl with the rubber spatula. Add the whole egg and process for about 5 seconds to incorporate.

With the machine running, add the milk through the feed tube until a dough ball forms. (You may not need to use all the milk.) Continue to process until the dough ball has made 15 revolutions.

Remove the dough to a ceramic or glass bowl, cover with a dry dish towel, and set aside in a warm spot for about 1$^{1}/_{2}$ hours, until the dough has doubled in size.

Lightly coat cookie sheets with vegetable oil cooking spray.

Punch the dough down and transfer it to a lightly floured work surface, turning to coat the dough with flour. Roll out to a $^{1}/_{4}$-inch-thick circle, about 12 inches across. Cut out circles with a 2$^{1}/_{2}$-inch cutter. Gather the scraps of dough, roll out again, and cut out additional circles.

Mound 1 teaspoon of the poppyseed filling in the center of each circle. Fold the dough up around the filling to form a triangle, overlapping the folds of dough a bit at each of the 3 corners and pinching them closed. Place 1 inch apart on the prepared cookie sheets. Set aside, uncovered, for 30 minutes, until puffy.

Preheat the oven to 375 degrees.

Whisk the egg white and water in a small bowl and paint the exposed dough with the wash. Sprinkle with the poppyseeds.

Bake for about 12 minutes, until golden.

Transfer the hamantaschen to wire racks to cool.

For homemade Poppyseed Filling, first crush 1 cup poppyseeds. Put the seeds on a large sheet of wax paper and work a rolling pin back and forth over the seeds until they crack and darken.

Combine with ¹/₂ cup water, ¹/₄ cup honey, and 2 tablespoons light corn syrup in a small saucepan. Cook over medium-low heat for about 10 minutes, stirring occasionally, until thick. Cool before filling the hamantaschen.

Apricot Hamantaschen

These little "Haman's hats" have a wonderfully flaky crust that boasts a hint of citrus lent by the orange zest. Be sure to buy apricot *filling* if you don't make your own, not the thinner apricot preserves. Kosher households should omit the milk wash.

1 large egg
$\frac{1}{2}$ teaspoon orange extract
$\frac{1}{4}$ cup canola oil
$1\frac{1}{3}$ cups all-purpose flour
$\frac{1}{4}$ cup granulated sugar
$\frac{1}{2}$ teaspoon orange zest
1 teaspoon baking powder
$\frac{1}{8}$ teaspoon salt
$1\frac{1}{2}$ tablespoons water
1 cup apricot filling (see box)
$\frac{1}{4}$ cup milk

In a mixing bowl, whisk together the egg, orange extract, and oil until well blended.

Combine the flour, sugar, orange zest, baking powder, and salt in the bowl of a food processor fitted with the steel blade. With the machine running, pour in the egg mixture through the feed tube. Process for a few additional seconds, until incorporated. Drizzle in the water.

Turn the dough out onto a very lightly floured work surface. With floured hands, knead and work it into a ball, being sure to incorporate all the bits of dough. Cover and refrigerate for 25 minutes.

Preheat the oven to 350 degrees.

Lightly coat cookie sheets with vegetable oil cooking spray.

Remove the dough to a lightly floured work surface and roll it out to a thickness of about $\frac{1}{8}$ inch. Cut out $2\frac{1}{2}$-inch circles. Put 1 teaspoon of the apricot filling in the center of each and lightly moisten the outer border with water.

Fold each circle up around the filling to form a triangle. Pinch the 3 corners closed. Place on the prepared cookie sheets. Paint the dough with milk.

Gather up the residual bits of dough into a ball, roll out again, and repeat the process.

Bake for about 15 minutes, until lightly browned. Cool on the sheets on wire racks.

To make Apricot Filling, combine 12 ounces dried apricots, 1 1/4 cups water, and 1 cup granulated sugar in a small saucepan. Bring to a boil over high heat. Reduce the heat to medium-low and simmer, uncovered, for 15 to 20 minutes, until fork tender.

Transfer the contents of the pan to the bowl of a food processor fitted with a steel blade and process until smooth. If a ring of water forms around the edge of a small amount spooned onto a plate, simmer for 3 to 5 minutes more. Let cool at room temperature before using.

Marian Packer's Norwegian Sugar Cookies

YIELD – ABOUT 4 DOZEN COOKIES

These buttery Scandinavian treats were a childhood favorite of our friend Ann Bloomstrand. Her family's neighbor, Marian Packer, made them at Eastertime, since the recipe calls for hard-boiled egg yolks.

The cookies have a very delicate, but readily discernible hint of almond, provided by the addition of a little extract. For variety, top each cookie with a glacé cherry instead of a pecan half.

Easter

1 cup (2 sticks) unsalted butter, at room temperature, cut into pieces
1 cup granulated sugar
2 large hard-boiled egg yolks, mashed
2 large eggs, separated
1 teaspoon almond extract
2$\frac{1}{2}$ cups all-purpose flour
1 cup pecan halves

Preheat the oven to 325 degrees.

Cream the butter and sugar in a large bowl with an electric mixer at medium speed. Add the mashed egg yolks, raw egg yolks, and almond extract. Mix until thoroughly blended. Stir in the flour with a wooden spoon, just to incorporate.

Divide the dough into quarters. On a lightly floured work surface, roll a quarter of the dough out to a 9-inch circle about $\frac{1}{8}$ inch thick. Cut out 2$\frac{1}{2}$-inch rounds with a cookie cutter and transfer them to ungreased cookie sheets. Gather and reroll the scraps of dough for additional cookies. Repeat the process for the remaining 3 pieces of dough.

Top each cookie with a pecan half. Lightly beat the egg whites and brush over the cookies. Bake for about 12 minutes, until lightly browned.

Remove the cookies to wire racks to cool.

1 cup (2 sticks) unsalted butter, melted
¼ cup plus 2 tablespoons confectioners' sugar
1 tablespoon bourbon
½ tablespoon vanilla extract
1 large egg yolk
2 cups cake flour
½ teaspoon baking powder
3 dozen whole cloves

Preheat the oven to 350 degrees.

Coat cookie sheets with vegetable oil cooking spray.

Combine the butter and ¼ cup of the confectioners' sugar in a large mixing bowl. Whisk until smooth. Whisk in the bourbon and vanilla, then the egg yolk. Add the flour and baking powder and stir with a wooden spoon to incorporate.

Using 1 tablespoon of dough for each cookie, roll into balls and place on the prepared sheets. Make a well in the center of each cookie with your little finger and stick a clove into each well.

Bake for about 12 minutes, until firm to the touch.

Cool on the sheets for 1 minute, then remove to wire racks. Dust with the remaining confectioners' sugar through a sieve and allow to cool. Remove the cloves just before serving.

John Koulias's Greek Easter Cookies

YIELD = ABOUT 3 DOZEN COOKIES

We tinkered a bit with the execution, but the basic recipe for these traditional cookies comes from John Koulias, one of Kevin's oldest friends. (Um, we don't mean that quite the way it sounds, John.)

Baking these cookies with whole cloves embedded in the dough intensifies their rich spice flavor; be sure to remove the cloves before serving the cookies to guests or packing them to give as gifts.

Partially Ellie's Apricot Marmalade Bars

YIELD = 36 BARS

This recipe came to us by way of Barry's sister-in-law, Eleanor, in California, who got it from her friend Margie, who got it from a friend in the Midwest. Along the way, everyone's tinkered a bit with the recipe—for the better, we think. Now we pass it along for you to add your special touch.

These bars defy those who are skeptical of Passover sweets. The trick to successful baking with matzo meal is to work quickly to keep the dough from drying into a paste; have all your ingredients ready and within easy reach before you begin.

Passover

1 1/2 cups matzo meal
3/4 cup potato starch
1 teaspoon ground cinnamon
1 teaspoon salt
6 large eggs
1 1/2 cups plus 1 tablespoon granulated sugar
1 cup canola oil
2 large peaches, peeled, stoned, and thinly sliced
7 apricots, peeled, stoned, and thinly sliced
1/2 cup orange marmalade

Preheat the oven to 350 degrees.

Lightly coat a 9-by-13-inch baking pan with vegetable oil cooking spray.

Put the matzo meal in the bowl of a food processor fitted with the steel blade. Process for 1 minute. Add the potato starch, cinnamon, and salt and process for another 15 seconds.

Combine the eggs and 1 1/2 cups of the sugar in a mixing bowl. Beat with an electric mixer at medium speed until light and frothy. At low speed, beat in the oil, mixing until well combined. Add the matzo mixture and stir with a wooden spoon until incorporated.

Pour two thirds of the batter (about 3 cups) into the prepared baking pan. Layer the peaches and apricots on top of the batter. Dollop the marmalade over the fruit by the tablespoonful. Pour the remaining batter on top.

Bake for 55 to 60 minutes, until the cake is golden, springs back to the touch, and is beginning to pull away from the sides of the pan.

Remove to a wire rack, dust the top with the remaining 1 tablespoon sugar, and cool in the pan.

Cut into bars measuring 1 1/2 inches by a little over 2 inches.

1¾ cups matzo meal
1 tablespoon potato starch
½ cup unsweetened cocoa powder
½ cup chopped walnuts
¾ cup currants
3 large eggs
⅔ cup granulated sugar
½ cup canola oil

Preheat the oven to 350 degrees.

Coat a large baking sheet with vegetable oil cooking spray.

Have all the ingredients ready and within easy reach before you begin.

Put the matzo meal into the bowl of a food processor fitted with the steel blade. Process for about 1 minute, until finely ground.

Transfer it to a large mixing bowl and add the potato starch, cocoa powder, nuts, and currants. Whisk and set aside.

Combine the eggs and sugar in a bowl. Beat with an electric mixer at low speed until the mixture is pale. Add the oil and continue to beat until blended and slightly thickened. Add to the large bowl and stir just to combine.

Working with moistened hands, divide the dough in half and form each half on the baking sheet into a 10-by-3-by-¾-inch loaf. Bake for 30 minutes.

Cut into ½-inch slices, stand the slices up on the baking sheet, and toast in the oven for 10 minutes.

Chocolate Mandel Bread

YIELD = ABOUT
3½ DOZEN COOKIES

In the style of a mandelbrot, but made with matzo meal instead of flour and with walnuts replacing almonds. The cocoa and currants add a novel touch.

*To chocolate-dip
the mandel bread, melt 8 ounces bittersweet chocolate
in a glass measuring cup in a microwave oven at full power or
melt in the top of a double boiler over gently boiling water.
Remove from the heat and stir until smooth.*

*Line a large baking sheet with lightly oiled wax paper. Dip each
Mandel bread slice about halfway into the melted chocolate
and place on the prepared baking sheet. Refrigerate
until the chocolate hardens.*

Almond Biscotti

YIELD = ABOUT
2 ¹/₂ DOZEN BISCOTTI

Brimming with slivered almonds, this Passover treat is actually a cross between a traditional biscotti and a mandelbrot. The result is a cookie that is crisp yet tender.

1¹/₂ cups matzo meal
1 cup slivered blanched almonds
1 tablespoon potato starch
³/₄ cup granulated sugar
4 large eggs
¹/₂ tablespoon almond extract

Preheat the oven to 350 degrees.

Coat a large baking sheet with vegetable oil cooking spray.

Have all your ingredients ready and within easy reach before you begin.

Finely grind the matzo meal in a food processor fitted with a steel blade, about 1 minute. Add the almonds and potato starch and process for about 15 seconds to break up the almonds and mix. Transfer to a large mixing bowl and whisk in the sugar.

In a small bowl, combine the eggs and almond extract. Whisk until the eggs are beaten and the mixture is well blended. Add to the dry ingredients in the large bowl. Stir just to combine.

Divide the dough in half. With moistened hands, form each half on the prepared baking sheet into a 9-by-2¹/₂-by-³/₄-inch log.

Bake for about 30 minutes, until golden.

Remove from the oven, leaving the oven on. Cut on a 45-degree angle into ¹/₂-inch slices. Place standing up on the sheet and bake for 15 minutes more to toast.

BASE:
1½ cups sweetened flaked coconut
¼ cup pecan pieces
¼ cup (½ stick) unsalted butter, melted

FILLING:
8 ounces cream cheese, at room temperature
¾ cup granulated sugar
1 large egg
2 teaspoons vanilla extract
4 ounces semisweet chocolate, broken up

Preheat the oven to 325 degrees.

Line each well of a 24-well mini muffin tin (¼-cup wells) with a 2¼-inch paper cup.

Combine the coconut, pecans, and butter in a bowl. Mix well with a fork. Put 1 tablespoon of the mixture into each well of the tin and press down to cover the bottom of the cup. Bake for about 10 minutes, until just beginning to brown.

Remove the tin from the oven, leaving the oven on.

To make the filling, combine the cream cheese and sugar in a mixing bowl. Cream with an electric mixer at medium speed. Beat in the egg, then the vanilla and chocolate.

Put 4 heaping teaspoons of the mixture into each cup and bake for about 20 minutes, until puffed up and slightly cracked on top.

Cool the cheesecakes in the tin for 1 hour, then refrigerate for at least 3 hours. Remove the cheesecakes from the tin and peel off the paper cups.

Chocolate Cheese Cups

YIELD = 24 INDIVIDUAL CHEESECAKES

Individual chocolate cheesecakes, with the indulgent addition of coconut and pecans. We developed this unique Passover finale in the tradition of Barry's mother's family, who believe the seder should end with a *very* rich dessert.

Miniature Mocha Nut Cheesecakes

YIELD = 24 MINIATURE CHEESECAKES

A creamy medley of coffee and chocolate in a hazelnut and brown sugar cup, this makes a unique addition to the Passover table. Use a tin with $1/4$-cup wells.

BASE:

2 cups hazelnuts
3 tablespoons firmly packed light brown sugar
$1/4$ cup ($1/2$ stick) unsalted butter, melted

FILLING:

8 ounces cream cheese, at room temperature
$3/4$ cup granulated sugar
1 large egg
$1/4$ cup boiling water
1 tablespoon instant coffee granules
$1/2$ tablespoon unsweetened cocoa powder
$1/2$ cup sour cream

To decorate the cheesecakes, melt 2 ounces bittersweet chocolate in the top of a double boiler over gently boiling water. Remove the top of the pan from the boiling water and add 1 tablespoon unsalted butter, stirring until melted and combined. Drizzle a little over each cheesecake in a random pattern.

Preheat the oven to 325 degrees.

Lightly coat a 24-well mini muffin tin with vegetable oil cooking spray.

In a food processor fitted with a steel blade, finely chop the hazelnuts. Combine in a mixing bowl with the brown sugar and melted butter. Mix well with a fork. Put 2 tablespoons into each well of the prepared tin, spreading the mixture over the entire surface of each well with the back of a teaspoon.

Bake for 15 minutes and remove from the oven, leaving the oven on.

To make the filling, cream the cream cheese and granulated sugar in a bowl with an electric mixer at medium speed. Beat in the egg.

In a small bowl, combine the boiling water, coffee granules, and cocoa powder. Mix well.

Add the sour cream to the cream cheese mixture and beat in at medium speed. Beat in the coffee mixture.

Put a scant 5 teaspoons of the mixture into each cup. Bake for about 20 minutes, until the cheesecakes have puffed up.

Remove the tin from the oven and allow the cheesecakes to cool for 1 hour before refrigerating for at least 3 hours. Gently pry the cheesecakes from the wells with the tip of a knife.

1 cup chopped dates
¼ cup freshly squeezed orange juice
3 large eggs
1 cup granulated sugar
¾ cup matzo meal
½ teaspoon potato starch
⅛ teaspoon salt
¼ cup canola oil
1 teaspoon grated orange zest
1 cup chopped walnuts

Preheat the oven to 350 degrees.

Coat a 2-quart rectangular glass baking dish with vegetable oil cooking spray.

Have all your ingredients ready and within easy reach before beginning.

Combine the dates and orange juice in a small bowl and set aside.

Put the eggs and sugar in the bowl of a stationary electric mixer fitted with the paddle attachment. Beat at low speed for 10 minutes.

Meanwhile, fit a food processor with the steel blade and turn the machine on. Add the matzo meal through the feed tube and process for 1 minute. Add the potato starch and salt. Process for a few seconds to combine. Set aside.

Add the oil to the mixture in the stationary mixer and beat for 10 minutes more. Add the orange zest, dates and orange juice, walnuts, and matzo mixture. Mix at low speed just to incorporate. Pour into the prepared baking dish.

Bake for 20 to 25 minutes, until puffy and golden.

Cool in the pan on a wire rack. Cut into 2-by-1¾-inch bars.

Passover Date Nut Bars

YIELD = 24 BARS

These treats came to us by way of Eleanor Bluestein's mom, who also contributed *Ruth Gold's Date Nut Squares* (page 99). We like them equally as much. That Mrs. Gold really knows her date nut bars!

Although metal baking pans are usually our preference, here we call for a glass baking dish, which will produce a crisper base.

Chocolate Macaroon Wafers

YIELD = ABOUT
7 DOZEN WAFERS

Thin and elegant, these chewy wafers have an intense chocolate flavor. The recipe yields enough macaroons to last through the holiday if they're kept in an airtight container.

2 cups almonds
$^3/_4$ cup unsweetened cocoa powder
2 cups granulated sugar
$^1/_4$ cup light corn syrup
$^1/_4$ cup boiling water
4 large egg whites, at room temperature
$^1/_2$ teaspoon cream of tartar

In a food processor fitted with the steel blade, process the almonds for about 30 seconds, until finely ground.

Combine the cocoa powder and $1^1/_3$ cups of the sugar in a bowl and mix. Add the corn syrup and water. Whisk until smooth and glossy. Mix in the almonds thoroughly. Set aside.

Process the remaining $^2/_3$ cup sugar to a superfine consistency, about 2 minutes.

In a stationary electric mixer fitted with the whisk, beat the egg whites at medium speed for about 2 minutes, until frothy. Add the cream of tartar and beat just until peaks begin to form, about 2 minutes. Raise the speed to high and gradually add the superfine sugar. Continue to beat until very stiff, shiny peaks are formed, about 2 minutes.

Switch to the paddle attachment and add the chocolate mixture to the meringue. Mix at low speed for about 30 seconds, until incorporated. Chill for 15 minutes.

Meanwhile, preheat the oven to 375 degrees.

Lightly coat cookie sheets with vegetable oil cooking spray and set on top of the oven to warm slightly.

Drop by the half tablespoonful onto the prepared cookie sheets, about 2 inches apart. Bake for 10 minutes, until the edges are firm.

Cool on the cookie sheets on wire racks.

2 cups sweetened flaked coconut
1/2 cup sweetened condensed milk
1 teaspoon vanilla extract
1/3 cup granulated sugar
2 large egg whites, at room temperature
1/4 teaspoon cream of tartar

Preheat the oven to 350 degrees.

Lightly coat cookie sheets with vegetable oil cooking spray.

Combine the coconut, condensed milk, and vanilla in a bowl. Mix and set aside.

Process the sugar to a superfine consistency in a food processor fitted with the steel blade, about 2 minutes.

Beat the egg whites with an electric mixer at medium speed until frothy, about 2 minutes. Add the cream of tartar and mix about 2 minutes more, just until peaks begin to form.

Raise the speed to high and gradually add the superfine sugar to the mixture. Continue to mix for an additional 2 minutes or until very stiff, shiny peaks form.

Fold the coconut mixture into the meringue. Drop by the half tablespoonful onto the prepared cookie sheets, leaving about 2 inches between cookies. Bake for about 10 minutes, until the edges are brown.

Cool on the sheets on wire racks.

Coconut Macaroons

YIELD = ABOUT
5 DOZEN MACAROONS

These tasty morsels have a crisp meringue shell and a chewy macaroon center.

To make Cocoa Coconut Macaroons, add 1 tablespoon unsweetened cocoa powder to the coconut mixture and proceed according to recipe directions.

While the macaroons are baking, combine 1 cup confectioners' sugar, 1 tablespoon cocoa powder, and 2 tablespoons hot water in a bowl. Whisk thoroughly and drizzle about 1/2 teaspoon over each macaroon while still warm.

Harry's Honey Madeleines

YIELD = 24 MADELEINES

We developed this recipe for Barry's brother, whose work often takes him to Paris for extended periods of time. When he's back home, these remind him of the madeleines sold in a little neighborhood bakery in the Marais, the city's old Jewish neighborhood.

Moist and sweet, these are sure to add a stylish note to your seder. Like most madeleines, they're best freshly made. They can be kept for a day or two, wrapped loosely in aluminum foil and stored at room temperature; they will become too soft if kept in an airtight container.

6 tablespoons unsalted butter
1/2 cup matzo meal
1/2 teaspoon ground cinnamon
1/2 teaspoon ground ginger
1 tablespoon potato starch
5 large egg whites, plus 2 egg yolks
3/4 cup granulated sugar
2 tablespoons honey

Preheat the oven to 350 degrees.

Coat madeleine plaques well with vegetable oil cooking spray.

Have all your ingredients ready and within easy reach before you begin.

Heat the butter in a small frying pan or saucepan over medium-high heat just until it begins to brown, 3 to 4 minutes, taking care not to burn it. Transfer to a small bowl and set aside.

Fit a food processor with the steel blade and turn the machine on. Add the matzo meal through the feed tube and process for 1 minute. Add the cinnamon, ginger, and potato starch and process for another 15 seconds.

Put the egg whites in a large mixing bowl and beat until frothy with an electric mixer at medium speed. Add the sugar and mix until incorporated.

In a small bowl, combine the egg yolks and the honey. Whisk to lightly beat and combine. Add to the egg white mixture and beat in at low speed. Beat in the butter, then the matzo mixture.

Fill each mold of the prepared madeleine plaques almost to the top with the batter.

Bake for 13 to 14 minutes, until dark golden.

Unmold the madeleines by tilting the plaques over a work surface and banging lightly so that they pop out. Cool the madeleines on wire racks.

For Honey Lemon Madeleines, leave out the ground cinnamon and ginger and add 1/2 tablespoon grated lemon zest to the matzo meal.

Halloween

¹/₂ cup (1 stick) unsalted butter, at room temperature
¹/₂ cup firmly packed dark brown sugar
1 large egg yolk
1 cup creamy peanut butter
¹/₂ teaspoon vanilla extract
¹/₂ teaspoon baking soda
¹/₄ teaspoon salt
1 cup all-purpose flour

Cream the butter in a large bowl with an electric mixer at medium speed. Add the brown sugar and beat until the mixture is light and fluffy. Beat in the egg yolk, peanut butter, and vanilla.

Whisk together the baking soda, salt, and flour. Add to the butter mixture and stir with a wooden spoon to form a stiff dough. Turn the dough out onto half of a long sheet of wax paper. Flatten the dough by hand, fold the wax paper over it to cover, and freeze for 30 minutes.

Preheat the oven to 375 degrees.

Lightly coat cookie sheets with vegetable oil cooking spray.

Divide the dough in half. Re-cover and refrigerate half of it.

Transfer the other half to a work surface that has been lined with wax paper and lightly floured. Roll out to a ¹/₄-inch-thick circle about 10 inches in diameter. Cut out 2¹/₂-inch cookies and transfer them to the prepared cookie sheets. Gather and reroll the scraps of dough for additional cookies.

Remove the second batch of dough from the refrigerator and repeat the process.

Bake for about 10 minutes, until lightly browned around the edges.

Let the cookies cool for 2 minutes on the sheets, then remove them to wire racks to finish cooling.

Peanut Butter Jack-O'-Lanterns

YIELD = ABOUT 2¹/₂ DOZEN JACK-O'-LANTERNS

Let your imagination run amok in fashioning these edible jack-o'-lanterns. We suggest appropriately eerie facial features sculpted in black and orange cake decorating gel and black gumdrop eyes (fastened with the gel).

Mary McLaughlin's Shortbread Ghosts

YIELD = ABOUT
4 DOZEN GHOSTS

The essence of Halloween is ghouls, goblins, and ghosts—in this case deathly white shortbread ghosts sure to elicit squeals of terrified delight from your household's coven-in-training. True to her Scottish heritage, Mary's been baking these for years.

1 cup (2 sticks) unsalted butter, at room temperature, cut into pieces
$^1/_2$ cup granulated sugar
$^1/_2$ teaspoon vanilla extract
1$^3/_4$ cups all-purpose flour
4 ounces white chocolate, broken up
8 dozen mini chocolate chips

Cream the butter and sugar in a bowl with an electric mixer at medium speed. Beat in the vanilla. Stir in the flour with a wooden spoon. Gather the dough into a ball, wrap it in wax paper, and refrigerate for 30 minutes.

Preheat the oven to 400 degrees.

Divide the dough in half. Place half on a lightly floured work surface and turn the dough to coat it with flour. Roll it out to a 9-by-8-inch rectangle $^1/_4$ inch thick.

Using miniature people-shaped cookie cutters, cut out cookies and place them about 1 inch apart on ungreased cookie sheets. (We used cutters that fashioned shortbread figures about 2 inches tall and 1$^1/_2$ inches across at the widest point.)

Gather the scraps of dough, roll again, and cut out additional cookies. Repeat the process with the remaining half of the dough.

Bake for about 8 minutes, until just beginning to brown around the edges.

Let the cookies cool on the sheets for 2 minutes before removing them to wire racks.

For the frosting, melt the white chocolate in a microwave at full power for 1 minute and stir until melted and smooth, or in the top of a double boiler over simmering water, stirring constantly.

Frost the cookies, adding 2 mini chocolate chip eyes. Allow the cookies to harden in the refrigerator for at least 30 minutes.

Pumpkins are so prevalent at this time of year that you might well be tempted to make your own fresh pumpkin puree instead of using the prepared variety.

First, preheat the oven to 350 degrees and line a baking sheet with aluminum foil. Cut the pumpkin in half lengthwise. Clean out the seeds and veins. Place cut side down on the prepared baking sheet. Bake 45 to 50 minutes, until fork tender. Scoop out the pulp and puree it in a food processor fitted with the steel blade. The puree can be frozen for up to 3 months in heavy-duty, airtight plastic storage bags.

Pumpkins are so prevalent at this time of year that you might well be tempted to make your own fresh pumpkin puree instead of using the prepared variety.

First, preheat the oven to 350 degrees and line a baking sheet with aluminum foil. Cut the pumpkin in half lengthwise. Clean out the seeds and veins. Place cut side down on the prepared baking sheet. Bake 45 to 50 minutes, until fork tender. Scoop out the pulp and puree it in a food processor fitted with the steel blade. The puree can be frozen for up to 3 months in heavy-duty, airtight plastic storage bags.

Mark's and Don's Cranberry Cookies

YIELD = ABOUT
5 1/2 DOZEN COOKIES

This dense, chewy little cookie, somewhat reminiscent of a hermit, is a specialty of our friends Mark Stahr and Don Houck. Because they feature dried cranberries, these can be enjoyed all year round.

Thanksgiving

2$^1/_4$ cups all-purpose flour
$^3/_4$ teaspoon ground cinnamon
$^1/_2$ teaspoon ground allspice
$^1/_4$ teaspoon ground nutmeg
$^1/_2$ teaspoon baking soda
$^1/_2$ teaspoon salt
1 cup dried cranberries
$^1/_4$ cup boiling water
$^1/_2$ cup (1 stick) unsalted butter, at room temperature
$^1/_2$ cup firmly packed dark brown sugar
$^1/_2$ cup granulated sugar
$^1/_2$ teaspoon orange extract
1 cup natural unsweetened applesauce

Preheat the oven to 375 degrees.

Whisk together the flour, cinnamon, allspice, nutmeg, baking soda, and salt.

Combine the cranberries and boiling water in a small bowl. Mix and set aside to plump.

In a large mixing bowl, cream the butter and sugars with an electric mixer. Mix in the orange extract and applesauce at low speed.

Drain and add the cranberries, along with the flour mixture. Stir with a wooden spoon to incorporate. Cover with plastic wrap and refrigerate for 20 minutes.

Drop the dough by the tablespoonful onto ungreased cookie sheets, leaving about 2 inches between cookies. Flatten each cookie a bit with lightly floured hands.

Bake for about 15 minutes, until lightly browned and firm to the touch.

Remove the cookies to wire racks to cool.

1 cup all-purpose flour

$^1\!/_2$ teaspoon ground allspice

$^1\!/_2$ teaspoon ground cloves

$^1\!/_2$ teaspoon ground cinnamon

$^1\!/_4$ teaspoon baking soda

$^1\!/_4$ teaspoon salt

$^1\!/_2$ cup golden raisins

$^1\!/_2$ cup chopped walnuts

1 cup prepared mincemeat, commercial or homemade (page 244)

1 large egg

2 tablespoons unsalted butter, at room temperature

$^3\!/_4$ cup firmly packed dark brown sugar

2 tablespoons dark molasses

$^1\!/_2$ teaspoon grated orange zest

$^1\!/_2$ teaspoon orange extract

$^1\!/_2$ teaspoon vanilla extract

1 tablespoon confectioners' sugar

Preheat the oven to 375 degrees.

Coat a 9-by-13-inch baking pan with vegetable oil cooking spray and flour lightly.

Whisk together the flour, spices, baking soda, and salt in a mixing bowl. Stir in the raisins, walnuts, and mincemeat. Set aside.

Combine the egg, butter, brown sugar, and molasses in a large bowl. Beat thoroughly with an electric mixer at medium speed until the mixture is thick and smooth. At low speed, beat in the orange zest and extracts. Add the flour mixture and stir with a wooden spoon to incorporate.

Turn the batter into the prepared pan and spread it evenly. Bake for about 15 minutes, until the cake is firm to the touch and a toothpick inserted at the edge comes out clean.

Remove from the oven and dust with the confectioners' sugar. Cool in the pan on a wire rack.

Cut into bars measuring $1^1\!/_2$ inches by a generous 2 inches.

Claudia Clark Potter's Mincemeat Bars

YIELD = 36 BARS

We think Claudia's moist and rich bars make a nice change from mincemeat pie. The addition of pungent ground cloves provides an interesting juxtaposition to the sweetness of the raisins, producing a flavor medley every bit as intriguing and complex as Ms. Potter herself.

Easy Meatless Mincemeat

YIELD = ABOUT 2 CUPS

2 cups cored and coarsely chopped tart, firm apple, unpeeled
1 cup cored and coarsely chopped pear
3/4 cup seedless raisins
1/2 cup diced dried apricots
1 tablespoon freshly squeezed orange juice
1/4 teaspoon ground allspice
1/4 teaspoon ground nutmeg
1/2 teaspoon ground cinnamon
1/3 cup firmly packed dark brown sugar
1 tablespoon white wine vinegar
1 tablespoon water

Combine all the ingredients in a medium nonreactive saucepan. Bring to a boil over medium heat, reduce the heat to low, and simmer, uncovered, for about 30 minutes, until all the liquid has been absorbed and the mixture has thickened. Stir often to prevent scorching. The mincemeat can be stored in an airtight container for 1 month in the refrigerator or for up to 3 months in the freezer.

2 cups all-purpose flour
1 teaspoon baking powder
$^1/_4$ teaspoon baking soda
$^1/_4$ teaspoon salt
$^1/_2$ teaspoon ground cinnamon
$^1/_2$ teaspoon ground allspice
$^1/_2$ teaspoon ground nutmeg
$^1/_2$ cup slivered blanched almonds
$^1/_2$ cup (1 stick) unsalted butter, at room temperature, cut into pieces
$^3/_4$ cup firmly packed dark brown sugar
2 large eggs
$^1/_2$ teaspoon rum extract
1 cup prepared mincemeat, commercial or homemade (see box, page 244)

RUM FROSTING:
3 tablespoons unsalted butter, at room temperature
$2^1/_4$ cups confectioners' sugar
$^1/_4$ cup plus $^1/_2$ tablespoon golden rum

Preheat the oven to 375 degrees.

Coat cookie sheets with vegetable oil cooking spray.

Whisk together the flour, baking powder, baking soda, salt, and spices in a mixing bowl. Stir in the almonds and set aside.

In a large bowl, cream the butter and brown sugar with an electric mixer at medium speed. Scrape down the sides of the bowl with a rubber spatula. Beat in the eggs until fluffy, then the rum extract. At low speed, beat in the mincemeat. Add the flour mixture and stir to incorporate with a wooden spoon.

Using about 2 tablespoons of dough for each, drop the cookies about 2 inches apart onto the prepared sheets. Bake for about 15 minutes, until golden and firm to the touch.

Remove the cookies to wire racks to cool completely.

For the frosting, combine the butter, confectioners' sugar, and rum in a mixing bowl. Beat until smooth with an electric mixer at medium speed and spread a little over each cookie.

Mincemeat Mounds with Rum Frosting

YIELD = ABOUT
$2^3/_4$ DOZEN COOKIES

These cookies have a more subtle flavor than our Mincemeat Bars (page 243), which allows the rich rum frosting to shine. Prepared mincemeat can be found in most supermarkets, either ready to use or in the condensed form, which is boiled with water for 1 minute and then set aside for 1 hour to cool and thicken. To make your own mincemeat at home, see page 244.

Doubleday Sweet Potato Dollops

YIELD = ABOUT
2 1/2 DOZEN DOLLOPS

We can't think of a better finale for the Thanksgiving banquet than these incredibly scrumptious and generously portioned treats. They received rave revues when we sent a batch off to our publisher. One caller reported munching the cookie en route to her office and turning right around for more, only to find the tin empty by the time she got back down the hall.

(cont.)

1 sweet potato (about 1 pound)
8 ounces canned crushed pineapple
1/3 cup golden raisins
1/3 cup seedless raisins
1/4 cup bourbon
1 3/4 cups all-purpose flour
1 cup quick oats
1/2 tablespoon baking powder
1/2 teaspoon salt
1/2 tablespoon ground cinnamon
1/2 teaspoon ground nutmeg
3/4 cup chopped pecans
1/2 cup (1 stick) unsalted butter, at room temperature
1 1/2 cups firmly packed light brown sugar
1 large egg

GLAZE:
1/2 cup confectioners' sugar
1 1/2 tablespoons bourbon

Preheat the oven to 350 degrees.

Coat cookie sheets with vegetable oil cooking spray.

Bake the sweet potato in a microwave oven at full power for 7 minutes. Remove, wrap in aluminum foil, and set aside for 5 minutes. (The sweet potato can also be baked in a conventional oven, preheated to 375 degrees, until fork tender, about 45 minutes. If cooking by this method, dispense with the foil and just allow the potato to cool sufficiently to be handled.)

Cut the potato in half and scoop out the insides. (You should have about 1 cup.) Set aside to cool.

Drain the pineapple in a colander, pressing out the excess liquid with the back of a wooden spoon.

Combine the raisins and bourbon in a small bowl and set aside to soak.

Whisk together the flour, oats, baking powder, salt, cinnamon, nutmeg, and pecans.

In a large bowl, cream the butter and brown sugar with an electric mixer at low speed. Add the egg and mix at medium speed until fluffy. Mix in the sweet potato and pineapple. Stir in the raisins, along with any residual soaking liquid. Add the flour mixture and stir to incorporate.

Using 2 tablespoons of dough for each cookie, drop 2 inches apart onto the prepared sheets. Flatten the cookies with the back of a spoon.

Bake for about 15 minutes, until the cookies are golden brown and firm to the touch.

Meanwhile, combine the confectioners' sugar and bourbon for the glaze in a bowl. Stir the mixture until smooth.

Remove the cookies to wire racks. Cool for 3 minutes, brush with the glaze, then cool completely.

The cookies become somewhat more redolent of bourbon as they age. (Come to think of it, it's probably just as well they didn't sit for days on a proofreader's desk.) Use canned pineapple, which lends more moisture than would fresh.

Healthy Cookies

Cookies are a treat by definition. In most cases, we don't worry a lot about the amounts of sugar, butter, and eggs involved. We think of cookies as an indulgence to be worked into a sensible diet that includes some restraint as well.

However, for those whose lifestyle or specialized dietary requirements do not allow for such indulgences, we offer a variety of nonfat (less than $^1/_2$ gram of fat per cookie) or low-fat (less than 3 grams of fat per cookie) options, along with cookies prepared without sugar and cookies prepared without wheat.

In *The 99% Fat-Free Cookbook* and *The 99% Fat-Free Book of Appetizers and Desserts,* we showed that reducing the amount of fat does not have to compromise quality or taste. We use applesauce and spreadable fruits to produce moist baked goods and often add buttermilk or banana for extra richness. Nonfat liquid egg substitute or egg whites replace the yolks, corn syrup or fruit butters do the job of butter, and cocoa powder mixtures yield flavorful chocolate treats that contain no fatty cocoa butter.

Preparing cookie sheets to prevent sticking is particularly important in reduced-fat baking. Line cookie sheets with baker's parchment or nonstick plastic ovenware liner or use *light* vegetable oil cooking spray. Spray once quickly and spread the oil evenly over the surface of the cookie sheet to coat.

Reduced-fat cookies are in their prime for 3 days if stored in cookie jars or cookie tins and for 5 days if wrapped in aluminum foil and refrigerated. They may be frozen for up to 6 weeks.

Our sugarless recipes are offered for those on restricted diets and for parents who want to limit their children's intake. We eschew sugar, honey, and molasses, sweetening the cookies with natural fruit juice concentrates or spreadable fruit fillings. We do not claim, however, to provide recipes that can be safely used by all diabetics, who should follow their individual physician's guidelines closely.

Sugarless cookies remain fresh and flavorful for 3 to 5 days wrapped loosely in aluminum foil and stored at room temperature. They don't take to the refrigerator particularly well, but may be frozen for up to 3 months.

Gluten-free recipes are included for the gluten intolerant and for those who may wish to avoid wheat at times for religious reasons.

Many of our gluten-free cookies have a meringue base. While meringues can be made with a hand-held electric mixer—or even manually with a large balloon whisk—a stationary electric mixer will produce the best results. It's necessary to work with a certain mass of egg white (we usually use the whites of 4 large eggs) to produce stiff enough peaks, hence the rather large yields of some smaller meringue cookies. Try to avoid making meringues on very humid days.

Gluten-free cookies should be stored in cookie jars or cookie tins, where they will remain in top form for at least 5 days. With the exception of the brownie, the crisp texture of these cookies will be compromised in the refrigerator. We don't recommend freezing these cookies.

Nonfat

½ cup natural unsweetened applesauce
¼ cup plus two tablespoons unsweetened Dutch-processed
  cocoa powder
2 tablespoons light corn syrup
1 cup granulated sugar
¼ teaspoon instant coffee granules
2 large egg whites
3 tablespoons nonfat sour cream
1 teaspoon vanilla extract
½ cup all-purpose flour

Preheat the oven to 350 degrees.

Lightly coat an 8-by-8-inch baking pan with light vegetable oil cooking spray, spreading the oil evenly to cover the surface.

Combine the applesauce, cocoa powder, corn syrup, sugar, and coffee granules in a large mixing bowl. Stir with a wooden spoon until blended and smooth. Stir in the egg whites, sour cream, and vanilla. Add the flour and stir just to incorporate. Pour into the prepared baking pan.

Bake for about 18 minutes, until a tester inserted into the center comes out with a few moist crumbs clinging. (The center of the brownie should still be underbaked.)

Cool in the pan on a wire rack for 30 minutes. Cut into 2-inch squares.

Fat per brownie = 0.25 g
Calories = 82.4

We developed a Nonfat Coffee Frosting for those folks who prefer their brownies fully dressed. Combine ½ cup confectioners' sugar, ½ tablespoon instant coffee granules, and 1 tablespoon hot water in a bowl. Whisk until smooth and spread over the whole brownie in the pan (after cooling, but before cutting). Refrigerate for about 15 minutes until the frosting is firm before cutting.

Newfangled Cocoa Brownies

YIELD = 16 BROWNIES

We struggled to come up with another plain chocolate brownie as good as the Old-Fashioned Cocoa Brownies featured in our original 99% *Fat-Free Cookbook,* which received lots of accolades. By jove, I think we finally got it . . . and reduced the fat even further in the process!

This rendition has less flour and no leavening agent, yielding a denser, less cakey brownie with an intense chocolate flavor. We think the substitution of sour cream for the yogurt used in the original lends a bit of added zip as well.

The recipe is simple and quick. The brownie should appear slightly underbaked when removed from the oven; it will firm up while cooling.

John Vranicar's Savory Biscotti

YIELD = ABOUT
2 1/2 DOZEN BISCOTTI

We created this complex and sophisticated cookie (which is nonfat, to boot) for our equally sophisticated friend John, whose favorite flavors are pear and ginger.

In place of egg yolks, we use pear butter. A nice flavor counterpoint is provided by flecks of crystallized ginger, which soften while baking. For crisper biscotti, toast the slices on their sides rather than standing up, and flip them after 10 minutes.

2 1/2 cups all-purpose flour
2/3 cup granulated sugar
1 teaspoon baking powder
3/4 teaspoon baking soda
1/4 teaspoon salt
1/4 cup finely chopped crystallized ginger
4 large egg whites
1/3 cup natural pear butter
1 teaspoon vanilla extract

Preheat the oven to 375 degrees.

Line 1 large or 2 small baking sheets with baker's parchment and flour lightly.

Sift the flour, sugar, baking powder, baking soda, and salt together into a large mixing bowl. Add the ginger and whisk thoroughly. Create a well in the center.

In another bowl, whisk the egg whites until frothy. Whisk in the pear butter and vanilla to combine. Pour into the well of the flour mixture and mix with a wooden spoon until incorporated. Set aside for 7 minutes to thicken.

Divide the dough in half and place each half on the prepared baking sheet(s). With lightly floured hands, shape them into 10-by-2-inch loaves about 3/4 inch high.

Bake for about 30 minutes, until the dough has risen and the loaves are golden brown and lightly cracked on top. Remove the loaves to a work surface, leaving the oven on.

Cut with a serrated knife into generous 1/2-inch slices. Stand the slices upright on the baking sheet(s), leaving a small space between each. Return to the oven for about 20 minutes more to toast.

Remove to wire racks to cool.

Fat per cookie = 0.09 g
Calories per cookie = 64.2

1¼ cups rolled oats
1 cup whole wheat flour
¼ teaspoon salt
¼ teaspoon baking soda
½ teaspoon ground mace
1 cup mashed banana (about 2 bananas) (see box)
1 cup firmly packed light brown sugar
¼ cup nonfat sour cream
1 teaspoon banana extract

Preheat the oven to 375 degrees.

Lightly coat cookie sheets with light vegetable oil cooking spray, distributing the oil evenly over the surface.

Put the oats into the bowl of a food processor fitted with the steel blade. Process for about 1¼ minutes, to a fine powder. Add the flour, salt, baking soda, and mace. Process for 1 minute.

Combine the banana and brown sugar in a large mixing bowl and whisk thoroughly. Whisk in the sour cream and banana extract. Add the flour mixture. Stir well with a wooden spoon.

Drop by the tablespoonful onto the prepared cookie sheets about 1 inch apart. Bake for about 13 minutes, until the cookies are firm to the touch and have begun to brown on top.

Remove to wire racks to cool.

Fat per cookie = 0.33 g
Calories per cookie = 52.1

Use very ripe, dark bananas to make Banana Bread Cookies; the ones you would otherwise toss are perfect. You can also "ripen" firmer bananas by warming them in the oven at the lowest setting for about a half-hour.

Banana Bread Cookies

YIELD = ABOUT
3 DOZEN COOKIES

Moist little morsels that taste a lot like Mom's banana bread, these cookies hold up well if stored in an airtight container. We mix ground oats with the flour for added texture. If you don't have a food processor, grind the oats in a blender and then whisk them with the other dry ingredients to combine.

Orange Madeleines

No butter or egg yolk in these elegantly sculptured little cakes, just corn syrup and egg white. Best served the day they are made.

Use a madeleine plaque with 3-inch molds.

2 large egg whites
$1/4$ cup plus 2 tablespoons confectioners' sugar
2 tablespoons light corn syrup
$1/2$ teaspoon orange extract
3 tablespoons all-purpose flour
1 teaspoon finely grated orange zest

Preheat the oven to 350 degrees.

Lightly coat a 12-mold madeleine plaque with light vegetable oil cooking spray, taking care to work the oil into the crevices of the molds.

Put the egg whites in a mixing bowl and whisk until frothy. Add the confectioners' sugar, corn syrup, and orange extract, whisking to combine thoroughly. Stir in the flour and orange zest with a wooden spoon, just to incorporate. Put about a tablespoonful of the batter into each mold.

Bake for about 12 minutes, until golden brown.

Invert the plaque over a wire rack and tap the madeleines out onto the rack to cool.

Fat per cookie = 0.18 g
Calories per cookie = 35.0

To convert Orange Madeleines into Lemon Madeleines, simply use equal amounts of lemon extract and lemon zest in place of the orange extract and zest.

1 cup currants
$\frac{1}{2}$ cup boiling water
$1\frac{3}{4}$ cups all-purpose flour
$\frac{3}{4}$ cup quick oats
1 teaspoon ground allspice
$\frac{1}{2}$ teaspoon ground cinnamon
$\frac{1}{2}$ teaspoon baking soda
$\frac{1}{2}$ teaspoon salt
$\frac{1}{2}$ cup natural apple butter
$\frac{1}{2}$ cup firmly packed light brown sugar
2 tablespoons light corn syrup
1 cup natural unsweetened applesauce

Preheat the oven to 375 degrees.

Lightly coat cookie sheets with light vegetable oil cooking spray, distributing the oil evenly over the surface.

Combine the currants and boiling water in a small bowl and set aside to soak.

Whisk together the flour, oats, allspice, cinnamon, baking soda, and salt.

In a large mixing bowl, combine the apple butter, brown sugar, and corn syrup. Whisk until smooth. Stir in the applesauce with a wooden spoon, just to combine. Stir in the flour mixture. Drain the currants and fold them in.

Using 2 tablespoons for each cookie, drop the dough onto the prepared sheets about 1 inch apart. Bake for about 15 minutes, until lightly browned and firm.

Transfer the cookies to wire racks to cool.

Fat per cookie = 0.26 g
Calories per cookie = 58.9

Apple Currant Cookies

YIELD = ABOUT
$2\frac{1}{2}$ DOZEN COOKIES

No mistaking the primary flavor in this cookie—we use applesauce, apple butter, and apple pie spices. The combination of apple butter and corn syrup allows us to dispense with butter. Soaking the currants a bit makes them plump and soft.

For Peach Currant Cookies, substitute an equal amount of peach butter for the apple butter and reduce the amount of ground allspice used to $\frac{3}{4}$ teaspoon.

Big Chocolate Cake Cookies

YIELD = ABOUT
2 1/2 DOZEN COOKIES

Don't worry that this dough is very soft, rather like a thick pudding. The cookies bake up into dense, chewy mounds. Oats provide the crunch usually supplied by fatty nuts, while brown sugar intensifies the rich chocolate taste lent by the cocoa powder.

1/2 cup rolled oats
2 1/4 cups all-purpose flour
1 1/4 teaspoons baking powder
1/4 teaspoon salt
1/2 cup unsweetened Dutch-processed cocoa powder
1 teaspoon instant coffee granules
1/2 cup boiling water
1 cup natural unsweetened applesauce
1 cup firmly packed light brown sugar
1/4 cup nonfat liquid egg substitute
1/4 cup buttermilk
1 teaspoon vanilla extract

Preheat the oven to 375 degrees.

Lightly coat cookie sheets with light vegetable oil cooking spray, spreading the oil evenly over the surface.

Whisk together the oats, flour, baking powder, and salt. Set aside.

Combine the cocoa powder, coffee granules, and boiling water in a small bowl. Stir until smooth.

In a large mixing bowl, combine the applesauce and brown sugar. Beat with an electric mixer set at medium speed until the sugar is completely dissolved and the mixture is smooth, 15 to 20 seconds. Add the liquid egg substitute, buttermilk, and vanilla. Beat for about 20 seconds more, until frothy.

Scrape in the cocoa mixture and beat at low speed for 20 to 25 seconds. Stir in the flour mixture with a wooden spoon. Using 2 tablespoons of dough for each cookie, drop 2 inches apart onto the prepared cookie sheets.

Bake for about 8 minutes, until firm to the touch.

Remove the cookies to wire racks to cool.

Fat per cookie = 0.32 g
Calories per cookie = 71.7

*How can you possibly top a nonfat cookie that tastes
like a hunk of old-fashioned chocolate cake?
Why, with a* Nonfat Chocolate Icing, *of course:*

1 cup confectioners' sugar
1 tablespoon plus 1 teaspoon unsweetened Dutch-
   processed cocoa powder
1 tablespoon light corn syrup
2 tablespoons hot water

   Combine the ingredients in a mixing bowl and whisk until
thoroughly blended and smooth. Top each cooled cookie with about
1 teaspoon of the icing.

YIELD = ABOUT 1 ¹/₄ CUPS

Orange Nutty Cookies

YIELD = ABOUT
3 DOZEN COOKIES

These cookies are based on a recipe a friend of ours makes for her infant son. They're not only virtually fat-free, but sugarless as well. Orange juice concentrate and cranberries provide more than sufficient sweetness, while applesauce lends moisture and Grape Nuts cereal provides a nutty crunch.

You can use 2 tablespoons nonfat liquid egg substitute for the egg white, if desired.

$^{1}/_{2}$ cup rolled oats
$^{3}/_{4}$ cup all-purpose flour
$^{1}/_{4}$ cup plus 2 tablespoons Grape Nuts cereal
$^{3}/_{4}$ teaspoon baking soda
1 teaspoon ground cinnamon
$^{1}/_{4}$ teaspoon salt
6 ounces orange juice concentrate, thawed, undiluted
3 tablespoons natural unsweetened applesauce
1 large egg white
$^{1}/_{2}$ teaspoon grated orange zest
$^{1}/_{2}$ cup dried cranberries

Preheat the oven to 350 degrees.

Lightly coat cookie sheets with light vegetable oil cooking spray, distributing the oil evenly over the sheets.

Whisk together the oats, flour, Grape Nuts, baking soda, cinnamon, and salt.

Combine the orange juice concentrate, applesauce, egg white, orange zest, and cranberries in the bowl of a blender. Blend at low speed for 30 seconds. Pour over the flour mixture and stir with a wooden spoon just to incorporate.

Using a rounded $^{1}/_{2}$ tablespoon of dough for each, drop the cookies onto the prepared cookie sheets.

Bake for about 10 minutes, until light golden brown and firm to the touch.

Remove the cookies to wire racks to cool.

Fat per cookie = 0.16 g
Calories per cookie = 34.5

For a bit of indulgence, replace the Grape Nuts with $^{1}/_{2}$ cup chopped walnuts. This will boost the fat content somewhat, but the cookie will still be a low-fat treat.

Fat per cookie=1.19 g
Calories per cookie=41.0

DOUGH:

1¾ cups all-purpose flour

¾ cup quick oats

1 teaspoon baking powder

½ teaspoon baking soda

½ cup honey

¼ cup dark molasses

⅓ cup firmly packed light brown sugar

2 tablespoons water

1 teaspoon finely grated orange zest

FILLING:

1 pound Calimyrna figs, stemmed

⅓ cup granulated sugar

1 cup water

2 tablespoons light corn syrup

2 tablespoons freshly squeezed orange juice

Fig Bars

YIELD = 48 BARS

The addition of oats adds crunch to the shell of these tasty bars. They can also be cut before baking, but we prefer the moister results produced by cutting afterward.

Preheat the oven to 350 degrees.

Line a large baking sheet with baker's parchment.

Put the flour, oats, baking powder, and baking soda in a large mixing bowl and combine with a whisk.

Combine the honey, molasses, and brown sugar in a small saucepan over medium-low heat. Simmer for about 2 minutes, stirring constantly, until the sugar has dissolved. Remove from the heat and stir in the water and orange zest.

Add to the flour mixture and stir with a wooden spoon to incorporate fully. Gather the dough, wrap it in wax paper, and refrigerate until firm, about 20 minutes.

For the filling, combine the figs, sugar, water, corn syrup, and orange juice in a medium saucepan. Bring to a boil over medium heat. Reduce the heat to low, cover, and simmer for about 20 minutes, until the figs are fork tender. Transfer to a food processor fitted with the steel blade and puree. (You should have about 2¼ cups of thick puree.)

Put the chilled dough onto a work surface that has been lined with wax paper and floured lightly. Divide into 4 equal pieces. With lightly floured hands, flatten each piece into a strip about 3 inches wide and 15 inches long. Spread a generous $\frac{1}{2}$ cup of the fig filling lengthwise down the middle of each strip.

Using the wax paper as an aid, roll a long side of each strip of dough over to enclose the filling. Pinch the seams to seal and flatten. When finished, the strips should have spread to about 18 inches long.

Roll the strips off the wax paper onto the prepared baking sheet, seam sides down. Bake for about 15 minutes, until lightly browned and puffed.

Remove the baking sheet to a wire rack and cool for 20 minutes. Cut the strips into $1\frac{1}{2}$-inch bars.

Fat per cookie = 0.23 g
Calories per cookie = 72.1

2 tablespoons all-purpose flour
1 tablespoon unsweetened Dutch-processed cocoa powder
$\frac{1}{2}$ teaspoon ground cinnamon
$\frac{1}{2}$ teaspoon instant coffee granules
1 large egg white
2 tablespoons granulated sugar
1 tablespoon unsalted butter, melted

Preheat the oven to 375 degrees.

Very lightly coat 2 large nonstick baking sheets with light vegetable oil cooking spray, spreading the oil evenly over the surface of the pans. Flour lightly.

Whisk together the flour, cocoa powder, cinnamon, and coffee granules in a mixing bowl.

In another bowl, combine the egg white and sugar. Beat for about 15 seconds with an electric mixer at medium speed, until the sugar is dissolved and the mixture is thick and frothy. At low speed, beat in the butter. Add the dry ingredients and beat at low speed, just to incorporate.

Using a tablespoon of batter for each cookie, form thin 4- to $4\frac{1}{2}$-inch circles on the prepared baking sheets by working the batter in a circular motion with the back of a measuring spoon. Leave $2\frac{1}{2}$ inches between cookies.

Bake for about 6 minutes, until very firm to the touch and slightly browned around the edges.

Working very fast, before the cookies harden, drape each one around a rolling pin or wine bottle laying on its side, press it into place, leave for a few seconds to cool, and slip off. If the cookies become too firm to shape before you've finished, put them back into the oven for a few seconds to soften.

Fat per cookie = 0.40 g
Calories per cookie = 35.4

Cappuccino Tuiles

YIELD = 8 TUILES

Crisp, festive cookies with a lingering cappuccino flavor. We like giant ($4\frac{1}{2}$-inch) tuiles; for smaller cookies, use only $\frac{1}{2}$ tablespoon of batter for each. In addition to working the batter into free-form circles on lightly greased and floured baking sheets, you can also draw circles on the bottom of sheets of baker's parchment cut to fit the pans, flip the paper over, and spread the batter within the guidelines. (If you use baker's parchment, you don't need to grease and flour the baking sheets.)

(cont.)

Prepare all the cookies before baking; don't let the batter sit. Once baked, the cookies must be shaped into tuiles as quickly as possible upon removal from the oven. It's easier if you've recruited a few extra hands to help expedite the process.

The tuiles can easily become the base for
Filled Chocolate Tacos, *a real party delight.*

Instead of shaping the warm cookies around a thick rolling pin or wine bottle, fold them over the handle of a clean broom or mop that has been suspended between two chairs. Once hardened, fill them with hulled, chunked, and chilled strawberries (you'll need about a pint to fill 8 tacos) and top them with a silky, rich nonfat Crème Anglaise we developed for The 99% Fat-Free Book of Appetizers and Desserts. *For about 1 1/2 cups Crème Anglaise:*

1 cup skim milk
1/2 cup nonfat liquid egg substitute
3 tablespoons granulated sugar
1 teaspoon vanilla extract

Warm the milk in a small saucepan over low heat just until it begins to give off steam. Remove from the heat.

Put the egg substitute and sugar in a mixing bowl, whisking to combine thoroughly. While continuing to whisk, slowly pour in the warm milk. Return the mixture to the saucepan over low heat. Cook for 3 to 4 minutes, stirring constantly, until thickened just enough to lightly coat the back of a spoon. Stir in the vanilla and drizzle over the berries in each taco.

Low-Fat

½ cup all-purpose flour
1½ cups rolled oats
½ teaspoon baking soda
¼ teaspoon baking powder
½ teaspoon ground cinnamon
¼ teaspoon salt
½ cup natural pumpkin butter
½ cup firmly packed light brown sugar
1 large egg white
1 tablespoon light corn syrup
½ teaspoon vanilla extract
¼ cup buttermilk
⅓ cup butterscotch chips

Preheat the oven to 350 degrees.

Lightly coat cookie sheets with light vegetable oil cooking spray, distributing the oil evenly over the surface.

Combine the flour, oats, baking soda, baking powder, cinnamon, and salt in a mixing bowl. Whisk thoroughly.

In a large mixing bowl, combine the pumpkin butter, brown sugar, egg white, and corn syrup. Beat with an electric mixer at high speed until smooth and frothy. Add the vanilla and buttermilk and mix at low speed for a few seconds more to combine.

Add the flour mixture and mix thoroughly with a wooden spoon. Fold in the butterscotch chips and refrigerate for at least 5 minutes.

Drop dough by the tablespoonful onto the prepared cookie sheets about 2 inches apart. Bake for 8 to 10 minutes, until lightly browned.

Remove the cookies to wire racks to cool.

Fat per cookie = 0.75 g
Calories per cookie = 47.9

Brown Sugary Butterscotch Chip Cookies

YIELD = ABOUT
3 DOZEN COOKIES

These flaky, chewy cookies are really quite wonderful, with a rich brown sugar flavor heightened by bits of butterscotch. The pumpkin butter boosts the taste of both the brown sugar and the butterscotch. We use buttermilk for added richness and moisture, while a little corn syrup lends silkiness.

Susan's Orange Chippers

YIELD = ABOUT
2 DOZEN COOKIES

We developed the recipe for these generously stuffed goodies with our literary agent, Susan Ramer, in mind. Orange and chocolate are her favorite flavor combination, and she's dedicated to low-fat eating.

We think they'll please a lot of other folks too. We use mini chocolate chips so that you get a mouthful with each bite. Banana provides the moisture and richness of butter, while sunflower seeds provide added crunch.

1½ cups rolled oats
1⅔ cups whole wheat pastry flour
½ teaspoon salt
1 teaspoon baking powder
½ teaspoon baking soda
¼ cup sunflower seeds
¾ cup mashed banana (about 2 bananas)
1 cup firmly packed dark brown sugar
½ cup nonfat liquid egg substitute
1 teaspoon grated orange zest
½ teaspoon orange extract
¼ cup semisweet mini chocolate chips

Preheat the oven to 375 degrees.

Line cookie sheets with baker's parchment.

Whisk together the oats, pastry flour, salt, baking powder, baking soda, and sunflower seeds in a bowl.

In a large bowl, combine the banana and brown sugar. Beat with an electric mixer at medium speed until the sugar is dissolved. Mix in the liquid egg substitute, orange zest, and orange extract.

Add the flour mixture and mix thoroughly with the electric mixer at low speed. Fold in the chocolate chips.

Drop the dough about 3 inches apart onto the prepared sheets, using 2 tablespoons for each cookie. Bake for about 10 minutes, until lightly browned.

Remove the cookies to wire racks to cool.

Fat per cookie = 1.28 g
Calories per cookie = 100.0

Purists can produce a more traditional chocolate chip cookie by substituting 1 teaspoon vanilla extract for the ½ teaspoon orange extract and omitting the orange zest and sunflower seeds.

½ cup quick oats
1½ cups whole wheat flour
1 teaspoon baking powder
½ teaspoon salt
¾ cup natural unsweetened applesauce
¾ cup granulated sugar
1 cup shredded carrots (about 4 carrots)
¼ cup unsweetened finely shredded coconut
¼ cup currants
1 teaspoon vanilla extract
¾ teaspoon ground cinnamon
1 teaspoon orange zest

FROSTING:
4 ounces nonfat cream cheese, at room temperature
1 cup confectioners' sugar
½ teaspoon vanilla extract
½ tablespoon freshly squeezed lemon juice

Preheat the oven to 375 degrees.

Lightly coat cookie sheets with light vegetable oil cooking spray.

Combine the oats, whole wheat flour, baking powder, and salt in the bowl of a food processor fitted with the steel blade. Process until finely ground, about 30 seconds.

In a mixing bowl, combine the applesauce and sugar. Stir with a wooden spoon to dissolve the sugar. Stir in the carrots. Add the coconut, currants, vanilla, cinnamon, and orange zest. Mix thoroughly. Add the oat mixture and stir to combine.

Drop the dough 2 inches apart onto the prepared sheets, using 2 tablespoons for each. Bake 12 to 15 minutes, until firm to the touch, but do not brown. Remove the cookies to wire racks to cool.

Meanwhile, prepare the frosting. Cream the cream cheese in a bowl with an electric mixer at medium speed. Sift the confectioners' sugar on top. Beat in the sugar until the mixture is smooth and fluffy. Stir in the vanilla and lemon juice. Let sit for 2 minutes before frosting the cookies.

Return the cookies to the sheets and chill at least 1 hour.

Fat per cookie = 0.75 g
Calories per cookie = 94.6

Carrot Cake Cookies

YIELD = ABOUT
2 DOZEN COOKIES

Dense and satisfying, with a rich, creamy frosting. The frosting will have thickened after an hour in the refrigerator, but will still be a bit tacky to the touch. For a firmer frosting, chill the frosted cookies overnight. The carrots can be shredded by hand or in a food processor fitted with the grating disk.

Nutty Biscotti

YIELD = ABOUT
2 DOZEN BISCOTTI

In *The 99% Fat-Free Cookbook,* we used Grape Nuts cereal to replace the nuts in a much-acclaimed flourless chocolate cake. It seemed like a good idea then, and it still does. For this low-fat cookie, we use Grape Nuts once again, adding just enough slivered almonds to boost the flavor.

$\frac{1}{4}$ cup slivered blanched almonds
$\frac{3}{4}$ cup Grape Nuts cereal
$\frac{3}{4}$ cup granulated sugar
$2\frac{1}{2}$ cups all-purpose flour
$\frac{1}{2}$ tablespoon baking powder
$\frac{1}{2}$ teaspoon baking soda
$\frac{1}{4}$ teaspoon salt
1 cup nonfat liquid egg substitute
$\frac{1}{2}$ teaspoon almond extract

Preheat the oven to 350 degrees.

Line a baking sheet with baker's parchment and flour a 4-inch-wide strip down the middle.

Combine the almonds, Grape Nuts, and sugar in the bowl of a food processor fitted with the steel blade. Process to a coarse grind, about 15 seconds. Add the flour, baking powder, baking soda, and salt. Process for a few seconds more, just to combine. Transfer to a large mixing bowl and make a well in the center.

In a small bowl, whisk together the liquid egg substitute and almond extract until slightly frothy. Pour the mixture into the well of the dry ingredients. Stir with a wooden spoon to form a dough.

Turn the dough out onto the strip of flour on the prepared baking sheet. With lightly floured hands, shape it into a 12-by-3$\frac{1}{2}$-inch loaf about $\frac{3}{4}$ inch high; add more flour to your hands as necessary.

Bake for about 30 minutes, until puffed, crusty, and cracked along the bottom. Remove the loaf to a wire rack and allow it to cool for 15 minutes, leaving the oven on.

At a slight angle, cut crosswise into $\frac{1}{2}$-inch slices. Stand the slices upright on the baking sheet, return them to the oven, and toast for about 15 minutes.

Cool on wire racks.

Fat per cookie = 0.68 g
Calories per cookie = 88.5

1 cup whole wheat flour
1 teaspoon ground cinnamon
1 teaspoon baking soda
$^1/_4$ teaspoon salt
$^3/_4$ cup natural unsweetened applesauce
1 cup unpacked dark brown sugar
1 tablespoon light corn syrup
$^1/_2$ tablespoon vanilla extract
$^1/_4$ cup buttermilk
1 large egg white
$2^3/_4$ cups rolled oats
1 cup chopped dates

Preheat the oven to 375 degrees.

Lightly coat cookie sheets with light vegetable oil cooking spray, spreading the oil evenly over the surface.

Whisk together the flour, cinnamon, baking soda, and salt in a mixing bowl and set aside.

Combine the applesauce and brown sugar in a large bowl. Beat with an electric mixer at high speed until the sugar is dissolved and the mixture is smooth, about 30 seconds. Add the corn syrup, vanilla, buttermilk, and egg white. Beat for about 30 seconds more, until frothy.

At low speed, beat in the flour mixture, just to incorporate. With a wooden spoon, stir in the oats, then the dates.

Using 2 tablespoons of dough for each cookie, drop the dough onto the prepared cookie sheets about 2 inches apart. Flatten gently into patties.

Bake for about 12 minutes, until firm and lightly browned.

Transfer the cookies to wire racks to cool.

Fat per cookie = 0.62 g
Calories per cookie = 84.2

Oatmeal Date Cookies

YIELD = ABOUT
$2^1/_2$ DOZEN COOKIES

These soft, chewy cookies derive their moist, silky texture from applesauce instead of butter and their richness from buttermilk used in lieu of egg yolks.

Raspberry Rugalach

YIELD = ABOUT
3 DOZEN RUGALACH

We use nonfat cream cheese in this dough, and replace some of the butter with nonfat sour cream. The result is a surprisingly rich crust with less than half the fat. The dough is best if refrigerated overnight before rolling.

6 tablespoons (³/₄ stick) unsalted butter, at room temperature
4 ounces nonfat cream cheese, at room temperature
2 tablespoons nonfat sour cream
³/₄ cup granulated sugar
1 cup all-purpose flour
2 teaspoons ground cinnamon
¹/₂ cup plus 1 tablespoon seedless raspberry spreadable fruit

In a large bowl, cream the butter and cream cheese with an electric mixer at high speed. At medium speed, mix in the sour cream and ¹/₂ cup of the sugar. At low speed, mix in the flour, just to incorporate. Work the dough into a ball with a rubber spatula, wrap it in plastic wrap, and refrigerate for at least 4 hours or overnight.

Lightly coat a cookie sheet with light vegetable oil cooking spray, spreading the oil evenly over the surface.

Combine the cinnamon and the remaining ¹/₄ cup sugar. Sprinkle 1¹/₂ tablespoons of the mixture onto a work surface that has been lined with wax paper.

Divide the dough in thirds. Place 1 piece on the prepared work surface, turn to coat it with the sugar and cinnamon mixture, and cover with a second sheet of wax paper. Roll out to about 8 by 4 inches. Remove the top sheet, coat again in the sugar and cinnamon mixture, and re-cover. Roll out to 12 by 6 inches, and remove the top sheet.

Spread 3 tablespoons of the raspberry filling evenly over the dough, leaving a ¹/₂-inch border on 1 long side. Starting with the long side without the border, roll the dough into a log. Cut it into 1-inch pieces and transfer them with a spatula to the prepared cookie sheet, seam side down. Refrigerate for 10 minutes more.

Repeat the process for the remaining 2 pieces of dough. Meanwhile, preheat the oven to 350 degrees.

Bake for about 12 minutes, until light golden brown.

Transfer to wire racks to cool.

Fat per cookie = 2.02 g
Calories per cookie = 56.7

Sugarless

1 1/3 cups all-purpose flour
1/2 teaspoon salt
1/2 cup (1 stick) unsalted butter, well chilled, cut into 8 pieces
1/4 cup skim milk, well chilled
3 ounces unsweetened chocolate, chopped
1/4 cup chopped hazelnuts
1/2 cup apricot spreadable fruit

Combine the flour and salt in the bowl of a food processor fitted with the steel blade. Turn the machine on and add the butter through the feed tube, 1 piece at a time. Process for a few seconds until the mixture is a pebbly consistency. Pour in the milk through the feed tube and continue to process to form a dough ball. Wrap the ball in wax paper and refrigerate for 30 minutes.

Melt the chocolate in a double boiler, stirring constantly with a wooden spoon. Remove from the heat and stir in the hazelnuts.

Divide the dough in half. Re-cover half and return it to the refrigerator. Put the other half on a work surface lined with wax paper and lightly floured. Roll it out to a thickness of 1/8 inch, working it into a 12-by-9-inch rectangle.

Spread 1/4 cup of the spreadable fruit on the dough. Spread half of the chocolate mixture (about 6 tablespoons) over the spreadable fruit. Starting with a long end, roll the dough into a log. Repeat the process for the second piece of dough. Wrap the logs in wax paper and refrigerate until firm, about 1 hour.

Preheat the oven to 350 degrees.

Slice the logs into 1-inch pieces and place them on ungreased cookie sheets. Bake for about 23 minutes, until lightly browned.

Transfer the cookies to wire racks to cool.

Some of the components of this filling also make a smashing sugarless, low-fat hot fudge sauce.

Melt the chocolate in a double boiler as directed. Whisk in the apricot spreadable fruit until smooth. Remove from the heat and serve immediately.

YIELD = ABOUT
1 CUP SAUCE

Fat per cookie = 6.48 g
Calories per cookie = 79.3

Chocolate Snails

YIELD = ABOUT
2 DOZEN SNAILS

It's hard to believe these scrumptious and pretty little party cookies are made without sugar. The apricot spreadable fruit lends just the right degree of sweetness without adding any discernible flavor. The butter and milk combination promotes browning in the absence of sugar.

Fruit Bars

YIELD = 36 BARS

As pretty as a fruitcake, which is basically what this is. By simmering the dried fruit in water and port, we're in essence creating a simple syrup without using sugar.

This is the exception to our general rule that sugarless cookies are best stored at room temperature; it will remain fresh and flavorful for up to a week in the refrigerator. Cut the bars only as you're ready to serve them and store the rest intact in the pan, covered with aluminum foil.

$^1\!/_2$ cup port
$1^1\!/_2$ cups water
1 cup currants
$^1\!/_2$ cup golden raisins
1 cup chopped dried apricots
$^3\!/_4$ cup chopped pecans
$^1\!/_2$ cup chopped dates
$^1\!/_2$ cup chopped dried pears
$^1\!/_2$ cup chopped dried peaches
$^1\!/_2$ cup chopped Calimyrna figs
$1^3\!/_4$ cups all-purpose flour
$^1\!/_4$ teaspoon ground nutmeg
$^1\!/_4$ teaspoon ground cloves
$1^1\!/_4$ teaspoons ground cinnamon
1 teaspoon baking soda
$^1\!/_2$ teaspoon salt
$^1\!/_2$ cup (1 stick) unsalted butter, melted

Preheat the oven to 350 degrees.

Coat a 9-by-13-inch baking pan with light vegetable oil cooking spray and flour lightly.

In a medium saucepan, combine the port, water, currants, raisins, apricots, pecans, dates, pears, peaches, and figs. Bring to a boil over high heat. Lower the heat and simmer, uncovered, for about 3 minutes, until the fruit is fork tender. Remove from the heat and cool.

In a large mixing bowl, whisk together the flour, nutmeg, cloves, cinnamon, baking soda, and salt. Add the melted butter and mix thoroughly with a wooden spoon. Stir in the fruit mixture, including the liquid.

Combine thoroughly and turn into the prepared baking pan, spreading the batter evenly with a rubber spatula. Bake for about 40 minutes, until firm to the touch and golden brown.

Cool completely in the pan on a wire rack. Cut into bars measuring $1^1\!/_2$ inches by a generous 2 inches.

Fat per bar = 4.40 g
Calories per bar = 112.2

1 cup sliced almonds
1 teaspoon baking powder
2¼ cups all-purpose flour
½ cup (1 stick) unsalted butter, at room temperature
¼ cup buttermilk
1 teaspoon almond extract
1 large egg white, beaten
¼ cup plus 2 tablespoons seedless blackberry spreadable fruit

Preheat the oven to 375 degrees.

Combine ½ cup of the almonds, the baking powder, and ¼ cup of the flour in the bowl of a food processor fitted with the steel blade. Process for about 15 seconds, until the nuts are finely chopped.

Add the butter and the remaining 2 cups flour. Turn on the machine and drizzle the buttermilk and almond extract through the feed tube. Continue to process until a dough ball forms. Using 1 tablespoon for each cookie, roll the dough into balls and set aside.

Put the remaining ½ cup almonds into the food processor and pulse 2 to 3 times to chop coarsely. Transfer to a shallow bowl.

Roll the balls in the beaten egg white and then in the chopped nuts to coat. Place on ungreased cookie sheets. Make a well in the center of each cookie with your thumb and fill it with ½ teaspoon of the spreadable fruit.

Bake for about 15 minutes, until firm to the touch and very lightly browned.

Fat per cookie = 3.99 g
Calories per cookie = 71.3

For Almond Butter Thumbprints, put ¼ teaspoon almond butter in the well of each cookie in place of the blackberry spreadable fruit.

Blackberry Thumbprints

YIELD = ABOUT
3 DOZEN THUMBPRINTS

The buttermilk adds extra richness, while still allowing us to cut down on the butter. Use natural rather than blanched almonds to add flecks of color to the dough. In addition to the almond butter variation noted below, try other spreadable fruits for variety; we particularly like apricot.

Raspberry Triangles

YIELD = 24 TRIANGLES

Nonfat ricotta cheese is responsible for the rich, creamy taste of these cookies. Be sure to cut a deep slit in the top to keep the dough from closing up while baking. We paint the cookies with a whole egg; replace it with nonfat liquid egg substitute if you are concerned about cholesterol.

1 cup all-purpose flour
$\frac{1}{8}$ teaspoon baking powder
$\frac{1}{2}$ cup (1 stick) unsalted butter, at room temperature
$\frac{1}{2}$ cup nonfat ricotta cheese
$\frac{1}{4}$ cup plus 2 tablespoons seedless raspberry spreadable fruit
1 large egg, beaten

Whisk together the flour and baking powder in a small bowl.

In another bowl, cream the butter with an electric mixer at low speed. Add the ricotta cheese and mix until well blended. Add the flour mixture and stir with a wooden spoon to form a dough. Wrap the dough in wax paper and refrigerate for 1 hour.

Preheat the oven to 425 degrees.

Divide the dough in half. Rewrap half and return it to the refrigerator. On a work surface that has been lined with wax paper and lightly floured, roll out the other half to a thickness of $\frac{1}{8}$ inch, shaping it into a 10-by-7$\frac{1}{2}$-inch rectangle. Cut it into twelve 2$\frac{1}{2}$-inch squares.

Put $\frac{3}{4}$ teaspoon spreadable fruit in the bottom left-hand corner of each square. Moisten the edges with water. Fold the top right-hand corner over the filling to create a triangle and crimp the edges closed. Make a deep $\frac{3}{4}$-inch-long slit in the top of each triangle to expose the filling. Transfer the triangles to ungreased cookie sheets. Repeat the process with the other half of the dough.

Brush the cookies with the beaten egg and bake for about 10 minutes, until lightly browned.

Remove the cookies to wire racks to cool.

Fat per cookie = 4.09 g
Calories per cookie = 67.5

¾ cup all-purpose flour
¾ cup whole wheat pastry flour
1 cup wheat germ
¾ cup rolled oats
1 tablespoon baking powder
2 teaspoons ground cinnamon
One 12-ounce can apple juice concentrate, thawed, undiluted
⅓ cup (⅔ stick) unsalted butter, melted
1 large egg
1 cup golden raisins
½ cup chopped pecans

Preheat the oven to 375 degrees.

Lightly coat cookie sheets with light vegetable oil cooking spray, working the oil evenly over the surface.

In a large mixing bowl, whisk together the flours, wheat germ, oats, baking powder, and cinnamon.

Combine the juice concentrate, butter, egg, raisins, and pecans in a blender. Run at low speed just until the raisins and pecans are coarsely chopped. Add the mixture to the dry ingredients and stir to combine thoroughly.

Drop the dough by the half tablespoonful onto the prepared cookie sheets. Bake for 8 to 10 minutes, until the cookies are a light golden brown.

Transfer the cookies to wire racks to cool.

Fat per cookie = 2.12 g
Calories per cookie = 52.5

Oatmeal Raisin Pecan Cookies

YIELD = ABOUT
5 DOZEN COOKIES

Soft and redolent of cinnamon, these cookies are healthy and kid-friendly. We recommend baking a bunch to ensure that there will be cookies left for the kids after the grown-ups in the house have had their fill.

Apricot Swirls

YIELD = ABOUT
3 1/2 DOZEN SWIRLS

The use of nonfat cream cheese and liquid egg substitute allows us to add some rich, creamy butter and still keep down the total fat content of these healthy cookies.

Use a serrated knife to facilitate slicing the roll into rounds. While baking, the flaky dough opens up like the petals of a flower, and the filling oozes out to create an attractive glaze.

$^3/_4$ cup (1$^1/_2$ sticks) unsalted butter, at room temperature
4 ounces nonfat cream cheese, at room temperature
$^1/_4$ cup nonfat liquid egg substitute
1$^3/_4$ cups all-purpose flour
$^3/_4$ cup apricot spreadable fruit

Cream the butter and cream cheese in a bowl with an electric mixer at low speed. Add the liquid egg substitute and beat at medium speed until the mixture is smooth. Beat in the flour at low speed to form a dough. Gather the dough into a ball, wrap it in wax paper, and refrigerate for at least 2 hours.

Preheat the oven to 350 degrees.

Lightly coat cookie sheets with light vegetable oil cooking spray, spreading the oil evenly over the surface.

Cover a work surface with a sheet of wax paper and flour lightly. Divide the dough in half. Roll half out to a $^1/_8$-inch-thick rectangle measuring about 9 by 12 inches. Spread 6 tablespoons of the spreadable fruit over the dough.

Starting at a long end, roll the dough up like a jelly roll. Trim the ragged ends and cut the roll into $^1/_2$-inch slices. Transfer the slices to the prepared cookie sheets. Repeat the process with the remaining piece of dough and the remaining fruit.

Bake for 18 to 20 minutes, until lightly browned. Remove the cookies to a wire rack to cool.

Fat per cookie = 3.37 g
Calories per cookie = 60.3

For Strawberry Swirls, substitute an equal amount of strawberry spreadable fruit for the apricot spreadable fruit.

¹/₃ cup currants
¹/₂ cup (1 stick) unsalted butter, well chilled,
    cut into 16 pieces
¹/₄ teaspoon vanilla extract
¹/₈ teaspoon ground cinnamon
1 cup all-purpose flour
2 teaspoons cornstarch

Preheat the oven to 325 degrees.

Combine the currants and butter in the bowl of a food processor fitted with the steel blade. Process for about 10 seconds, until the currants are chopped and the butter is lightly creamed. Add the remaining ingredients in the order listed. Pulse 8 to 10 times until the mixture is pebbly in consistency and free of any unincorporated flour.

Press evenly into an 8-inch-round cake pan. Crimp the edge all around with the tines of a fork.

Bake for 15 minutes, prick the surface a few times with a fork, and bake for about 20 minutes more, until the edge is just beginning to brown.

Cool in the pan on a wire rack for 10 minutes. Then unmold the shortbread, cut it into 12 wedges, and cool completely.

Fat per wedge = 7.75 g
Calories per wedge = 113.3

Jill Van Cleave's Currant Shortbread

YIELD = 12 WEDGES

You won't even miss the sugar in this elegant shortbread, which we developed with a little help from Jill Van Cleave—baker extraordinaire, fellow cookbook author, and provider of moral support and endless encouragement when we're on a deadline!

Little bits of currant scattered throughout the shortbread provide more than sufficient sweetness. Bake it in an 8-inch-round cake pan or in a decorative mold (page 57).

Double Chocolate Fudgies

YIELD = 64 FUDGIES

Question: Remove all the flour from a brownie recipe and what do you have left?

Answer: A fudgie, an almost sinfully dense and rich concoction with an intense chocolate flavor and a mouthful of nuts in each bite.

Gluten-Free

1$^3/_4$ cups chopped walnuts
$^3/_4$ cup granulated sugar
6 ounces bittersweet chocolate, chopped
3 tablespoons unsalted butter
3 tablespoons milk
2 large eggs
$^1/_2$ teaspoon salt
1 cup semisweet chocolate chips

Preheat the oven to 325 degrees.

Lightly grease an 8-by-8-inch baking pan with butter.

Put $^3/_4$ cup of the walnuts and $^1/_4$ cup of the sugar in the bowl of a food processor fitted with the steel blade. Process to a fine grind, about 1 minute.

Combine the bittersweet chocolate, butter, and remaining $^1/_2$ cup sugar in the top of a double boiler over boiling water. Cook, stirring constantly, until the chocolate and butter are melted and the mixture is smooth. Remove from the heat and stir in the milk. Transfer to a large heat proof ceramic or glass bowl and cool for 3 to 4 minutes.

Whisk in the eggs, one at a time. Stir in the ground nut mixture and the salt. Fold in the remaining 1 cup walnuts and the chocolate chips. Pour into the prepared pan.

Bake for about 35 minutes, until the fudgie is set in the center and pulling away from the sides of the pan, or until a tester comes out almost clean.

Cool in the pan on a wire rack for 30 minutes. Cut into 1-inch squares.

Fat per fudgie = 4.24 g
Calories per fudgie = 64.4

1 cup chopped dates
2 tablespoons plus 2 teaspoons finely chopped orange zest
1 cup chopped walnuts
1⅓ cups firmly packed dark brown sugar
⅔ cup granulated sugar
4 large egg whites, at room temperature
½ teaspoon cream of tartar

Preheat the oven to 300 degrees.

Lightly coat cookie sheets with light vegetable oil cooking spray, working the oil evenly over the surface.

Combine the dates, orange zest, walnuts, and brown sugar in a bowl and mix thoroughly. Set aside.

Put the granulated sugar into a food processor fitted with the steel blade. Process to a superfine consistency, about 2 minutes.

Fit a stationary electric mixer with the whisk. Beat the egg whites at medium speed for about 2 minutes, until frothy. Add the cream of tartar and beat just until peaks begin to form, about 2 minutes. Raise the speed to high and gradually add the superfine sugar. Continue to mix for about 2 minutes more, until very stiff, shiny peaks form.

Fold the date mixture into the meringue. Drop by the half tablespoonful onto the prepared cookie sheets, leaving at least 1 inch between cookies. Bake for about 15 minutes, until very lightly browned.

Cool on the sheets on wire racks for at least 15 minutes, until the sheets are cool to the touch.

Fat per cookie = 0.77 g
Calories per cookie = 31.0

Fruit and Nut Kisses

YIELD = ABOUT
8 DOZEN KISSES

Based on an old Victorian recipe, these contain enough luscious brown sugar and dates to make them a favorite of kids and sweet lovers of more advanced years.

Dutch Kisses

YIELD = ABOUT
5 DOZEN KISSES

The first step in this recipe is grinding granulated sugar to superfine consistency in the food processor. While baking, the superfine sugar will melt, creating tiny little air pockets that lend crispness to the meringue.

1 cup granulated sugar
4 large egg whites, at room temperature
$^1/_2$ teaspoon cream of tartar
$^1/_4$ cup unsweetened Dutch-processed cocoa powder
1 tablespoon hazelnut liqueur
1 tablespoon boiling water
1 cup chopped hazelnuts

Preheat the oven to 300 degrees.

Lightly coat cookie sheets with light vegetable oil cooking spray, distributing the oil evenly.

Put $^2/_3$ cup of the sugar into a food processor fitted with the steel blade. Process to superfine consistency, about 2 minutes.

Fit a stationary electric mixer with the whisk. Beat the egg whites at medium speed for about 2 minutes, until frothy. Add the cream of tartar and beat just until peaks begin to form, about 2 minutes. Raise the speed to high and gradually add the superfine sugar. Continue to mix for about 2 minutes more, until very stiff, shiny peaks form.

Combine the cocoa powder and the remaining $^1/_3$ cup sugar in a mixing bowl. Add the liqueur and boiling water. Stir until smooth. Stir in 1 tablespoon of the prepared meringue, blending thoroughly.

Fold the cocoa mixture and the nuts into the meringue with a rubber spatula. Drop onto the prepared cookie sheets by the tablespoonful, about 1$^1/_2$ inches apart. Bake for about 15 minutes or just until firm to the touch.

Cool on the sheets on wire racks.

Fat per cookie = 1.28 g
Calories per cookie = 27.8

For Dutch Almond Kisses, substitute $^3/_4$ cup blanched almonds for the cup of hazelnuts and 4 teaspoons almond liqueur for the tablespoon of hazelnut liqueur.

1²/₃ cups granulated sugar
4 large egg whites, at room temperature
¹/₂ teaspoon cream of tartar
2 cups sweetened flaked coconut

Preheat the oven to 325 degrees.

Lightly coat cookie sheets with light vegetable oil cooking spray, distributing the oil evenly over the surface.

Put ²/₃ cup of the sugar into a food processor fitted with the steel blade. Process to a superfine consistency, about 2 minutes.

Fit a stationary electric mixer with the whisk. Beat the egg whites at medium speed for about 2 minutes, until frothy. Add the cream of tartar and beat just until peaks begin to form, about 2 minutes. Raise the speed to high and gradually add the superfine sugar. Continue to beat for about 2 minutes more, until very stiff, shiny peaks form.

Combine the remaining 1 cup sugar and the coconut in a bowl and mix well. Add to the meringue and mix thoroughly with a slotted spoon.

Drop by the teaspoonful onto the prepared cookie sheets, about 1¹/₂ inches apart. Bake for about 20 minutes, until golden.

Cool on the sheets on wire racks.

Fat per cookie = 0.58 g
Calories per cookie = 19.1

Mini Coconut Meringues

YIELD = ABOUT
10 DOZEN MERINGUES

These crunchy little cookies have a chewy center. Dropped by the teaspoonful, the recipe yields sufficient cookies (which hold up well for days in an airtight container) to feed party crowds. You can also use 2 teaspoons of dough per cookie for everyday baking.

Cashew Pralines

YIELD = ABOUT
2 1/2 DOZEN PRALINES

The only trick to preparing this crisp, nutty confection is blind faith. Although the sugar and water mixture will go through a dry, sandy phase while heating—one that hints strongly of failure—persevere and you will be rewarded with a rich, smooth syrup in the end.

We prefer to toast the cashews ourselves for maximum taste, but you can use unsalted dry-roasted cashews.

1 cup whole raw cashews
2 cups granulated sugar
$\frac{1}{2}$ cup water
$\frac{1}{4}$ cup firmly packed dark brown sugar
$\frac{1}{8}$ teaspoon salt
$\frac{1}{4}$ cup heavy cream
1 teaspoon vanilla extract

Preheat the oven to 350 degrees.

Line a baking sheet with aluminum foil for toasting the cashews, and evenly coat nonstick baking sheets with light vegetable oil cooking spray for preparation of the pralines.

Arrange the cashews in a single layer on the lined baking sheet. Bake for 5 minutes, shake the pan, and return it to the oven for 3 minutes more. Shake the pan once more and set aside to cool.

Combine the granulated sugar and water in a large, heavy-bottomed frying pan. Bring to a boil over high heat. Reduce the heat to medium and cook for about 15 minutes, stirring constantly with a wooden spoon, until a smooth golden brown syrup forms. Remove from the heat and stir in the brown sugar and salt.

Scald the cream in a small saucepan over high heat, just until bubbles begin to form around the edge. Stir immediately into the mixture in the frying pan. Stir in the vanilla and the toasted nuts.

Ladle by the tablespoonful onto the prepared baking sheets, leaving about 3 inches between cookies. Allow to cool at room temperature.

Fat per cookie = 2.79 g
Calories per cookie = 91.3

For Peanut Pralines, substitute $1\frac{1}{2}$ cups blanched peanuts for the cashews. Use raw peanuts and toast them per recipe directions.

2 cups sweetened flaked coconut
$^1/_3$ cup semisweet mini chocolate chips
$^1/_2$ cup chopped macadamia nuts
$^3/_4$ cup sweetened condensed milk
1 teaspoon lemon extract

Preheat the oven to 350 degrees.

Coat cookie sheets well with light vegetable oil cooking spray, working the oil evenly over the surface.

In a bowl, mix the coconut, chocolate chips, and nuts. Add the condensed milk and lemon extract. Mix thoroughly with a wooden spoon.

Drop onto the prepared cookie sheets by the half tablespoonful, about 2 inches apart. Bake for about 10 minutes, until very lightly browned.

Immediately remove the cookies to a wire rack to cool.

Fat per cookie = 2.74 g
Calories per cookie = 44.2

Macadamia Macaroons

YIELD = ABOUT
4 $^1/_2$ DOZEN MACAROONS

This is a traditional soft and chewy macaroon, with the thoroughly modern addition of macadamia nuts. It's a great recipe to prepare for unexpected company because it's made in a matter of minutes from pantry staples. Somewhat higher in fat than most recipes in this chapter, consider it an indulgence.

Ginger Squiggles

YIELD = ABOUT 6 DOZEN 3-INCH
SQUIGGLES OR 1½ DOZEN
12-INCH BATONS

These free-form meringue ribbons contain virtually no fat. For an interesting presentation, form 12-inch Ginger Batons and serve them in a basket like bread sticks.

1 ounce crystallized ginger, cut into three 1½-by-1-inch pieces
1 cup firmly packed light brown sugar
⅔ cup granulated sugar
4 large egg whites, at room temperature
½ teaspoon cream of tartar

Line baking sheets with baker's parchment.

Combine the crystallized ginger and brown sugar in the bowl of a food processor fitted with the steel blade. Process for about 30 seconds, until all the ginger has been broken up, leaving a powdery mixture. Remove to a bowl and set aside.

Put the granulated sugar into the food processor. Process to superfine consistency, about 2 minutes.

Fit a stationary electric mixer with the whisk. Beat the egg whites at medium speed for about 2 minutes, until frothy. Add the cream of tartar and beat just until peaks begin to form, about 2 minutes. Raise the speed to high and gradually add the superfine sugar. Continue to mix for about 2 minutes more, until very stiff, shiny peaks form.

Scrape the ginger mixture into the meringue. Fold it in with a balloon whisk. (The whisk from the stationary electric mixer used to make the meringue will work well.)

Using a pastry bag with a ribbon tip, squeeze 3-inch ribbons onto the prepared baking sheets, leaving about 1 inch between cookies. Let sit at room temperature for at least 45 minutes to dry.

Preheat the oven to 250 degrees.

Bake for 45 to 50 minutes, until lightly colored. Remove from the oven and set the sheets aside for 1 minute. Peel the cookies from the parchment and cool them on wire racks for at least 10 minutes more.

Fat per squiggle = 0.01 g
Calories per squiggle = 24.7

Fat per baton = 0.04 g
Calories per baton = 99.0

To chocolate-dip Ginger Squiggles,
Ginger Batons, or Orange Teardrops
(page 286):

Put 6 ounces bittersweet chocolate, broken up,
into a small, shallow microwave-proof bowl. Heat
in a microwave oven at full power for 1 minute and
stir. Heat for about 2 minutes more in 30-second intervals,
stirring after each interval, until fully melted. (You can
also melt the chocolate in the top of a double boiler
over boiling water.)

Gently twist a toothpick into the center of the bottom of a
cookie. Dip the cookie into the chocolate, swirling it to cover
one end of a Ginger Squiggle or the upper half of an
Orange Teardrop. Turn the cookie right side up, slide it onto
the tines of a fork, and pull out the toothpick. Slide the
cookie from the fork onto wax paper and allow the
chocolate to dry and harden at room temperature
for 30 minutes.

Ginger Batons can be dipped without the aid of a
toothpick; just submerge them in the melted
chocolate to the desired level of coating and
allow them to dry thoroughly on
wax paper.

Orange Teardrops

YIELD = ABOUT
10 DOZEN TEARDROPS
OR 2 DOZEN GIANT TEARDROPS

We serve these tasty nonfat citrus morsels year round, but they make a particularly nice, light finish to a Passover seder.

You can also make giant teardrops by tracing 4- to 5-inch circles on the back of the baker's parchment used to line the baking sheets and covering each circle with a mound of dough about 1/2 inch high.

1 cup confectioners' sugar
2 tablespoons finely chopped orange zest
2/3 cup granulated sugar
4 large egg whites, at room temperature
1/2 teaspoon cream of tartar

Line baking sheets with baker's parchment.

Combine the confectioners' sugar and orange zest in a small bowl and mix well. Set aside.

Put the granulated sugar into a food processor fitted with the steel blade. Process to superfine consistency, about 2 minutes.

Fit a stationary electric mixer with the whisk. Beat the egg whites at medium speed for about 2 minutes, until frothy. Add the cream of tartar and beat just until peaks begin to form, about 2 minutes. Raise the speed to high and gradually add the superfine sugar. Continue to mix for about 2 minutes more, until very stiff, shiny peaks form.

Fold in the orange zest mixture with a rubber spatula. Transfer to a heavy-duty 1-quart plastic storage bag. Seal tightly and cut a whole in a bottom corner. Squeeze circles about 1 1/4 inches in diameter and 1/2 inch high onto the prepared baking sheets, about 1 inch apart. Let sit at room temperature for 1 hour to dry.

Preheat the oven to 250 degrees.

Bake for 50 to 55 minutes, until the cookies are just beginning to crack.

Cool for 1 minute on the sheets before peeling the cookies from the parchment. Transfer to wire racks and cool for 10 to 15 minutes more.

Fat per teardrop = 0
Calories per teardrop = 8.7

Fat per giant teardrop = 0
Calories per giant teardrop = 43.3

Make a great summertime dessert that's light and refreshing by layering giant orange teardrops with whipped cream and raspberries. (For a red, white, and blue Fourth of July extravaganza, make one of the layers blueberry!)

1 cup heavy cream
$^1/_2$ teaspoon vanilla extract
$^1/_2$ tablespoon granulated sugar
24 giant teardrops
1 pint raspberries, picked over
8 sprigs fresh mint

Combine the cream, vanilla, and sugar in a bowl and beat with an electric mixer at medium speed to soft peaks. On each of 8 teardrops, spread $1^1/_2$ tablespoons of the whipped cream and scatter 2 tablespoons raspberries.

Add a second teardrop, then another layer of whipped cream and raspberries. Top with a third teardrop and a sprig of fresh mint.

YIELD = 8 SERVINGS

Toppings

Sometimes you just can't get enough of a good thing!

When you need a little extra pampering and a plain cookie simply won't do, head toward the pantry to whip up a topping.

Whether a delicate yet satisfying glaze, or a hearty frosting, or an icing thick enough to really sink your sweet tooth into, toppings add a festive finishing touch.

We offer a selection of our favorites, along with suggested pairings, but we also encourage experimentation. To further broaden the creative possibilities, remember that many toppings also work well as fillings for sandwich cookies.

Our Maple Glaze, Chocolate Glaze, and Orange Glaze may be added when the cookies are still warm or after they have cooled. Apply the other toppings after allowing the cookies to cool. Cookies topped with Lemon Cream Cheese Icing, Strawberry Cream Cheese Frosting, or Creamy Candied Ginger Frosting should be stored in the refrigerator.

Unused topping will keep for a day, covered and refrigerated.

Shelf life and wrapping procedures for frosted cookies depend upon the type of cookie beneath the frosting. (See individual chapter introductions for specific directions.) Whenever possible, we prefer to store frosted cookies in a single layer; if you stack the cookies, put a sheet of wax paper between each layer to prevent cookie crumbs from sticking to the frosting of the layer below.

Lemon Cream Cheese Icing

YIELD = ³/₄ CUP
PLUS 1 TABLESPOON

Lemon Cream Cheese Icing adds a refreshing accent to Very Vanilla Wafers (page 178); top each one with about ³/₄ teaspoon. To finish Lemon Sour Cream Cookies (page 153) in style, prepare a double recipe and use 1 teaspoon icing for each cookie.

³/₄ cup confectioners' sugar
3 ounces cream cheese, at room temperature
1 tablespoon heavy cream
1 teaspoon freshly squeezed lemon juice
¹/₂ tablespoon grated lemon zest

Sift the confectioners' sugar into a bowl. Add the cream cheese and beat with an electric mixer at low speed to a pebbly consistency. Beat in the cream and lemon juice, continuing to beat until the mixture is smooth and spreadable. Stir in the lemon zest.

1 cup confectioners' sugar
1 teaspoon grated orange zest
1/2 teaspoon vanilla extract
3 tablespoons freshly squeezed orange juice

Put the confectioners' sugar in a mixing bowl. Whisk in the orange zest. Add the vanilla and orange juice and continue to whisk until thoroughly combined.

Orange Glaze

YIELD = ABOUT 1/2 CUP
PLUS 1 TABLESPOON

We especially like this delicate topping on Orange Walnut Jumbles (page 152) and German Spice Cookies (page 129); use about 3/4 teaspoon for each cookie. Try a scant 1 teaspoon on a Big Chocolate Cake Cookie (page 258) or 1/2 teaspoon drizzled over a Pumpkin Cookie (page 240).

Chocolate Glaze

YIELD = ABOUT ½ CUP
PLUS 3 TABLESPOONS

Chocolate Glaze adds a glossy finish and a satisfying taste twist to so many cookies! Use a generous ½ teaspoon atop each White Russian (page 130) or Macadamia Macaroon (page 283), or 1 teaspoon for each Cashew Macaroon (page 188). For a real indulgence, spoon 1 tablespoon over a wedge of Scottish Shortbread (page 81).

Select top-quality chocolate with a high cocoa butter content. An optional ½ teaspoon brandy stirred into the glaze will boost the chocolate flavor.

4 ounces semisweet chocolate, broken up
¼ cup plus 1 tablespoon heavy cream

Finely chop the chocolate in a food processor fitted with the steel blade. Transfer it to a small bowl.

Scald the cream in a small saucepan over medium-low heat until bubbles form around the edge, 30 to 40 seconds. Pour over the chocolate and allow the mixture to sit for 1 minute. Stir until smooth.

¼ cup unsalted butter, at room temperature
2 tablespoons heavy cream
2 cups confectioners' sugar
2 teaspoons rum extract
¼ cup finely chopped walnuts

Cream the butter in a bowl with an electric mixer at low speed. Beat in the cream. Sift in the confectioners' sugar and beat at low speed until the mixture is pebbly. Beat in the rum extract.

Stir in the walnuts with a rubber spatula.

Rum Walnut Butter-cream

YIELD = ABOUT 1 CUP
PLUS 2 TABLESPOONS

This scrumptious frosting pairs regally with Kevin's Eggnog Cookies (page 214). Kevin approves thoroughly and recommends using about ½ tablespoon to top each cookie.

Rum Walnut Buttercream can also be used to finish New England Farmhouse Cookies (page 140)—top each with about 1¼ teaspoons frosting—or Fruit and Nut Kisses (page 279)—use a scant ¾ teaspoon for each kiss.

Strawberry Cream Cheese Frosting

YIELD = ABOUT 1 CUP
PLUS 2 TABLESPOONS

This flavorful topping adds a nice accent to plainer cookies. Try 1 teaspoon atop a Very Vanilla Wafer (page 178) or $\frac{1}{2}$ tablespoon spread on an Old-Fashioned Sugar Cookie (page 124).

3 ounces cream cheese, at room temperature
$\frac{1}{3}$ cup ricotta cheese
$\frac{1}{3}$ cup strawberry spreadable fruit
$\frac{1}{4}$ teaspoon orange extract
$\frac{1}{4}$ cup confectioners' sugar

Combine the cream cheese and ricotta cheese in a bowl and beat with an electric mixer at medium speed until creamy and smooth. Beat in the spreadable fruit and orange extract. Sift in the confectioners' sugar and beat at medium speed until the mixture is well combined and thick.

4 ounces cream cheese, at room temperature
2 tablespoons unsalted butter, at room temperature
2 tablespoons chopped candied ginger
¾ cup confectioners' sugar

Cream the cream cheese and butter in a bowl with an electric mixer at medium speed until soft. Beat in the candied ginger. Sift in the confectioners' sugar and beat at medium speed until thoroughly mixed.

Creamy Candied Ginger Frosting

YIELD = ABOUT 1 CUP

Those of us who simply can't get enough ginger top Gingersnaps (page 182) with this kindred delight; use a generous 1 teaspoon on each. Creamy Candied Ginger Frosting complements Molasses Spice Cookies (page 166) and German Spice Cookies (page 129) as well; top each cookie with a generous teaspoonful.

Brown Butter Frosting

YIELD = ABOUT 1 CUP

A scant teaspoon of Brown Butter Frosting will intensify the taste of a Double Butterscotch Cookie (page 193). Brown Butter Frosting will also provide a flavor boost to Bernice Solomon's Brown Sugar Cookies (page 160) or Macadamia Butters (page 122); top each cookie with 1 teaspoon of the frosting.

$^{1}/_{4}$ cup ($^{1}/_{2}$ stick) unsalted butter
2 cups confectioners' sugar
$^{1}/_{2}$ tablespoon vanilla extract
2 tablespoons hot water

Melt the butter in a small saucepan over medium heat. Shaking the pan constantly, continue to cook for about 30 seconds more, until the butter is just beginning to brown. Remove from the heat and set aside.

Sift the confectioners' sugar into a bowl. Add the vanilla, hot water, and melted butter. Whisk until well combined.

1 cup confectioners' sugar
2 tablespoons almond butter
2 tablespoons water

Combine the confectioners' sugar and almond butter in a bowl. Mix thoroughly with a wooden spoon. Add the water and continue to stir until the mixture is smooth and creamy.

Almond Butter Frosting

YIELD = ABOUT ¹/₂ CUP
PLUS 2 TABLESPOONS

This nut butter–based topping is a natural atop Graham Crackers (page 136); use about ¹/₂ tablespoon on each. It adds an almost sinful accent to the already rich Double Chocolate Fudgies (page 278); spread the entire frosting yield over the brownie before cutting it into individual squares.

Café Mocha

Try frosting a Java Jive Mocha Snap (page 174) with ½ tablespoon Café Mocha—a marriage made in heaven! This coffee lover's delight boosts the basic flavor component of White Russians (page 130) as well; use about 1 ¼ teaspoons for each. For an interesting spin on Devil's Food Cookies (page 163), top each one with a teaspoon of Café Mocha.

¼ cup plus 2 tablespoons unsweetened
    Dutch-processed cocoa powder
¼ cup (½ stick) unsalted butter, at room temperature
¼ cup hot, strong brewed coffee
2 teaspoons instant coffee granules
2 teaspoons vanilla extract
1 teaspoon ground cinnamon
2 cups confectioners' sugar

Combine the cocoa powder, butter, coffee, and coffee granules in a bowl. Beat with an electric mixer at medium speed until well blended. Beat in the vanilla and cinnamon. Sift in the confectioners' sugar and beat at medium speed until the mixture is smooth.

2 ounces bittersweet chocolate, broken up
2 tablespoons unsalted butter
3 tablespoons plus 1 teaspoon milk
1 teaspoon vanilla extract
2 cups confectioners' sugar

Combine the chocolate, butter, and milk in a microwave-safe bowl. Microwave at full power for 1 minute, then whisk until smooth. (You can also combine and melt the ingredients in the top of a double boiler over boiling water.)

Add the vanilla and sift in the confectioners' sugar. Whisk the mixture until smooth.

Chocolate Butter- cream

YIELD = ABOUT 1 1/4 CUPS

Chocoholics will find true happiness biting into a Devil's Food Cookie (page 163) topped with a generous 3/4 teaspoon of Chocolate Buttercream. We've also found that it goes well with Orange Walnut Jumbles (page 152) and Thelma Houston's Vanilla Sugar Tea Cookies (page 147); frost each cookie with about 1/2 tablespoon.

White Chocolate Icing

YIELD = ABOUT ¹/₂ CUP
PLUS 2 TABLESPOONS

For a treat, spread a scant ³/₄ teaspoon of this rich and creamy icing on a Very Vanilla Wafer (page 178) or a generous ³/₄ teaspoon on one of Thelma Houston's Vanilla Sugar Tea Cookies (page 147). Each of our generously proportioned Graham Crackers (page 136) will accommodate ¹/₂ tablespoon of the icing nicely.

2 ounces white chocolate, broken up
1 cup confectioners' sugar
1 teaspoon vanilla extract
3¹/₂ teaspoons milk

Put the white chocolate in a glass measuring cup and microwave at full power for about 1 minute to melt. (You can also melt the chocolate in the top of a double boiler over boiling water.)

Sift the confectioners' sugar into a bowl. Add the melted chocolate, vanilla, and milk. Stir well with a rubber spatula.

2¹/₂ cups confectioners' sugar
6 tablespoons (³/₄ stick) unsalted butter
1 teaspoon orange oil
2 tablespoons milk

Sift the confectioners' sugar into a mixing bowl. Add the butter, orange oil, and milk. Beat with an electric mixer at medium speed until smooth and fluffy.

Orange Butter Icing

YIELD = ABOUT 1¹/₂ CUPS

Orange Butter Icing adds an extra flavor dimension and a bit of seasonal color to Pumpkin Oat Cookies (page 158)—top each cookie with about ¹/₂ tablespoon icing; or Mark's and Don's Cranberry Cookies (page 242)—top each with about 1 teaspoon. For variety, we like it on Dried Fruit Hermits (page 189); use about 1¹/₄ teaspoons for each hermit.

Look for the orange oil in gourmet shops.

Lemon Butter Frosting

YIELD = ABOUT 1 CUP

For extra richness and sweetness, top Lemon Sour Cream Cookies (page 153) with a scant 3/4 teaspoon of this frosting. It also works well on Chewy Honey Cookies (page 134); use about 3/4 teaspoon on each. To finish Old-Fashioned Sugar Cookies (page 124), top each one with about 1 teaspoon of the frosting.

2$^1/_2$ tablespoons unsalted butter
1$^1/_2$ cups confectioners' sugar, sifted
$^1/_2$ teaspoon lemon extract
1 tablespoon finely grated lemon rind

Combine all the ingredients in a mixing bowl. Beat with an electric mixer at medium speed until the mixture is smooth and creamy.

1⅓ cups pure maple syrup
¼ cup (½ stick) unsalted butter
1 teaspoon maple extract
¾ cup confectioners' sugar

Combine the maple syrup and butter in a glass measuring cup. Microwave at full power until the butter is melted and the mixture is bubbly, about 1 minute. (This can also be done in a small saucepan over low heat.)

Whisk in the maple extract. Sift in the confectioners' sugar, using a small, fine-mesh sieve. Whisk until the sugar is fully incorporated. Refrigerate for 10 minutes.

Top the cookies and allow about 15 minutes at room temperature for the glaze to set.

Maple Glaze

YIELD = ABOUT 1¼ CUPS

We find this adds a nice finishing touch to Dried Fruit Hermits (page 189), Bernice Solomon's Brown Sugar Cookies (page 160), New England Farmhouse Cookies (page 140), or Banana Bread Cookies (page 255). Use about 1 teaspoon to top each cookie.

Source Guide

THE BRIDGE COMPANY
214 E. 52nd St.
New York, NY 10022
(212) 688-4220
(bakeware, including cookie
cutters, madeleine plaques,
cookie presses, and molds)

DEAN & DELUCA
560 Broadway
New York, NY 10012
(800) 221-7714 or (212) 431-1691
(chocolate, extracts, flours,
spices; bakeware, including
madeleine plaques)

FRESH FIELDS
2484 N. Elston Ave.
Chicago, IL 60647
(312) 862-5300
(dried fruit, fruit butters,
nut butters)

KING ARTHUR CATALOG
P.O. Box 876
Norwich, VT 05055
(800) 827-6836
(flours; bakeware,
including cookie cutters)

KITCHEN BAZAAR
4455 Connecticut Ave., N.W.
Washington, D.C. 20008
(202) 363-4600
(bakeware)

KOZLOWSKI FARMS
5566 Gravenstein Highway
Forrestville, CA 95436
(707) 887-1587
(fruit butters)

LA CUISINE
323 Cameron St.
Alexandria, VA 22314
(800) 521-1176 or (703) 836-4435
(chocolate, extracts; bakeware,
including cookie cutters
and madeleine plaques)

MOON SHINE TRADING
P.O. Box 896
Winters, CA 95694
(916) 753-0601
(nut butters)

SPICELAND, INC.
P.O. Box 34378
Chicago, IL 60634
(312) 736-1000
(spices, extracts)

SWEET CELEBRATIONS
7009 Washington Ave. S.
Edina, MN 55416
(800) 328-6722
(chocolate, extracts; bakeware
and baking supplies, including
foil and paper cups)

WAX ORCHARD
22744 Wax Orchard Rd., S.W.
Vashon, WA 98070
(800) 634-6132
(fruit butters)

WILLIAMS-SONOMA
P.O. Box 7456
San Francisco, CA 94120
(415) 421-4242
(chocolate, extracts; bakeware,
including cookie cutters,
cookie presses, shortbread
and gingerbread molds)

WILTON ENTERPRISES
2240 W. 75th St.
Woodridge, IL 60517
(630) 963-7100
(baking supplies, including
pastry bags and tips)

Index

All-purpose flour, 10
Almond Apricot Pillows, 162
Almond Biscotti, 230
"Almond bread" (mandelbrot), 62
Almond Brownies, Roasted, 92–93
Almond Butter Frosting, 299
Almond Butter Thumbprints (sugarless), 273
Almond Cookies, 155
Almond Crescents, Brandy, 68
Almond-Filled Strips, 42–43
Almond Kisses, Dutch (gluten-free), 280
Almond Medallions, Cocoa, 40
Almond Pralines, 198
Almonds, 11
Almond Spritz, 76
Aluminum foil, 17, 90. *See also* Cookie storage
Amaretti, 196–97
Amish Letter Cookies, 43
Anise, 75, 79, 142
Anise Madeleines, 78
Anise Pizzelles, 74
Apple Currant Cookies (nonfat), 257
Apple Honey Pillows, 39

Apple Oatmeal Wheat Fingers, 104
Applesauce (in healthy cookies), 251
Apricot Bars, Quick, 113
Apricot Butter Bars, 112–13
Apricot-Filled Chocolate Thumbprints, 34
Apricot Filling, 225
Apricot Hamantaschen, 224–25
Apricot Linzer Cookies, 48–49
Apricot Marmalade Bars, 228
Apricot Oatmeal Wheat Fingers, 104
Apricot Pillows, Almond, 162
Apricots, 104, 189, 272
Apricot Swirls (sugarless), 276

Babka. *See* Chocolate Currant Crescents
Baker's parchment, 13, 20, 70, 251
Bakeware, sources for, 306–7
Baking chocolate, 8–9
Baking pans, 13, 17, 20, 87, 90, 233
Baking tips, 21. *See also* Cookies, baking

Baklava, Honey Cakes compared with, 212
Banana (in healthy cookies), 251
Banana Bread Cookies (nonfat), 255, 305
Bar cookies, 85–114
    Ann's Key Lime Bars, 102
    Apple Oatmeal Wheat Fingers, 104
    Apricot Butter Bars, 112–13
    Apricot Oatmeal Wheat Fingers, 104
    baking, 88
    Blackberry Linzer Squares, 106
    Blackberry Streusel Bars, 105
    Blueberry Streusel Bars, 105
    Brandied Candied Fruit Bars, 103
    Cappuccino Cream Cheese Bars, 109
    Caramel Cashew Bars, 100–1
    Chocolate-Covered Cashew Butter (or Peanut Butter) Bars, 108
    Chocolate Orange Bars, 94
    cutting, 88, 97
    English Walnut Toffee Fingers, 89

equipment for, 13, 17, 87–88, 97
Fig Port Bars, 95
fillings for, 87
Hazelnut Chocolate Squares, 114
Peach Crumb Bars, 96
Pear Caramel Bars, 90–91
Pecan Toffee Fingers, 89
Quick Apricot Bars, 113
Raspberry Linzer Squares, 106
Roasted Almond Brownies, 92–93
Ruth Gold's Date Nut Squares, 99
Sour Cherry Coconut Squares, 107
spatula and, 17
storing, 22, 88
Susan Felber's Three-Layer Brownies, 110–11
Three-Citrus Bars, 94
Ultimate Brownies, 93
White Chocolate Brownies, 98
See also Healthy cookies; Holiday cookies
Biscotti, 57
Almond, 230
Chocolate Hazelnut, 60–61
equipment for, 13
Ginger Pear, 59
Nutty (low-fat), 268
Savory (nonfat), 254
Bitter chocolate, 8–9
Bittersweet chocolate, 8–9
Blackberry Linzer Squares, 106
Blackberry Streusel Bars, 105
Blackberry Tarts, 38
Blackberry Thumbprints (sugarless), 273
Bleached flour, 10

Blueberry Streusel Bars, 105
Blue Cheese Wedges, Nutty, 84
Bohemian kolacky. See Kolacky
Bourbon Balls, Chocolate, 179
Bowls, 14
Bow ties, 57, 66
Brandied Candied Fruit Bars, 103
Brandy Almond Crescents, 68
Brandy Frosting, 214
Brandy snap (variation on), 174
Brown Butter Frosting, 298
Brownies
    Cappuccino Cream Cheese Bars compared with, 109
    equipment for, 13
    freezing/refrigerating, 88, 252
    gluten-free version of, 278
    Newfangled Cocoa (nonfat), 253
    Roasted Almond, 92–93
    Three-Layer, 110–11
    Ultimate, 93
    White Chocolate, 98
Brown sugar, 7, 19, 258, 265, 279
Brown Sugar Cookies, 160, 298, 305
Brown Sugary Butterscotch Chip Cookies (nonfat), 265
Butter, 5, 19–20, 251. See also Fruit butters; Nut butters
Buttermilk
    in healthy cookies, 251
    sour milk versus, 193
Butterscotch Chip Cookies, Brown Sugary (nonfat), 265
Butterscotch Cookies, Double, 193, 298

Café Mocha frosting, 300
Cake flour, 10

Cake pans, 58, 83. See also Baking pans
Candied fruit, 103
Candy thermometer, 17
Cannoli shells, 73, 74
Cappuccino Cream Cheese Bars, 109
Cappuccino-Filled Hazelnut Sandwiches, 26–27
Cappuccino Thumbprints, Hazelnut, 27
Cappuccino Tuiles (nonfat), 263
Caramel Bars, Pear, 90–91
Caramel Cashew Bars, 100–1
Caramel Meringue-Filled Oatmeal Sandwich Cookies, 36–37
Caraway Cookies, 142
Cardamom Cookies, 167
Carob powder, 5
Carrot Cake Cookies (low-fat), 267
Cashew Bars, Caramel, 100–1
Cashew Butter Bars, Chocolate-Covered, 108
Cashew Macaroons, 188, 294
Cashew Medallions, Cocoa, 41
Cashew Pralines (gluten-free), 282
Cashews, 11
Cashew Turtles, Chocolate, 64
Checkerboard Cookies, 168
Cheesecakes, 16
    Cappuccino Cream Cheese Bars compared with, 109
    Chocolate Cheese Cups, 231
    Individual Chocolate Chip Cheesecakes, 46
    Miniature Mocha Nut Cheesecakes, 232
    Orange Cheese Cups, 47
Cherries, 5, 107, 156, 181, 189

in Brandied Candied Fruit
Bars, 103
in Chocolate Works, 181
in Dried Fruit Hermits, 189
to top Almond Spritz, 76
Cherry Coconut Squares, Sour,
107
Cherry Pillows, Chocolate Sour,
156
Cherry Thumbprints, Chocolate,
35
Chewy Chocolate Chip Cookies,
Big, Soft, 176
Chewy cookies, storing, 22
Chewy Honey Cookies, 134, 304
Chinese five-spice powder, 79,
82
Chinese recipes, 148–49, 155
Chocolate, 8–9, 20, 306–7
brownies. See Brownies
in Devil's Food Cookies, 163
in Orange Chippers (low-fat),
266
in reduced-fat cookies, 251
See also entries beginning
Chocolate, Cocoa and Mocha
Chocolate and Peanut Butter
Cups, No-Bake, 29
Chocolate Bourbon Balls, 179
Chocolate Buttercream, 301
Chocolate Cake Cookies, Big
(nonfat), 258–59, 293
Chocolate Cashew Turtles, 64
Chocolate Cherry Thumbprints,
35
Chocolate Chip Cheesecakes, 46
Chocolate chip cookie (variation
of low-fat Orange Chippers),
266
Chocolate Chip Cookies, Big,
Soft, Chewy, 176

Chocolate Chip Cookies, Crunchy
Granola, 190–91
Chocolate Chip Cookies, Peanut
Butter, 185
Chocolate-Covered Cashew
Butter (or Peanut Butter)
Bars, 108
Chocolate Currant Crescents,
30–31
Chocolate-Dipped Chocolate
Hazelnut Biscotti, 61
Chocolate-dipped Chocolate
Mandel Bread, 229
Chocolate-dipped Ginger
Squiggles (or Ginger Batons)
(gluten-free), 285
Chocolate-dipped jumbles, 152
Chocolate-dipped Orange
Teardrops, 285
Chocolate-dipped sandwich
cookies, 33
Chocolate Fudgies, Double
(gluten-free), 278
Chocolate Ganache Filling, 54
Chocolate Glaze, 195, 294
Chocolate Grouchos, 70
Chocolate Hazelnut Biscotti,
60–61
Chocolate Icing, Nonfat, 259
Chocolate Macaroon Wafers, 234
Chocolate Madeleines, 77
Chocolate Mandel Bread, 229
Chocolate Mint Cookies, Cakey,
194–95
Chocolate Nut Pizzelles, 72–73
Chocolate Nut Revels, 219
Chocolate Nut Swirls, 150
Chocolate Oat Cookies, No-Bake,
187
Chocolate Orange Bars, 94
Chocolate Pancakes, 70

Chocolate Peanut Butter
Thingies, 131
Chocolate Pecan Tartlets, 45
Chocolate Raspberry Hazelnut
Ribbons, 168
Chocolate Raspberry Revels, 219
Chocolate Rugalach, 28
Chocolate Shots, 218
Chocolate Snails (sugarless), 271
Chocolate Sour Cherry Pillows,
156
Chocolate sprinkles, 76, 218
Chocolate Squares, Hazelnut, 114
Chocolate Tacos, Filled (nonfat),
264
Chocolate Thumbprints, Apricot-
Filled, 34
Chocolate Thumbprints, Cherry,
35
Chocolate toffee chips, 176
Chocolate Truffle Sandwich, 121
Chocolate Turtle Cookies, 64–65
Chocolate Walnut Truffles,
120–21
Chocolate–White Chocolate
Chunk Cookies, 181
Chocolate Works, 181
Cholesterol, 5, 274
Christmas cookies, 76. See also
Holiday cookies
Cigar cookies, 70–71, 186
Cinnamon cookies. See
Snickerdoodles
Cinnamon Crescents, Sugar 'n',
31
Cinnamon Horns, Pecan, 141
Cinnamon Puffs, 216
Cinnamon Raisin Swirls, 159
Cinnamon Swirls, 159
Citrus Bars, Three-, 94
Citrus Mandelbrot, 62

Clove Cookies, Lemon, 127
Cocoa Almond Medallions, 40
Cocoa Brownies, Newfangled
   (nonfat), 253
Cocoa Cashew (or Peanut)
   Medallions, 41
Cocoa Coconut Macaroons, 235
Cocoa Mint Crisps, 157
Cocoa powder, 5, 251, 253, 258,
   280
Coconut
   in Chocolate Cheese Cups, 231
   in Key Lime Bars, 102
Coconut Crisps, 139
Coconut Macaroons, 235
Coconut Meringues, Mini (gluten-
   free), 281
Coconut Squares, Sour Cherry,
   107
Coffee Frosting, Nonfat, 253
Cognac Dreams (and Cognac
   Frosting), 126
Commercy cupcakes (Anise
   Madeleines), 78
Cones, 57, 72–73, 74
Confectioners' sugar, 7, 16, 21
Cookie/baking sheets, 13–14, 17,
   20–21, 118, 172
   reduced-fat baking and, 251
   spacing cookies on, 16, 21,
   172
Cookie cups. *See* Cups
Cookie cutters, 14, 48, 118, 130
   for bar cookies, 97
   Christmas, 209
   homemade, 123
   sources for, 306–7
   for spritz cookies, 57
Cookie dough(s)
   chilling, 17, 57, 117
   dry, 16, 19

food processors and, 19. *See
   also* Food processors
frozen/freezing, 17, 22, 117,
   145
liners for. *See* Liners/lining
overbeating, 20
rolling out, 57, 117, 118, 124.
   See also Rolling pins
rubber spatula and, 17
spreading of, during baking,
   20, 21, 172
sticky, 16, 117, 162, 172, 205
thick, 15
wooden spoons and, 18
yeast, 17
Cookie gun, 14
Cookie jars, 22, 58, 118, 145, 171,
   172
healthy cookies and, 251, 252
Cookie presses, 14, 57, 75, 120,
   210
sources for, 306–7
Cookies
baking, 21, 88
bar. *See* Bar cookies
Christmas, 76. *See also* Holiday
   cookies
cooling of/wire racks for, 17,
   18, 21, 57, 172
drop. *See* Drop cookies
equipment for, 13–18, 306–7.
   *See also specific types of
   equipment*
filled. *See* Filled cookies
freezing. *See* Frozen/freezing
   cookies
frosted, 291. *See also* Toppings
gluten-free, *See* Gluten-free
   cookies; Healthy cookies
healthy. *See* Healthy cookies
holiday. *See* Holiday cookies

ingredients for. *See* Ingredients
kid-pleaser (list of), 2–3
lacy, 20, 172, 186
low-fat. *See* Healthy cookies;
   Low-fat cookies
mastering techniques regarding,
   19–22
molded, 57, 58. *See also*
   Shaped, pressed, and molded
   cookies
no-bake, 29, 187
nonfat. *See* Healthy cookies;
   Nonfat cookies
overbaking, 14, 21
party (list of), 3–4
pressed, 57, 58. *See also* Cookie
   presses; Shaped, pressed, and
   molded cookies
quick and easy (list of), 1–2
refrigerator. *See* Refrigerator
   cookies
rolled. *See* Rolled cookies
shaped, 57, 58. *See also* Shaped,
   pressed, and molded cookies
shipping, 22
sources of ingredients and
   equipment for, 306–7
storing. *See* Cookie storage
sugarless. *See also* Healthy
   cookies; Sugarless cookies
tips regarding, 19–22
Cookie storage, 21–22, 58, 88
   of drop cookies, 172
   of frosted cookies, 291
   of granola cookies, 191
   of meringues, 281
   of reduced-fat cookies, 251
   of sugarless cookies, 252, 272
   See also Frozen/freezing
   cookies
Cookie tins, 22, 58, 118, 145, 172

healthy cookies and, 251, 252
Cooking spray, 20, 251
Cooling/wire racks, 17, 18, 21, 57, 172
Corn syrup (in healthy cookies), 251
Crackles, Orange Spice, 180
Cranberries, 5, 107, 199
    in Dried Fruit Hermits, 189
    in Orange Nutty Cookies (nonfat), 260
    in Pumpkin Cookies, 240
Cranberry Cookies, 242, 303
Cranberry Orange Oatmeal Cookies, 198
Cream cheese, 19, 20
    in Prune Pinwheels, 164–65
    in Raspberry Rugalach (low-fat), 270
Cream Cheese Bars, Cappuccino, 109
Cream Cheese Frosting, Strawberry, 296
Cream Cheese Icing, Lemon, 292
Creaming, 5, 15, 19–20
Creamy Candied Ginger Frosting, 297
Crème Anglaise, 137–38
    nonfat, 264
Creole Currant Nut Cookies, 161
Crescents, 57
    Brandy Almond, 68
    Chocolate Currant, 30–31
    Hazelnut Horn, 141
    Sugar 'n' Cinnamon, 31
Crisp cookies, storing, 22, 252
Crispy Chocolate Wafers, 149
Crunchy Granola Chocolate Chip Cookies, 190–91
Cups, 73, 74, 151

Chocolate and Peanut Butter Cups, No-Bake, 29
Chocolate Cheese Cups, 231
    Orange Cheese Cups, 47
Currant Cookies, Apple (or Peach), 257
Currant Crescents, Chocolate, 30–31
Currant Nut Cookies, 161
Currants
    in Chocolate Mandel Bread, 229
    in Fruit Bars (sugarless), 272
Currant Shortbread (sugarless), 277

Danish recipe, 127
Date Chews, 215
Date Cookies, Oatmeal (low-fat), 269
Date Nut Bars, Passover, 233
Date Nut Squares, 99
Date Pinwheels, 154
Dates
    in Dried Fruit Hermits, 189
    in Fruit and Nut Kisses (gluten-free), 279
    in Fruit Bars (sugarless), 272
Devil's Food Cookies, 163, 300, 301
Diabetics, 252
Dough. See Cookie dough(s)
Doughnut cutters, 118
Dried fruit, 5, 272, 306–7
Dried Fruit Hermits, 189, 303, 305
Drop cookies, 169–99
    Amaretti, 196–97
    Apricot Almond Pillows as, 162

Cakey Chocolate Mint Cookies, 194–95
Cashew Macaroons, 188, 294
Chocolate–White Chocolate Chunk Cookies, 181
Chocolate Works, 181
Cranberry Orange Oatmeal Cookies, 198
Crunchy Granola Chocolate Chip Cookies, 190–91
Double Butterscotch Cookies, 193, 298
Dried Fruit Hermits, 189, 303, 305
equipment for, 16, 17
Filbert Filigrees, 173
Gingersnaps, 182–83, 297
Java Jive Mocha Snaps, 174, 300
Large Lacies, 186
Lemon Poppyseed Wafers, 192
Macadamia Florentines, 173
No-Bake Chocolate Oat Cookies, 187
Oatmeal Lacies, 186
Orange Spice Crackles, 180
Peanut Butter Chocolate Chip Cookies, 185
Pistachio Pralines, 199
Sesame Wafers, 177
shaping, 17
Tahini Cookies, 184
Very Vanilla Wafers, 178–79, 296, 302
    See also Healthy cookies; Holiday cookies
Dusting, 21
Dutch Kisses (or Dutch Almond Kisses), (gluten-free), 280

Easter cookies, 226–27
Eastern European pastry
    (Raspberry Kolacky), 52–53
Eggnog Cookies, 214, 295
Eggs, 5, 17, 251
Egg whites, 5, 16, 17
    in healthy cookies, 251, 252
Electric mixers. *See* Mixers
English Walnut Toffee Fingers,
    89
Eurasian variation of Scottish
    Shortbread, 82
Exotic Shortbread, 82–83
Extracts, 6, 62, 306–7

Fennel Cookies, 142
Fig Bars (nonfat), 261–62
Fig Pinwheels, 154
Fig Port Bars, 95
Figs, in Fruit Bars (sugarless),
    272
Filbert Filigrees, 173
Filberts, 11. *See also* Hazelnuts
Filled cookies, 23–54
    Almond-Filled Strips, 42–43
    Apple Honey Pillows, 39
    Apricot-Filled Chocolate
        Thumbprints, 34
    Apricot Linzer Cookies, 48–49
    Blackberry Tarts, 38
    Cappuccino-Filled Hazelnut
        Sandwiches, 26–27
    Caramel Meringue-Filled
        Oatmeal Sandwiches, 36–37
    Chocolate Cherry
        Thumbprints, 35
    Chocolate Currant Crescents,
        30–31
    Chocolate Pecan Tartlets, 45
    Chocolate Rugalach, 28

Cocoa Almond Medallions, 40
Cocoa Cashew (or Peanut)
    Medallions, 41
Hazelnut Cappuccino
    Thumbprints, 27
Individual Chocolate Chip
    Cheesecakes, 46
Judy's No-Bake Chocolate and
    Peanut Butter Cups, 29
Marie Novosad's Poppyseed
    Kolacky, 50–51
Orange Cheese Cups, 47
Orange Marmalade Triangles,
    44
Peanut Thumbprints with
    Chocolate Ganache Filling,
    54
Prune Pastries, 165
Raisin Nut Rugalach, 28
Raspberry Kolacky, 52–53
Raspberry Tarts, 38
Strawberry Tarts, 38
Sugar 'n' Cinnamon Crescents,
    31
toppings used as fillings for,
    291
Viennese Raspberry
    Sandwiches, 32–33
See also Holiday cookies
Fingers
    Apple (or Apricot) Oatmeal
        Wheat, 104
    English Walnut Toffee, 89
    hazelnut (Viennese Raspberry
        Sandwiches), 32–33
    Pecan Toffee, 89
Five-spice powder, 79, 82
Five-Spice Springles, 79
Flour, 10, 16, 17, 19
    and rolling out cookies, 117, 124
    sources for, 306–7

Folding, 17
Food processors, 5, 15, 124, 162,
    176
    grinding nuts in, 19
    rolled cookies and, 117
    superfine granulated sugar and,
    7
Fourth of July dessert (cookie
    recipe used for), 287
Frosted cookies, 291. *See also*
    Toppings
Frozen/freezing cookie dough,
    17, 22, 117
    refrigerator cookies and, 145
Frozen/freezing cookies, 17, 22,
    25, 88
    drop cookies, 172
    gluten-free cookies, 252
    reduced-fat cookies, 251
    rolled cookies, 118
Fruit
    candied, 103
    citrus. *See entries beginning*
        Citrus
    dried. *See* Dried fruit
    spreadable, in healthy cookies,
        251, 252
    See also specific fruits
Fruit and Nut Kisses (gluten-
    free), 279, 295
Fruit Bars (sugarless), 272
Fruit Bars, Brandied Candied,
    103
Fruit butters, 6, 251, 306–7
Fruit juices, 6, 252

German Spice Cookies, 129, 293,
    297
German springerle (version of),
    79

Ginger, in Savory Biscotti, 254
Ginger Batons (gluten-free), 284, 285
Ginger Bells, 205
Ginger Frosting, Creamy Candied, 297
Ginger Pear Biscotti, 59
Gingersnaps, 182, 297
   variation on, 174
Ginger Squiggles (gluten-free), 284–85
Gluten-free cookies, 252, 278–87. *See also* Healthy cookies
Graham Crackers, 136–37, 299, 302
Graham flour, 10
Granola Chocolate Chip Cookies, Crunchy, 190–91
Granulated sugar, 7
Grape Nuts cereal
   in Nutty Biscotti (low-fat), 268
   in Orange Nutty Cookies (nonfat), 260
Graters, 15
Greek recipes, 212–13, 227

Halloween cookies
   Peanut Butter Jack-o'-Lanterns, 237
   Pumpkin Cookies, 240–41, 293
   Shortbread Ghosts, 238
Hamantaschen
   Apricot, 224–25
   Poppyseed, 222–23
   Prune, 220–21
Hanukkah cookies, 28
Hazelnut Biscotti, Chocolate, 60–61

Hazelnut Cappuccino Thumbprints, 27
Hazelnut Chocolate Squares, 114
Hazelnut fingers (Viennese Raspberry Sandwiches), 32–33
Hazelnut Horns, 141
Hazelnut Ribbons, Chocolate Raspberry, 168
Hazelnuts, 11. *See also* Filberts
Hazelnut Sandwiches, Cappuccino-Filled, 26–27
Healthy cookies, 249–87
   Almond Butter Thumbprints (sugarless), 273
   Apple Currant Cookies (nonfat), 257
   Apricot Swirls (sugarless), 276
   Banana Bread Cookies (nonfat), 255, 305
   Big Chocolate Cake Cookies (nonfat), 258–59, 293
   Blackberry Thumbprints (sugarless), 273
   Brown Sugary Butterscotch Chip Cookies (nonfat), 265
   Cappuccino Tuiles (nonfat), 263
   Carrot Cake Cookies (low-fat), 267
   Cashew Pralines (gluten-free), 282
   Chocolate-dipped Ginger Squiggles, Ginger Batons, or Orange Teardrops (all gluten-free), 285
   Chocolate Snails (sugarless), 271
   Crème Anglaise and, 264
   Double Chocolate Fudgies (gluten-free), 278

Dutch (or Dutch Almond) Kisses (gluten-free), 280
Fig Bars (nonfat), 261–62
Fruit and Nut Kisses (gluten-free), 279, 295
Fruit Bars (sugarless), 272
Ginger Batons (gluten-free), 284, 285
Ginger Squiggles (gluten-free), 284–85
Jill Van Cleave's Currant Shortbread (sugarless), 277
John Vranicar's Savory Biscotti (nonfat), 254
Lemon Madeleines (nonfat), 256
Macadamia Macaroons (gluten-free), 283
Mini Coconut Meringues (gluten-free), 281
Newfangled Cocoa Brownies (nonfat), 253
Nutty Biscotti (low-fat), 268
Oatmeal Date Cookies (low-fat), 269
Oatmeal Raisin Pecan Cookies (sugarless), 275
Orange Madeleines (nonfat), 256
Orange Nutty Cookies (nonfat), 260
Orange Teardrops (gluten-free), 286–87
Peach Currant Cookies (nonfat), 257
Peanut Pralines (gluten-free), 282
Raspberry Rugalach (low-fat), 270
Strawberry Swirls (sugarless), 276

Susan's Orange Chippers (low-fat), 266
traditional chocolate chip cookie (variation of Orange Chippers), 266
See also Low-fat cookies; Nonfat cookies; Sugarless cookies
Hermits, Cranberry Cookies compared with, 242
Hermits, Dried Fruit, 189, 303, 305
Holiday cookies, 201–47
  Almond Biscotti, 230
  Apricot Hamantaschen, 224–25
  Chocolate Cheese Cups, 231
  Chocolate Macaroon Wafers, 234
  Chocolate Mandel Bread, 229
  Chocolate Raspberry Revels, 219
  Cinnamon Puffs, 216
  Claudia Clark Potter's Mincemeat Bars, 243
  Cocoa Coconut Macaroons, 235
  Coconut Macaroons, 235
  Doubleday Sweet Potato Dollops, 246–47
  Elaine Barlas's Mexican Wedding Cookies, 211
  Evelyn West's Toffee Bars, 217
  Ginger Bells, 205
  Harry's Honey Madeleines, 236
  Helen Kalabsa's Chocolate Nut Revels, 219
  Honey Lemon Madeleines, 236
  Jeanne Troxell Munson's Raspberry Christmas Cookies, 208

John Koulias's Greek Easter Cookies, 227
K.C.'s Mom's Date Chews, 215
Kevin's Eggnog Cookies, 214, 295
Lisa Schumacher's Chocolate Shots, 218
Marian Packer's Norwegian Sugar Cookies, 226
Marie Koulias's Honey Cakes, 212–13
Mark's and Don's Cranberry Cookies, 242, 303
Mary McLaughlin's Shortbread Ghosts, 238
Mincemeat Mounds with Rum Frosting, 245
Miniature Mocha Nut Cheesecakes, 232
Ornament Cookies, 209
Partially Ellie's Apricot Marmalade Bars, 228
Passover Date Nut Bars, 233
Peanut Butter Jack-o'-Lanterns, 237
Pistachio Spritz Wreaths, 210
Poppyseed Hamantaschen, 222–23
Pumpkin Cookies, 240–41, 293
Sara Bluestein's Prune Hamantaschen, 220–21
Stained Glass Cookies, 206–7
See also specific holidays
Honey, 135
Honey Cakes, 212–13
Honey Cookies, Chewy, 134, 304
Honey Lemon Madeleines, 236
Honey Madeleines, 236
Honey Pillows, Apple, 39

Horns, 73, 74, 141
Hot fudge sauce (sugarless) (cookie recipe used for), 271

Icebox cookie (update of), 168
Ice cream cones (cookie recipes used for), 57, 72–74
Ice cream sandwiches (cookie recipe used for), 134
Ingredients
  combining dry and wet, 20
  handling dry, 19
  measuring, 15, 19
  selecting best, 5–7
  sources for, 306–7
Italian recipes, 196–97

Java Jive Mocha Snaps, 174, 300
Jewish recipes
  hamantaschen, 220–25
  Hanukkah cookies, 28
  mandelbrot. *See* Mandelbrot
  Passover cookies, 228–36, 286
  Purim cookies, 220–21
Jumbles
  Caraway Cookies as type of, 142
  Old-Fashioned Lemon, 152
  Orange Walnut, 152, 293, 301

Key Lime Bars, 102
Key Lime Pie Napoleons with Coconut Crème Anglaise (cookie recipe used for), 137–38
Kitchenware, 13–18
Kolacky

Poppyseed, 50–51
prune filling for, 220
Prune Pastries compared with, 165
Raspberry, 52–53
Kringlers, 67

Lackva, 220
Lemon Butter Frosting, 304
Lemon Clove Cookies, 127
Lemon Cream Cheese Icing, 292
Lemon Extract, 62
Lemon Glaze, 192
Lemon Jumbles, Old-Fashioned, 152
Lemon Madeleines (nonfat), 256
Lemon Poppyseed Wafers, 192
Lemon Sour Cream Cookies, 153, 292, 304
Lemon Yin-Yang Wafers, 149
Licorice flavor
    in Anise Madeleines, 78
    in Fennel Cookies, 142
Licorice Spritz, 75
Lime juice, 94, 102
Liners/lining, 13, 14, 17, 20
    of baking pans, 87, 90
    of cookie/baking sheets, 13, 14, 17, 20, 172
    for reduced-fat cookies, 251
Linzer cookies
    Apricot Linzer Cookies, 48–49
    Blackberry (or Raspberry) Linzer Squares, 106
Liquid egg substitute, 5, 251
Low-fat cookies, 5, 6, 251, 265–70. *See also* Healthy cookies

M & M's
    in Big, Soft Chewy Chocolate Chip Cookies, 176
    in Chocolate Shots, 218
Macadamia Butters, 122, 298
Macadamia Florentines, 173
Macadamia Macaroons (gluten-free), 283, 294
Macadamias, 11
Macaroons
    Amaretti as, 196
    Cashew, 188, 294
    Chocolate, 234
    Cocoa Coconut, 235
    Coconut, 235
    Coconut Crisps versus, 139
    Macadamia (gluten-free), 283, 294
Madeleine plaques, 15, 57, 77, 78, 256
    sources for, 306–7
Madeleines, 57
    Anise, 78
    Chocolate, 77
    Honey (or Honey Lemon), 236
    Orange (or Lemon), 256
Mandelbrot, 13, 57
    Almond Biscotti compared with, 230
    biscotti compared with, 60
    Chocolate Mandel Bread compared with, 229
    Citrus, 62
    Raisin (or Traditional), 63
Maple Glaze, 305
Marzipan, Almond-Filled Strips filling versus, 42
Measuring ingredients, 15, 17, 19, 87
Melomakarona, 212
Meringue, 16

caramel, 36
    in Cinnamon Puffs, 216
    in Coconut Macaroons, 235
    in Ginger Squiggles (gluten-free), 284–85
    in gluten-free cookies, 252
    Mini Coconut (gluten-free), 281
Mexican Wedding Cookies, 211
Milk chocolate, 8–9, 176
Mincemeat, Easy Meatless, 244
Mincemeat Bars, 243
Mincemeat Mounds with Rum Frosting, 245
Mint
    in Cakey Chocolate Mint Cookies, 194–95
    in Cocoa Mint Crisps, 157
    in Three-Layer Brownies, 110–11
Mixers, 15–16, 18
    creaming with, 19–20
    meringue and, 252
Mocha, Café, 300
Mocha Nut Cheesecakes, Miniature, 232
Mocha Snaps, Java Jive, 174, 300
Molasses Spice Cookies, 166, 297
Molded cookies, 57, 58
Molds, 15, 57, 80
    shortbreads and, 58, 83
    sources for, 306–7
    See also Madeleine plaques
Muffin tins, 16, 78, 151

Natural raw brown sugar, 7. *See also* Turbinado sugar

New England Farmhouse
Cookies, 140, 295, 305
New Year's Day cookies, 212–13,
214
No-Bake Chocolate and Peanut
Butter Cups, 29
No-Bake Chocolate Oat Cookies,
187
Nonfat Chocolate Icing, 259
Nonfat Coffee Frosting, 253
Nonfat cookies, 5, 6, 251,
253–64. *See also* Healthy
cookies
Nonstick plastic ovenware liner,
13, 20, 251
Norwegian Sugar Cookies,
226–27
Nut butters, 6, 92–93, 184, 306–7
Nutmeg, 6, 15, 214
Nuts, 10, 11
chopping and grinding, 19
toasting, 101
Nutty Biscotti (low-fat), 268
Nutty Blue Cheese Wedges, 84

Oat Cookies, No-Bake Chocolate,
187
Oat Cookies, Pumpkin, 158
Oatmeal Cookies, Cranberry
Orange, 198
Oatmeal Date Cookies (low-fat),
269
Oatmeal Lacies (or Lace Cigars),
186
Oatmeal Raisin Pecan Cookies
(sugarless), 275
Oatmeal Sandwich Cookies,
Caramel Meringue-Filled,
36–37

Oatmeal Wheat Fingers, Apple
(or Apricot), 104
Oats, toasting, 198
Orange Bars, Chocolate, 94
Orange Brown-Edge Cookies, 132
Orange Butter Icing, 303
Orange Cheese Cups, 47
Orange Chippers (low-fat), 266
Orange Clove Cookies, 127
Orange Extract, 62
Orange Glaze, 293
Orange Madeleines (nonfat), 256
Orange marmalade, in Apricot
Marmalade cookies, 228
Orange Marmalade Triangles, 44
Orange Nutty Cookies (nonfat),
260
Orange Oatmeal Cookies,
Cranberry, 198
Orange peel, dried, 132
Orange Spice Crackles, 180
Orange Teardrops (gluten-free),
286
Orange Wafers, 149
Orange Walnut Jumbles, 152,
293, 301
Ornament Cookies, 207, 209
Oven calibration, 17, 21

Pancakes, Chocolate, 70
Papaya, 5
Parmesan Pepper Rounds, 119
Passover cookies, 228–36, 286
Pastry
for hamantaschen, 220–25
for Individual Chocolate Chip
Cheesecakes, 46
for kolacky, 50–52
Pastry bag, 75, 120, 207, 306–7
Pastry cloths, 16, 17, 117, 205

Pastry crimper and cutting wheel,
97
Peach Crumb Bars, 96
Peach Currant Cookies (nonfat),
257
Peaches
in Apricot Marmalade Bars,
228
in Fruit Bars (sugarless), 272
Peanut Butter and Jelly
Thumbprints, 54
Peanut Butter Bars, Chocolate-
Covered, 108
Peanut butter chips, 176
Peanut Butter Chocolate Chip
Cookies, 185
Peanut Butter Cups, No-Bake
Chocolate and, 29
Peanut Butter Jack-o'-Lanterns,
237
Peanut Butter Thingies,
Chocolate, 131
Peanut Medallions, Cocoa, 41
Peanut Pralines (gluten-free), 282
Peanuts, 11
Peanut Thumbprints with
Chocolate Ganache Filling,
54
Pear Biscotti, Ginger, 59
Pear butter, in Savory Biscotti
(nonfat), 254
Pear Caramel Bars, 90–91
Pears, 59, 272
Pecan Cinnamon Horns, 141
Pecan Cookies, Oatmeal Raisin,
275
Pecans, 11
Pecan Tartlets, Chocolate, 45
Pecan Toffee Fingers, 89
Pecorino (as substitute for
Parmesan cheese), 119

Peppermint. *See* Mint
Peppermint patties, in Big, Soft
    Chewy Chocolate Chip
    Cookies, 176
Piecrust (cookie recipe used for),
    124
Piecrusts (prepared), in Quick
    Apricot Bars, 113
Pillows
    Almond Apricot, 162
    Apple Honey, 39
    Chocolate Sour Cherry, 156
    refrigerator cookies as, 145
    Sour Cream, with Slivered
        Almonds, 128
Pineapple, in Sweet Potato
    Dollops, 246–47
Pinwheels, 154, 164–65
Pistachio Pralines, 199
Pistachios, 11, 167
Pistachio Spritz Wreaths, 210
Pizza wheel, 97
Pizzelle irons, 57, 72, 73, 74
Pizzelles, 57
    Anise, 74
    Chocolate Nut, 72–73
    Vanilla, 74
Plastic ovenware liner, nonstick,
    13, 20
Plastic storage bags, 22
Plastic wrap, 17, 171, 191
Poppyseed Filling, 223
Poppyseed Hamantaschen,
    222–23
Poppyseed Kolacky, 50–51
Poppyseed Wafers, Lemon, 192
Port, in Fig Port Bars, 95
Pralines, 198, 199, 282
Pressed cookies, 57, 58. *See also*
    Cookie presses; Shaped,
    pressed, and molded cookies

Pretzels, 57, 67
Prune Butter, 221
Prune Hamantaschen, 220–21
Prune Pastries, 165
Prune Pinwheels, 164–65
Puff pastry, Almond-Filled Strips
    dough to substitute for, 42
Pumpkin Cheesecake (cookie
    recipe used for), 183
Pumpkin Cookies, 240–41, 293
Pumpkin Oat Cookies, 158, 303
Purim cookies, 220–21

Raisin Cookies, Rum, 128
Raisin Mandelbrot, 63
Raisin Nut Rugalach, 28
Raisin Pecan Cookies, Oatmeal,
    275
Raisins
    in Dried Fruit Hermits, 189
    in Fruit Bars (sugarless), 272
    in Mincemeat Bars, 243
    instead of currants, in Currant
        Nut Cookies, 161
    in Sweet Potato Dollops,
        246–47
Raisin Swirls, Cinnamon, 159
Raspberry Christmas Cookies,
    208
Raspberry Hazelnut Ribbons,
    Chocolate, 168
Raspberry Jam, 53
    in Raspberry Kolacky, 53
    in Viennese Raspberry
        Sandwiches, 32
Raspberry Kolacky, 52–53
Raspberry Linzer Squares, 106
Raspberry Revels, Chocolate, 219
Raspberry Rugalach (low-fat),
    270

Raspberry Sandwiches, Viennese,
    32–33
Raspberry Tarts, 38
Raspberry Triangles (sugarless),
    274
Ravioli cutter, 97
Refrigerator cookies, 143–68
    Almond Apricot Pillows, 162
    Almond Cookies, 155
    Bernice Solomon's Brown
        Sugar Cookies, 160, 298, 305
    Cardamom Cookies, 167
    Checkerboard Cookies, 168
    Chocolate Nut Swirls, 150
    Chocolate Raspberry Hazelnut
        Ribbons, 168
    Chocolate Sour Cherry Pillows,
        156
    Cinnamon Raisin Swirls, 159
    Cinnamon Swirls, 159
    Cocoa Mint Crisps, 157
    Cookie Cups (for custard and
        frozen desserts), 151
    Creole Currant Nut Cookies,
        161
    Crispy Chocolate Wafers, 149
    Date Pinwheels, 154
    Devil's Food Cookies, 163, 300,
        301
    Fig Pinwheels, 154
    Lemon Sour Cream Cookies,
        153, 292, 304
    Lemon Yin-Yang Wafers, 149
    Molasses Spice Cookies, 166,
        297
    Old-Fashioned Lemon
        Jumbles, 152
    Orange Wafers, 149
    Orange Walnut Jumbles, 152,
        293, 301
    Prune Pinwheels, 164–65

Pumpkin Oat Cookies, 158, 303
Thelma Houston's Vanilla Sugar Tea Cookies, 147, 157, 301, 302
Yin-Yang Wafers, 148–49
See also Healthy cookies; Holiday cookies
Roasted Almond Brownies, 92–93
Rolled cookies, 115–42
    Caraway Cookies, 142
    Chewy Honey Cookies, 134, 304
    Chocolate Peanut Butter Thingies, 131
    Chocolate Truffle Sandwich, 121
    Chocolate Walnut Truffles, 120–21
    Coconut Crisps, 139
    Cognac Dreams, 126
    Fennel Cookies, 142
    German Spice Cookies, 129, 293, 297
    Graham Crackers, 136–37, 299, 302
    Hazelnut Horns, 141
    Lemon Clove Cookies, 127
    Macadamia Butters, 122, 298
    New England Farmhouse Cookies, 140, 295, 305
    Old-Fashioned Sugar Cookies, 124, 296, 304
    Orange Brown-Edge Cookies, 132–33
    Orange Clove Cookies, 127
    Parmesan Pepper Rounds, 119
    Pecan Cinnamon Horns, 141
    refrigerator cookies as, 145
    Rum Raisin Cookies, 128

Sour Cream Pillows with Slivered Almonds, 128
White Russians, 130, 294, 300
See also Healthy cookies; Holiday cookies
Rolling pins, 16, 117, 142, 205
    springles and, 58, 79
Royal Icing, 205, 207, 209, 239
Rugalach, 28, 270
Rulers, 16
Rum Frosting, 240, 245
Rum Raisin Cookies, 128
Rum Walnut Buttercream, 295

Salt, 6
Sand dollars (Cocoa Almond Medallions), 40
Sandwich cookies
    Apricot Linzer, 48–49
    Cappuccino-Filled Hazelnut, 26–27
    Caramel Meringue-Filled Oatmeal, 36–37
    Chocolate Truffle, 121
    toppings used as fillings for, 291
    Viennese Raspberry, 32–33
Scandinavian recipes, 142, 226
Scoops, 16, 171
Scottish recipes, 81, 238, 294
Scottish Shortbread, 81, 294
Self-rising flour, 10, 126
Semisweet chocolate, 8–9
Sesame seeds, toasting, 177
Sesame Wafers, 177
    Tahini Cookies compared with, 184
Shaped, pressed, and molded cookies, 55–84
    Almond Spritz, 76

Anise Madeleines, 78
Anise Pizzelles, 74
Chocolate Cashew Turtles, 64
Chocolate-Dipped Chocolate Hazelnut Biscotti, 61
Chocolate Grouchos, 70
Chocolate Hazelnut Biscotti, 60
Chocolate Madeleines, 77
Chocolate Nut Pizzelles, 72–73
Chocolate Pancakes, 70
Chocolate Turtle Cookies, 64–65
Citrus Mandelbrot, 62
Exotic Shortbread, 82–83
Five-Spice Springles, 79
Ginger Pear Biscotti, 59
Kringlers, 67
Licorice Spritz, 75
Mary Ann Morrissey's Brandy Almond Crescents, 68
Nutty Blue Cheese Wedges, 84
Raisin Mandelbrot, 63
Scottish Shortbread, 81, 294
Snickerdoodles, 69
Strawberry Shortbread Cake, 81
Sugar Cookie Squares, 80
Traditional Mandelbrot, 63
Vanilla Pizzelles, 74
Walnut Bow Ties, 66
See also Holiday cookies
Shipping cookies, 22
Shortbread, 57, 58
    Currant (sugarless), 277
    Exotic, 82–83
    Ghosts, 238
    Hearts, 239
    Orange Walnut Jumbles compared with, 152
    molds for, 83
    Scottish, 81, 294

Strawberry, 81
in Three-Citrus Bars, 94
Sieve, fine-mesh, 21, 88
Sifters/sifting, 16, 19
Snickerdoodles, 69
Sour cherries, 107, 156, 181, 189
Sour Cherry Coconut Squares, 107
Sour Cherry Pillows, Chocolate, 156
Sour Cream Pillows with Slivered Almonds, 128
Sour milk, 193
Spatulas, 16–17, 19, 118, 172
Spice cookies
Cardamom Cookies, 167
German Spice Cookies, 129, 293, 297
Molasses Spice Cookies, 166, 297
Orange Spice Crackles, 180
Spice grinder, 142
Spices, 6, 79, 306–7
Springles, 57, 58, 79
Sprinkles, chocolate, 76, 218
Spritz cookies, 14, 57
Almond, 76
Licorice, 75
Pistachio Spritz Wreaths, 210
Stained Glass Cookies, 206–7
Star fruit, 5
Storing
of chocolate, 9
of cookie dough, 171. See also Frozen/freezing cookie dough
of cookies. See Cookie storage
of dried sour cherries, 107
of flour, 10, 19
of toppings, 291

Strawberries, in Peanut Butter and Jelly Thumbprints, 54
Strawberry Cream Cheese Frosting, 296
Strawberry Shortbread Cake, 81
Strawberry Swirls (sugarless), 276
Strawberry Tarts, 38
Streusel Bars, Blueberry (or Blackberry), 105
Substitutes, 5, 9, 251–52
Sugar, 7, 251
Sugar cookie base
for Apricot Butter Bars, 112
for Sour Cherry Coconut Squares, 107
Sugar Cookies, Brown, 160, 298, 305
Sugar Cookies, Norwegian, 226
Sugar Cookies, Old-Fashioned, 124, 296, 304
Sugar Cookie Squares, 80
Sugarless cookies, 6, 252, 271–77. See also Healthy cookies
Sugar 'n' Cinnamon Crescents, 31
Sugar Tea Cookies, Vanilla, 147, 157, 301, 302
Sunflower seeds, in Orange Chippers (low-fat), 266
Superfine granulated sugar, 7, 280
Swedish recipe (Cinnamon Swirls), 159
Sweet halvah, Tahini Cookies compared with, 184
Sweet Potato Dollops, 246–47

Tahini Cookies, 184
Tarts, 16, 38, 45
Tea cookies

Lemon Poppyseed Wafers as, 192
Vanilla Sugar, 147, 157, 301, 302
Temperature, measuring, 17
Thanksgiving cookies, 214, 240–47
Cranberry Cookies, 242, 303
Eggnog Cookies, 214
Pumpkin Cookies, 240–41, 293
See also Holiday cookies
Thermometers, 17, 21
Three-Citrus Bars, 94
Thumbprints
Almond Butter (sugarless), 273
Apricot-Filled Chocolate, 34
Blackberry (sugarless), 273
Chocolate Cherry, 35
Hazelnut Cappuccino, 27
Peanut, with Chocolate Ganache Filling, 54
Peanut Butter and Jelly, 54
Toffee Bars, 217
Toffee chips, in Chocolate Shots, 218
Toffee Fingers, English Walnut (or Pecan), 89
Toppings, 289–305
Almond Butter Frosting, 299
Brandy Frosting, 214
Brown Butter Frosting, 298
Café Mocha, 300
Chocolate Buttercream, 301
Chocolate Glaze, 195, 294
Cognac Frosting, 126
confectioners' sugar for, 16
Creamy Candied Ginger Frosting, 297
Crème Anglaise, 265

crumb (in Apricot Butter Bars), 112
Lemon Butter Frosting, 304
Lemon Cream Cheese Icing, 292
Lemon Glaze, 192
Macadamia Florentines, crumbled, as, 173
Maple Glaze, 305
Nonfat Chocolate Icing, 259
Nonfat Coffee Frosting, 253
Orange Butter Icing, 303
Orange Glaze, 293
Rum Frosting, 240, 245
Rum Walnut Buttercream, 295
spatula and, 17
Strawberry Cream Cheese Frosting, 296
White Chocolate Icing, 302
Tortoni, 197
Truffles, Chocolate Walnut, 120–21
Turbinado sugar, 7, 44, 130
Turtle Cookies, Chocolate, 64–65

Unbleached flour, 10
Unsweetened chocolate, 8–9

Valentine's Day cookies, 239
Vanilla Pizzelles, 74
Vanilla Sugar Tea Cookies, 147, 157, 301, 302
Vanilla Wafers, Very, 178–79, 296, 302
Vegetable oil cooking spray, 20, 251
Victorian snail cookie (version of), 150
Viennese Raspberry Sandwiches, 32–33

Wafers
    Chocolate Macaroon, 234
    Lemon Poppyseed, 192
    Macadamia Florentine, 173
    Sesame, 177
    Very Vanilla, 178–79, 296, 302
    Yin-Yang (Orange, Lemon, Chocolate), 148–49
Walnut Bow Ties, 66
Walnut Buttercream, Rum, 295
Walnut Jumbles, Orange, 152
Walnuts, 11
Walnut Toffee Fingers, English, 89

Walnut Truffles, Chocolate, 120–21
Wax paper, 17, 117, 145, 168, 291
Wheat, gluten-free cookies as a way to avoid, 252
Wheat germ, in Apricot Oatmeal Wheat Fingers, 104
Whisks/whisking, 17, 19, 252
White chocolate, 8–9
    in Chocolate Turtle Cookies, 64
    in Shortbread Ghosts, 238
White Chocolate Brownies, 98
White Chocolate Chunk Cookies, Chocolate–, 181
White Chocolate Icing, 302
White Russians, 130, 294, 300
Whole wheat flour, 10
Wooden spatula, 18, 19
Wooden spoons, 18, 19, 20

Yeast dough, thermometer and, 17
Yin-Yang Wafers, 148–49

Zest, 6, 15